DIGITAL HEALTH AND TECHNOLOGICAL PROMISE

What is 'digital health'? And what are its implications for medicine and healthcare, and for individual citizens and society? Digital health is of growing interest to policymakers, clinicians and businesses. It is underpinned by promise and optimism, with predictions that digital technologies and related innovations *will* soon 'transform' medicine and healthcare, and enable individuals to better manage their own health and risk and to receive more 'personalized' treatment and care.

Offering a sociological perspective, this book critically examines the dimensions and implications of digital health, a term that is often ill defined, but signifies the promise of technology to 'empower' individuals and improve their lives as well as generating efficiencies and wealth. The chapters explore relevant sociological concepts and theories; changing conceptions of the self, evident in citizens' growing use of wearables, online behaviours and patient activism; changes in medical practices, especially precision (or personalized) medicine and growing reliance on big data and algorithm-driven decisions; the character of the digital healthcare economy; and the perils of digital health.

It is argued that, for various reasons, including the way digital technologies are designed and operate, and the influence of big technology companies and other interests seeking to monetize citizens' data, digital health is unlikely to deliver much of what is promised. Citizens' use of digital technologies is likened to a Faustian bargain: citizens are likely to surrender something of far greater value (their personal data) than what they obtain from its use. However, growing data activism and calls for 'algorithmic accountability' highlight the potential for citizens to create alternative futures—ones oriented to fulfilling human needs rather than techno-utopian visions.

This ground-breaking book will provide an invaluable resource for those seeking to understand the socio-cultural and politico-economic implications of digital health.

Alan Petersen is Professor of Sociology, School of Social Sciences at Monash University in Melbourne. He researches and publishes in the sociology of health and medicine, science and technology studies, and gender studies. His recent books include *Hope in Health: The Socio-Politics of Optimism* (2015) and *Stem Cell Tourism and the Political Economy of Hope* (2017).

'This book is different from anything you have read about digital health before: Alan Petersen offers a novel, irreverent, and sobering take on digital health. Drawing upon debates from an impressively wide range of fields and disciplines, he teaches us to stop seeing technologies as the drivers of change, but instead to treat them as illustrations of political decisions that we have made, and of needs and inequities that we have ignored. In short, it tells the story of a political economy in which 'disruption' has become a word of praise.'

Barbara Prainsack, *Professor of Comparative Policy Analysis, Department of Political Science, University of Vienna, Austria*

'Alan Petersen provides an impressive overview of current challenges at the intersection of health, data and digital technologies. The book urges its readers to move beyond techno-utopian promises typically endorsed by policymakers and warns against entering what Petersen likens to a Faustian bargain, where citizens surrender their most intimate data in exchange for access to technologies that serve purposes other than their health, well-being and privacy.'

Klaus Høyer, *Professor of Medical Science and Technology Studies, Institute of Public Health, University of Copenhagen, Denmark*

'Petersen provides a nuanced sociological account of what digitalisation in its many guises might mean for the provision of healthcare. Resisting deterministic accounts from policy makers and those selling digital solutions, Petersen offers a way of understanding the present and the future that takes the past seriously. This book is important not only for those interested in digital health but for everyone concerned with the future of society in a world populated by people and digital technologies.'

Sally Wyatt, *Professor of Digital Cultures in Development, Technology and Society Studies, Maastricht University, Netherlands*

'In this insightful book Alan Petersen offers a timely sociological analysis of the dimensions and implications of "digital health". His conclusion is telling – that "digital health" is unlikely to deliver much of what is promised – but he also highlights the potential for citizens to create alternative futures aimed at meeting human needs rather than techno-utopian visions. For anyone interested in this key development in medicine and health care this book is highly recommended.'

Jonathan Gabe, *Professor of Sociology, Centre for Public Services and Policy, Royal Holloway, University of London, UK*

DIGITAL HEALTH AND TECHNOLOGICAL PROMISE

A Sociological Inquiry

Alan Petersen

LONDON AND NEW YORK

First published 2019
by Routledge
2 Park Square, Milton Park, Abingdon, Oxon OX14 4RN

and by Routledge
52 Vanderbilt Avenue, New York, NY 10017

Routledge is an imprint of the Taylor & Francis Group, an informa business

British Library Cataloguing in Publication Data
A catalogue record for this book is available from the British Library

Library of Congress Cataloging-in-Publication Data
Names: Petersen, Alan R., 1953- author.
Title: Digital health and technological promise : a sociological inquiry /
Alan Petersen.
Description: Milton Park, Abingdon, Oxon ; New York, NY : Routledge, 2019.
| Includes bibliographical references and index.
Identifiers: LCCN 2018035725| ISBN 9781138709676 (hardback) |
ISBN 9781138709690 (pbk.) | ISBN 9781315200880 (ebook)
Subjects: LCSH: Medical informatics. | Medical innovations.
Classification: LCC R858 .P484 2019 | DDC 610.285--dc23
LC record available at https://lccn.loc.gov/2018035725

ISBN: 978-1-138-70967-6 (hbk)
ISBN: 978-1-138-70969-0 (pbk)
ISBN: 978-1-315-20088-0 (ebk)

Typeset in Bembo
by Taylor & Francis Books

CONTENTS

Acknowledgements   *vi*

1   'Digital health', technology and promise   1

2   'Digital health' and networking of the self   24

3   The emergent algorithmic medicine   44

4   The digital healthcare economy   71

5   'Digital health', its promises and perils   95

References   *120*
Index   *138*

ACKNOWLEDGEMENTS

Many individuals and organizations have offered assistance or support during the preparation of this book. I have been fortunate in securing funding from the Australian Research Council, via two concurrent Discovery Projects (2017–2019), which has allowed relief from undergraduate teaching and time for research and writing. The first project, 'A sociological study of patients' use of digital media' (DP170100402), is undertaken in collaboration with Alison Anderson, Tim Caulfield and Allegra Schermuly, and I would like to thank them for their support and ideas. The second project, 'How do expectations shape testing in healthcare: a sociological study' (DP170100504), is undertaken in collaboration with Di Bowman, Kiran Pienaar and Stephen Derrick, and I would also like to thank them. The ideas for the book developed through various strands of previous work, but especially my research on stem cell tourism, again generously funded by the Australian Research Council (DP120100921), involving a long-standing and highly fruitful collaboration with Megan Munsie, which I would like to acknowledge. Claire Tanner and Casimir MacGregor were also involved in this project as postdoctoral fellows while Jane Brophy was the PhD student, and I thank them for their ideas, enthusiasm and collegiality. I am fortunate in working with wonderful colleagues in the Health and Biofutures Focus Program at Monash University: Mark Davis, Andrea Whittaker, Catherine Mills, John Gardner and Samuel Taylor-Alexander. Through our discussions and program-related events, including a workshop at Prato Monash and a panel of the 4S conference in Sydney, both in 2018, they have helped provide the ideal environment for intellectual work. Finally, as always, I am greatly indebted to Ros Porter, whose love and support has sustained me over the years.

1

'DIGITAL HEALTH', TECHNOLOGY AND PROMISE

'Disruptive', 'revolutionary' and 'transformative' are terms often used by policy-makers, health authorities, scientists and media commentators to describe the predicted implications of the development and applications of digital technologies in the near future. Health, medicine and healthcare, like other spheres of life, are anticipated to undergo rapid, profound change as a consequence of digitalization. This includes changes in how illness and wellness are understood, how medical research is undertaken, how healthcare practitioners are taught, how prevention, treatment and care are undertaken, and how related data is produced, stored and shared. Such change, it is argued, or simply assumed, *will* occur and be for the better. This generally implies more effective and efficient healthcare systems, more engaged and 'empowered' citizens, and greatly improved standards of community health and wellbeing. But are these promises likely to be fulfilled? If so, who will likely benefit and who will be disadvantaged? What are the implications of the growing application of digital technologies in health, medicine and healthcare for our conceptions of self, society and citizenship?

This book offers a sociological perspective on the shifting discourses and practices of 'digital health' (sometimes called 'e-health' or 'health informatics')—a field underpinned by promise and optimism, but accompanied by relatively little critical assessment of its social, economic, political and personal implications. As I explain, the question of what constitutes or could constitute digital health is far from settled. The term has been used variously in different countries and contexts to designate diverse phenomena. However, regardless of how it is defined, digital health tends to be viewed positively, conveying a conception of how health, medicine and healthcare *should* be practised, and of the roles and responsibilities of citizens as either 'consumers' of health; producers of information, products or services; or providers of treatments and care. Digital health designates an imagined medicine and healthcare that is predictive, 'personalized', timely, efficient and effective, and that has the potential, through related innovations, to contribute to economic growth. As I argue in Chapter 3, digital health designates a kind of healthcare that is increasingly *big data-driven*, using artificial intelligence (AI), algorithms and machine learning to undertake healthcare decisions. Digital technologies are seen as the means to facilitate self-responsibility in health by ensuring that citizens play an active role in their own risk management, health monitoring and care and thereby contribute to reducing burgeoning healthcare costs, associated in particular with the rising number of ageing-related chronic conditions. Predictions that personalized (or, increasingly, 'precision') medicine *will* be *the future* of healthcare intensified in the wake of the public announcement of the mapping of the human genome in 2000 (Chapter 3). However, recent developments, especially digital technologies, including AI, machine learning and data science, have led many scientists, policymakers and other influential authorities to suggest that this future may be much closer than many people have envisaged (Chapter 3). Consequently, governments have increased efforts to enhance 'digital literacy' in the population, to develop the necessary physical infrastructure and institutions, and to support programs of related research and development.

More and more governments, businesses and professional bodies have committed to advancing the use of digital technologies in medicine and healthcare. At the international level, many countries and jurisdictions have developed policies related to digital health and have invested in related infrastructure and personnel. Many refer to increasing the scale of digital transformation to enable the delivery of new models of healthcare (e.g. Queensland Government 2017: 27). Further, in policy and program statements, 'patient engagement' and 'community partnerships' figure prominently. In 2005, digital health received endorsement from the World Health Organization (WHO) which adopted a resolution on 'eHealth' that urged Member States to 'consider drawing up a longer-term strategic plan for developing and implementing eHealth services in the various fields of the health sector' (WHO, 2005). It defined e-health as 'the cost-effective and secure use of information and communications technologies in support of health and health-related fields, including health-care services, health surveillance, health literature, and health education, knowledge and research' (ibid.). The resolution called for an 'appropriate legal framework and infrastructure', and encouraged 'public and private partnerships' and efforts to 'reach communities, including vulnerable groups'. The WHO was also keen for Member States to establish and implement national electronic public health information systems and enhance the capacity for surveillance and rapid response to disease and public health emergencies (ibid.). Recent evidence suggests that Member States have responded positively to this call. A WHO survey undertaken in 2015 found that 58 percent of the 125 Member States that responded (of 194 in total) have national policies for e-health (WHO, 2016: 12). Since 2000, the number of countries with e-health policies has increased dramatically (ibid.: 14).

In Australia, the Australian Digital Health Agency was launched in 2016 with the aim of 'putting data and technology safely to work for patients, consumers and the healthcare professionals who look after them' (Australian Digital Health Agency, n.d.a). In a National Digital Health Strategy statement, released in August

2017, it was announced that from 2018 Australians would have to choose to opt out from the national My Health Record, which would increase participation from 20 percent to 98 percent of the population—making it 'the highest participation rate in a national health record system in the world' (ibid.: 10) (Chapter 4). The Agency identified a number of priority outcomes, including making health information 'available whenever and wherever it is needed', enabling health information to be 'exchanged securely', encouraging 'digitally-enabled models of care that drive improved accessibility, quality, safety and efficiency', and nurturing a 'thriving digital health industry' (ibid.: 5–7). The Agency sees both health consumers and providers as being able to access their health information 'at any time online and through mobile apps' (ibid.: 5). This kind of constant connection is central to the emerging future medicine and healthcare that is seen as personalized, timely, effective and more cost-efficient than currently offered (Chapter 3). Other countries likewise have made efforts to advance digital health (or eHealth) and invested in related programs of research and infrastructure, focusing on areas such as the establishment or updating of electronic health records, 'connected care', wearable technologies, big data analytics and predictive screening. The word connected figures prominently in policy statements and suggests the forging of links between citizens, such as patients and their families and health professionals, and between these different communities and various technologies.

This book explores the character of these purported connections and what they mean or may mean in the future for social relations, roles and citizen responsibilities. However, rapid developments in fields such as robotics and AI, and predictions that such technologies will replace or complement existing labour (Chapter 2), make it difficult to anticipate where digitalization is heading and how it will impact on different groups and societies more generally. With suggestions that the 'convergence' of 'technologies' will enable new ways of thinking about health and undertaking healthcare, it has become increasingly difficult to envisage how developments will play out in coming years; however, I discuss some trends and their likely implications (Chapter 5). As I explain in Chapter 2, there have been many predictions over the past five decades or more about automation and robotization and the question needs to be asked, *is this time different?* (Ford, 2016: 29). And, if so, to what extent, and how exactly is this difference manifest?

The book critically appraises a number of common claims about digital health and explores the socio-cultural, politico-economic and personal implications of the enactment of policies, programs and practices associated with digitally based or enabled health, medicine and healthcare. My starting premise is recognition that technologies *are always already social*. That is, what are taken to be technologies, and the ways in which they are conceived, developed and applied, inescapably reflects wider socio-political processes, including the priorities and values of those with particular investments in the future. Further, no matter where and how applied, technologies have socio-political consequences—shaping conceptions of society and social relations, and impacting unevenly on different sections of the population. The term socio-technical is often used to describe this inextricable link and complex interaction between technology and society.

As with many if not most new and emergent fields of technology, digital technologies are widely seen to hold great promise, which has underpinned the high hopes and expectations held by governments, businesses, professionals, investors and many lay citizens. As sociologists and science and technology studies scholars have argued, discourses of promise, hope and expectation play a major role in technological development, as seen in fields such as genetics, nanotechnologies and stem cell treatments (Brown, 2003; Nightingale and Martin, 2004). They are also play a crucial role in marketing healthcare products and services, as I will show. Such discourses may be described as *performative* in the sense of mobilizing actions, including investment decisions, in ways oriented to bringing about particular desired futures. Economists and economic sociologists increasingly have recognized the implications of such discourses in influencing decision-making in markets and whole economies (e.g. MacKenzie et al., 2007). The field of behavioural economics, which is attracting growing attention among scholars and policymakers, acknowledges the role of perceptions on economic activity. The rise of the 'digital economy', including the growth of direct-to-consumer advertising of diverse products and services and clinically unproven medical treatments, has arguably brought to the fore consideration of how representations may shape thinking and action; for example, how advertisers' promissory claims—namely optimistic stories about what products or services will offer—serve to manipulate and deceive consumers (Akerlof and Shiller, 2015). However, as histories of technological developments make clear, events rarely play out in ways imagined. Performativity may fail to produce what is promised—or 'misfire' as Butler (2010) puts it—and futures may unfold in ways unforeseen. Gartner's (2016) 'hype cycle', which charts the key phases of a technology's life cycle, involving peaks of inflated expectations and subsequent troughs of disillusionment that follow when promises fail to materialize, has characterized the development of many if not most fields of technological development. Gartner's hype cycle provides the basis for a whole new field of business of technology research and advice.

This book critically interrogates the claim that digital health will necessarily produce the outcomes or effects described in policy statements and in media depictions. In fact, the history of technology development suggests that, for various reasons, digital health is unlikely to materialize in ways envisaged. There are likely to be unforeseen and unintended consequences of technologies, which will be developed or used in ways unimagined by their designers and proponents (Chapter 5). However, the social and personal implications of efforts to *enact* digital health policies and programs are likely to be far reaching. Belief is a powerful motivator of human actions and has been shown to shape policies and programs in various technological fields in the past—such as genetics, nanotechnologies and stem cell treatments—all fields that I have researched over the past twenty years. As I argue, regardless of whether digital health evolves in ways imagined, related policies and programs are profoundly refashioning conceptions of self, society and citizenship, and impacting on related notions of truth, privacy, trust, rights and responsibilities.

That digitalization in general is reshaping conceptions of self, society and citizenship is evident in various areas of discourse and practice, including:

- interpersonal communications, where it has been noted that conversation is increasingly being substituted by electronic connection (Turkle, 2015);
- civil society and politics, where established forms of civic engagement and political activism are to some extent being replaced by 'slacktivism' (that is, citizens gaining a sense of doing something without making a substantial commitment) (Penny, 2017);
- business and policy making, with heightened concerns about cybersecurity (Lucas, 2015) including the hacking of personal (e.g. health) information (Chokshi, 2016);
- media and community debates, including about 'fake news' (Price, 2016), Facebook's and Google's tracking of users' web browsing activity (Solon, 2017), and 'sexploitation' and revenge porn; and
- patient activism, where individuals are playing an active role in shaping their futures by using the internet and social media to forge communities, share stories, raise funds for research, lobby for changes in policies, and gain access to clinically unproven treatments otherwise unavailable to them (Petersen et al., 2017).

Citizens' capacity to create their own content using the internet and social media—sometimes dubbed Web 2.0—has been associated with the purported decline of trust in mainstream media, as well as the failure of media commentators and electoral pundits to predict events such as Brexit in the UK and the outcome of the US elections (Sunstein, 2018). Individuals no longer necessarily defer to credentialed experts and expertise and established notions of truth. This has led some media and academic commentators to suggest that contemporary societies have moved to a 'post-truth' and 'post-trust' era (Baird, 2016).

In 2016, Oxford Dictionaries announced its Word of the Year 2016 was 'post-truth'—which it defined as 'relating to or denoting circumstances in which objective facts are less influential in shaping public opinion than appeals to emotion and personal belief' (Oxford Dictionaries, 2016). In its announcement, Oxford Dictionaries noted 'the word spiking in frequency this year in the context of the Brexit referendum in the UK and the presidential election in the US', and that '*Post-truth* has gone from being a peripheral term to being a mainstay in political commentary, now often being used by major publications without the need for clarification or definition in their headlines.' (ibid.) However, while growing digital media use has been associated with the erosion of truth, these same media provide the source of the data that is increasingly mined for various purposes via the use of tools such as Google Trends, Google AdWords and Google Ngram. In his book *Everybody Lies: What the Internet Can Tell Us About Who We Really Are*, Stephens-Davidowitz (2017) argues that these tools can reveal citizens' innermost secrets and information on such matters as racism, sexual practices, political intentions, sporting potential, and emotional and physical health. Stephen-Davidowitz's bold prediction is that the resulting big data will create a 'social science revolution' (ibid.: 273).

In the following chapters, I explore how digital media are shaping notions of fact, evidence, truth and trustworthiness, and of the role of emotions and personal beliefs in this context, and how the blurring of the line between truth and falsity and fact and fiction serves, intentionally or not, the interests of those seeking to profit from the application of digital technologies in health and healthcare. I step back from current debates about the purported disruptions or transformations wrought by digitalization, whether to the economy, healthcare or interpersonal communications, to take a critical perspective on digital health and its representations and implications. Specifically, I examine the socio-cultural and politico-economic contexts within which digital health has become salient, and in which digital technologies are ascribed value and find applications. I explore questions such as: What conceptions of self and citizenship are assumed by digital health initiatives? Will efforts to realize visions of digitally enabled or enhanced medicine and healthcare reinforce existing inequalities, or create new ones? What personal and interpersonal imperatives are implied by digital technologies and the development of related infrastructures such as electronic health record systems? How is knowledge being shaped by the growing reliance on data analytics for policies and decisions in medicine and healthcare?

A significant question for sociology is how digitalization is shaping the discipline itself and its ways of understanding the social. Sociologists frequently describe their discipline in terms of its capacity to debunk or demystify taken-for-granted assumptions about society. However, we are living in an era in which 'the social' itself and established ways of understanding are increasingly questioned. There are many schools of thought about the proper focus of sociology, many of which can be drawn upon to help make sense of digital health and its consequences; however, the discipline as a whole has been indelibly shaped by *modernist* conceptions of society mostly forged before the era of the internet and social media. As with other social science disciplines, such as anthropology and economics, sociology is largely oriented to documenting and explaining past events, and thus constitutes a *retrospective* rather than a prospective form of knowledge that offers insights into events as they unfold or are likely to unfold. Although encompassing a diverse array of perspectives, founded on different theories of knowledge, sociology is generally *diagnostic* in its orientation to the social, with a strong attachment to suffering; that is, analysing the conditions that give rise to inequalities, that limit human agency, that give rise to disease, that shorten lifespans, and so on. In this orientation, the discipline has failed to capture the social dynamics of knowledge production and the ever-shifting relations between knowledge and power (Miyazaki, 2004). For sociologists, shifting the focus from generating retrospective knowledge to developing prospective knowledge, and considering what this might entail for their research and action agendas, is challenging both conceptually and methodologically. What does such a shift entail in practice? What methods are appropriate for generating such knowledge? And, what might the implications be for social action and intervention?

While there is no straightforward answer to any of the above questions, I suggest that the rudiments for a new kind of sociology—one that is reflexive (self-questioning), and attentive to history and biography—is to be found in the work of seminal figures such as Karl Marx, Pierre Bourdieu and Michel Foucault, and their followers. Also useful in this regard are the writings of theorists such as Marshall McLuhan, Erich Fromm and Manuel Castells, who have written about and offered predictions in regard to techno-logical developments, especially electronic communication technologies, and their implications (Chapter 2). Contemporary sociology, I would suggest, has often been inattentive to history, despite its purported founders being either historians (e.g. Max Weber) or using historical methods in their work (Karl Marx). However, a socio-historical approach is urgently needed to make sense of digital and other technological developments, especially in understanding how questions of power and politics shape decisions. It is here that the work of the French philosopher and historian Michel Foucault is especially useful.

As Foucault observed many years ago, and long before the rise of the internet, there is an extricable link between knowledge and power, and discourse and practice. Using a particular historical perspective and method, namely genealogy, applied to areas such as medicine, crime and punishment, and sexuality, he revealed how discourses and practices reflect the workings of politics and power; for example, the shift from sovereign power, exercised by the king, to disciplinary power, represented in the penal system and other methods of controlling bodies and minds. His later work on governmentality highlighted the 'rationalities' by which humans govern themselves and others. This work has proved invaluable in analyses of the workings of neoliberal politics and power (e.g. Rose, 1999). The rise of the internet has enabled the development of previously unforeseen possibi-lities for reconstituting knowledge-power and governance, and for surveillance and control, including over life itself, and thus can be considered as integral to the workings of contemporary 'biopolitics' as articulated by Michel Foucault in a series of lectures delivered in 1978 and 1979 (Senellart, 2008). The 'Internet of Things', which envisages the linking of diverse devices, objects and people, may, if predic-tions are to be believed, enable new ways for people to connect and to achieve certain health and wellbeing outcomes—ones that are in accordance with ascribed ideals of healthy living and citizenship. Further, digitalization promises the collec-tion and analysis of health and medical data across whole populations—so-called big data analytics—including current health status, physical fitness, and engagement in health-promoting activities (e.g. exercise, eating patterns), offering new means for educating, surveilling and governing citizens, for monitoring behaviours and marketing health products and services. Personalized (or precision) medicine, which is based on whole-genome sequencing and aims to tailor or customize medicines to individuals based upon their genetic profiles, is one area where digital technologies are predicted to have their most immediate and far-reaching impacts (Chapter 3). Digitalization enables information otherwise deemed to be valueless to achieve value, namely to enable prediction and hence risk manage-ment or treatment. Digital health initiatives are oriented to citizens who are assumed to be willing and able to use the internet and other technologies to play an active role in the project of advancing health, and will strive to align their personal goals (for appearance, wellbeing) with wider social ideals such as eco-nomic growth and efficiency.

Developments in various technology fields, but especially biotechnologies (including genetics, stem cell technologies and neurotechnologies) and information and communication technologies, are converging in ways that are seen to effect a fundamental shift in conceptions of health, medicine and healthcare, involving citizens' active efforts to prevent illness and undertake treatment and care. This includes the use of wearable technologies to monitor and collect data on one's bodily functions that can be linked with other data, derived from medical records and potentially other sources, to allow diagnosis and personalized treatment or lifestyle management (Chapters 3 and 4). The term _bio-digital citizenship_, I suggest, usefully captures the forms of responsibility characterizing the recent mutation of healthy citizenship (Petersen et al., 2010), involving the intertwining of bio-based and digitally based identities, knowledge and practices. I also examine the related institutions and practices that have emerged or are emerging to enable this citizenship. In this chapter and those that follow, I begin to elaborate the historical background and contemporary context to these developments, whose implications, while potentially profound, are likely to be of a character very different from those envisaged.

This chapter begins by charting the rise of digital health, which tends to be either broadly defined or left undefined but is imbued with positive connotations, which I discuss. It introduces the key terms, theories and concepts that guide my argument and considers how these may help us understand recent manifestations and implications of digital health-related policies, programs and practices. My analysis is guided by a particular approach that I have developed through previous work, bringing together insights from diverse fields of research, including in the sociology of health and medicine, science and technology studies, gender studies, the sociology of the body, the sociology of risk and the sociology of emotions. In this work, which draws especially (although not exclusively) on the work of Michel Foucault, I have sought to cast light on the workings of politics and power, and related forms of governance, evident in many contemporary societies, broadly described as neoliberalism. While there has been considerable debate about the utility of the term neoliberalism, which is often used (and arguably overused) as a 'catch all' for what is in reality a diverse range of policies, programs and strategies, it describes well a general governing philosophy or 'rationality of rule' and related practical strategies that have found growing application in many contemporary societies. The neoliberal philosophy accords the market a primary role in meeting human needs, and prioritizes a particular form of reasoning, involving reference to competitive processes, small government, and individual volition, choice and accountability. These latter aspects are conveyed by the term 'responsibilization', that is, ascribing individuals' responsibility for a task or action that would previously have been undertaken by a state agency, such as a health department, or would not have been recognized as a responsibility at all (O'Malley, 2009).

Neoliberal rule relies heavily on techniques of governance involving forms of expertise, notably psychology, oriented to shaping individual subjectivity in specific ways, to make individuals responsible for self-care, including in health, education, financial security and other matters. As I have argued previously (Petersen, 2004), the emotions have become a key site for contemporary governance, and authorities have sought to guide choices and behaviours through the deployment of various 'nudges', using techniques developed in behavioural psychology and positive psychology. The philosophy is one of 'libertarian paternalism', whereby individuals should be free to do as they wish but it is also legitimate for authorities ('choice architects') to guide individuals in ways that will advance their health and longevity (Thaler and Sunstein, 2009). I examine some practical applications of libertarian paternalism in specific digital health initiatives, such as electronic health record systems (Chapter 4) and the architecture of the internet itself (Chapter 2).

As I will argue, the development and application of digital technologies, like all technologies, inevitably involves the generation or reinforcement of economic and social inequalities, a point that is rarely acknowledged in discussions about technological impacts, which are mostly imbued with optimism (Chapter 2). The history of the development of technologies has been shaped by a discourse of progress and improvement—the notion that things can always be done in a better way (Friedl, 2007). Some histories of technology development draw an analogy with Darwinian evolution, equating technologies with species and inventions with variations or mutations, and assume that societies determine which innovations are worthy of surviving and reproducing (ibid.: 10). The use of this analogy obscures the workings of politics and power; the creation of winners and losers from a particular distribution of economic and social resources; and the construction of histories as teleological, with events seen as inevitable and serving some ultimate purpose. I emphasize the ways in which expert knowledge and expertise, such as economics, psychology and marketing, are employed to advance digital health initiatives. Before proceeding further, however, I should clarify how digital health is conceived. While the term is often left undefined or only broadly defined in discussions, as noted, it is replete with mostly positive connotations.

The concept of digital health

The term digital health itself is historically recent, but its use has grown exponentially since 1990 according to the number of Google Scholar citations using this term over the period. The term digital health is sometimes used to describe what some commentators would consider to be part of e-health or 'bioinformatics'. However, these terms are also used in multiple ways. Whereas there were 99,300 references to digital health between 1990 and 1995, this had burgeoned to 1,600,000 references between 2005 and 2015. However, an increase in references to the term digital health tells us nothing about its meanings and applications. Digital health may be conceived or defined narrowly in terms of one domain of application, such as electronic health records, or widely to encompass a vast range of concepts and technologies, such as telehealth and telemedicine, personalized medicine, medical imaging, e-health and e-patient, mobile health, wearable computing, connected health, and health information technology.

The Australian Digital Health Agency offers a definition of digital health in its 2016–2017 Corporate Plan, to include the adoption of technology in healthcare and related concepts (e.g. eHealth, health IT, clinical and corporate information systems, telehealth) and infrastructure, along with 'mobile devices and applications, the way these are used, and the integrity and security of information that they capture, store, share, communicate and display' (Australian Digital Health Agency, n.d.b: 8). This definition is broad, encompassing technologies and modes of their use, related concepts and issues of security. References to 'integrity and security of information' are understandable in a context of growing concerns about identify theft and public access to personal data that are an inevitable component of patient healthcare records. I discuss this issue in more detail in later chapters, especially Chapter 5. In Australia, in recent years there have been reports of personal information being inadvertently released by authorities, such as the Red Cross, which unintentionally published the personal details, including the names, contact details, birthdates and medical details, of 550,000 Australian blood donors (Dudley-Nicholson, 2016).

In the early period of its operations, the Australian Digital Health Agency has focused strongly on the establishment of the national electronic health record system (My Health Record), a process that had stalled under its predecessor, the National Electronic Health Transition Authority, originally established in 2005 as a collaboration of the Australian Government and the State and Territory governments to establish the foundations for electronic health (eHealth) (Bajkowski, 2014). As in the UK and other countries, digital health, e-health or health informatics is seen to hold great promise for improving both standards of health, especially in establishing and maintaining an electronic health record of patients' medical histories as they move between different parts of the complex healthcare system, and economic efficiency. However, concerns among healthcare professionals and lay citizens about privacy and other issues have made this difficult in practice (Chapter 4).

The US Department of Health and Human Services has articulated a more detailed conception of and rationale for digital health. On the website of its Food and Drug Administration (FDA), it lists 'mobile health (mHealth), health information technology (IT), wearable devices, telehealth and telemedicine, and personalized medicine' within the 'broad scope of digital health' (US Food and Drug Administration, n.d.). The description goes on to note the benefits, which highlight economic efficiencies, access and quality issues, and personalization. Further, it is noted that 'The use of technologies such as smart phones, social networks and internet applications is not only changing the way we communicate, but is also providing innovative ways for us to monitor our health and well-being and giving us greater access to information.' From this and other descriptions on the webpage, it is evident that the FDA foresees digital health as encompassing applications enabled by converging technological developments in health, which are listed (e.g. wireless medical devices, mobile health apps, health IT, telemedicine), along with various stakeholders who are involved, 'including patients, healthcare practitioners, researchers, traditional medical device industry firms, and firms new to FDA regulatory requirements, such as mobile application developers' (ibid.).

In the UK, digital technologies are central to the future vision of the National Health Service (NHS). This is evident from its dedicated NHS Digital agency, established by an Act of Parliament in 2012, which is oriented to 'making better use of technology, data and information'; and the NHS's *Next Steps on the NHS Five Year Forward View* (National Health Service, 2017), which makes a number of references to the role of digital technologies in future healthcare. The latter report announces, among various initiatives, the establishment of an 'NHS Digital Academy' to 'train a new generation of Chief Information Officers and Chief Clinical Information Officers' so as to 'increase the chances of successful adoption of new information technology and its use to drive quality and efficiency', and a new 'online digital service … that will connect patients to their integrated Urgent Care via NHS 111' (ibid.). In 2018, the NHS released what it describes as a 'new digital roadmap' that outlines a number of major objectives in this area that are planned to be delivered by 2019–20. This includes the 'Citizen ID' project that is intended to facilitate access to patient records and online health services. The NHS is also planning to publish personal health record guidelines for local organizations to ensure that they are 'as high quality and connectable as possible' (National Health Service, 2018). The web blurb for this roadmap explains that the aim is to 'empower people to take control of their health and care through secure online access to clinicians, personalised and relevant health information, digital tools and advice that helps them to better manage their conditions' (ibid.). One of the stated goals is to create the Citizen ID; that is, an 'identity verification system that "will provide people with a simple log in for local and national NHS online services"' (Evenstad, 2018).

Digital health has also captured the imagination of marketers, established entrepreneurs and start-ups within particular cities or regions using the term as a means to market their city's or region's competitive edge, building on existing networks, hubs and expertise. For example, Digital Health London, a collaboration between three London Academic Health Science Networks, the Health Innovation Network, the Mayor of London, and two university–NHS collaborative ventures, describes its objectives in the following way: 'creating and supporting networks to build on London's existing mass of digital health expertise' and 'supporting the collaborative development of an environment that both meets the needs of the health system and allows businesses to develop, by tacking issues such as procurement and commissioning' (UCL Partners, 2018). Similarly, the City of Bradford Metropolitan District Council, UK, has partnered with the Department for Business, Innovation and Skills, BT, University of Bradford, and Digital Catapult Centre, to utilize digital technologies to develop the regional health economy and, it is claimed, 'make a significant contribution to the NHS, helping to reduce its funding gap of £30 billion by 2020' (Digital Health Enterprise Zone, n.d.). These initiatives are strongly steeped in the language of enterprise and innovation, and seek to establish a bridge between the worlds of business, government and the university. They reflect the optimism surrounding new digital technologies in delivering improved health and in creating new economic opportunities. This is not to say that digital health has been applied only to ventures that involve value creation and the delivery of medical treatments. Digital health has also been linked to the advancement of social inclusion and the reduction of health inequalities, which is evident in some NHS statements (National Health Service, 2016), although this is far less prominent. There exist various conceptions of digital health, which are shaped by national, regional and local healthcare priorities, but all are underpinned by a vision of what digital technologies can and in time *will* deliver. In short, digital health has become a signifier of an imagined future networked or connected health, medicine and healthcare, which transcends constraints of time and place, enabling human life to be more thoroughly monitored and health to be more economically exploited than in the past.

That this vision is widely shared is seen not just in national initiatives such as those described, but in transnational collaborations such as the New Global Digital Health Partnership, launched in February 2018. The media release announcing this initiative described it as 'a new global network to support best use of digital technology in modern healthcare' (Australian Digital Health Agency, 2018). The stated aims of the network are to 'collaborate on connected and interoperable healthcare', 'cybersecurity', 'policies that support digital health outcomes', 'clinician and consumer engagement', and 'evidence and evaluation of digital health' (ibid.). The Chief Executive Officer of the Australian Digital Health Agency, Tim Kelsey, was cited thus: 'Australia and its international partners can learn from each other and share information about what has worked in their health settings, and collaborate on initiatives together that will support digital health systems working more effectively in their countries' (ibid.).

One of the ways in which partners are able to learn is through specialized digital health publications, especially electronic newsletters distributed to interested individuals and organizations, and forums where developments are discussed. A number of publications now exist and are regularly updated, including *digitalhealth, Healthcare IT* and *Digital Health Age*. In addition, digital health has been the focus of international conferences, for example those of the Health Information and Management Systems Society (HIMSS), and exhibitions organized by the medical technology sector such as Medtec Live. The field has also given rise to opportunities in marketing research, such as the *Digital Health 2018: Trends, Opportunities and Outlook* report (Baers, 2018), which sells in electronic and hardcopy forms for up to US$7,500 depending on the number of users. Health informatics groups provide online resources to assist in distributing information about digital health, including links to blogs, commentaries, newsletters, associations, journals and news items (e.g. Health Informatics Society of Australia, n.d.).

Connecting bodies of knowledge with knowledge of bodies

Digitalization is seen to make information more accessible and thereby improve health and empower citizens. The promise is that by connecting specific bodies of knowledge with particular knowledge of bodies via big data, it will be possible to forge new understanding of health, risk, illness and care; in other words, to gain enhanced control over life itself. As I explain in Chapters 3 and 4, while this big data may include various types of information, such as on citizens' levels of physical activity, dietary practices and prescribing habits, in many countries biological data and especially genetic data is seen to hold most promise—reflecting a predominant genetic conception of health that prevails in the biosciences and biomedicine (Petersen, 2006). This reinforces a bias in health knowledge that both has inequitable effects and is vastly wasteful of healthcare resources (Chapter 3). However, while digital health is unlikely to deliver much of what is promised, as I discuss in Chapter 5, related policies and programs are having significant material effects in shaping social institutions, relations and roles, and consequently how health, illness and care are conceived and practiced. Investment in new digital platforms and expertise serves to lock in certain technological paths, and related inequalities, with some groups more advantaged than others in the emerging digital healthcare economy (Chapter 4). As with virtually all technologies, there will be winners and losers from the pursuit of policies and programs related to digital health, regardless of how developments play out in the future. In the following chapters I identify some of these groups and explain why they are likely to be differently positioned in the future healthcare economy.

Utopian and dystopian visions of digitalization

As noted, digital health is in general surrounded with great promise and optimism. However, in common with other new and emerging technologies, media and other public representations of digital technologies involve a mixture of optimistic/utopian and fearful/dystopian visions, and associated imagery and metaphors, which powerfully shape public and policy responses to particular developments. These competing visions can be seen in news reports on the applications of digital technologies, as well as expert predictions of future digital innovations (Chapter 2). In business news, it is common to see predictions of how digital technologies have the potential to positively transform how business is undertaken, including how healthcare is delivered, alongside other articles acknowledging significant and seemingly insurmountable issues of security. For example, a series of news articles published in *The Australian Financial Review* in 2017 on 'digitalizing government services' discussed issues such as how digital technologies will enhance consumer choice and enable individuals to compare prices of health services (Sherbon, 2017: 41), and how data analytics will assist both GPs and insurance companies to 'predict if someone's going to be hospitalized in the next two years', thereby advancing efforts to 'provide better patient care more efficiently' (Maguire, 2017: 41). However, another article in the same issue notes that 'most of the software companies cannot really guarantee our data's security', and cites a report from *The Economist* magazine referring to a list of 'data breaches in the last year alone including cyber thieves robbing the central bank of Bangladesh and Russian hackers interfering with the US elections' (Eggleton, 2017: 26). Concerns about cybersecurity have grown in prominence in recent years, in light of ransomware attacks (e.g. WannaCry in 2017) and evidence of phishing and hacking, as reported in various news media, and provide the context for health authorities' and technology companies' repeated assurances that they can be entrusted to secure citizens' health data.

Articles such as these are but part of a much longer history of competing utopian and dystopian visions of technological development, which can be found in popular cultural media and in social science and philosophical writings. Such images have been evident, for example, in news media reporting on genetics and medicine in the print news media, including articles published in the aftermath of the cloning of Dolly the sheep, which revealed widespread fears that humans would soon be replicated (Petersen, 2001, 2002). They have also been evident in news reporting and other popular media portrayals of nanotechnologies and the potential for self-replicating 'nano-bots' (Anderson et al., 2009). While bioscience and biotechnology have been rich sources for such imagery, given the ever-present fears of the consequences of 'tampering with nature'—visions of Mary Shelly's *Frankenstein* loom large—such images are evident to varying degrees in relation to many, if not most, new and emerging technologies, since the implications cannot be foreseen and thus controlled. Imagination and fear thrive in a context of uncertainty. However, as noted, technological developments rarely play out in ways imagined.

There is perhaps no clearer example of this than the internet and, more recently, social media. These technologies have profoundly shaped social relations in ways not envisaged by their founders. While the rise of internet has been enabled by various politico-economic and socio-cultural factors, like many areas of technological innovation, the guiding conception of a networked society (Castells, 2010 [1996]); Chapter 2) and a 'self-correcting information system' can be traced to the demands of warfare, specifically the Second World War, and military research (Keen, 2015: 14–21). Also, like other areas of technological development, the internet has been underpinned by technological optimism: namely the premise that a network of 'intelligent links' and the 'coupling of human brains and computing machines' will advance human welfare and security (ibid.: 18–20). Concerns about the vulnerability of the US's long-distance networks, heightened during the Cold War of the 1950s and 1960s, provided substantial impetus for investment in the development of digital technologies of communication, and in particular for the purported forerunner of the internet, ARPANET, which went live in 1969 (ibid.: 21–24). However, it was the embodiment of the idea of a 'single global information space' via the World Wide Web browser, launched by Tim Berners-Lee in 1990, that helped give form to the internet as a universal tool and heralded the birth of the 'Networked Computer Age' (ibid.: 30–32).

While, as Keen (ibid.) observes, Tim Berners-Lee was not motivated by money, and many like him saw the development of the World Wide Web as a means for enhancing national security and advancing civic goals such as democratizing knowledge, it signalled the beginnings of a new period of history dominated by transnational companies such as Google, Amazon and Facebook, and millions of new websites and businesses that were able to exploit the opportunities to create profit, especially via the scaling up of markets and the reinforcement of winner-takes-all economies associated with monopolization. It has generated new economic and social inequalities, arising from and manifest in the 'digital divide'—those who have access to and are able to utilize technologies and those who do not—as well as new kinds of surveillance.

Recently, Berners-Lee is reported to have expressed his alarm in relation the World Wide Web, including the compromising of personal data and the spread of 'fake news'. As he is quoted in one article (Swartz, 2017: 9), 'Even in countries where we believe governments have citizens' best interests at heart, watching everyone, all the time is simply going too far', in apparent reference to 'WikiLeaks' disclosure of what documents claim is a vast CIA surveillance operation.' According to Swartz, such surveillance 'creates a chilling effect on free speech and stops the web from being used as a space to explore important topics, like sensitive health issues, sexuality or religion' (ibid.). The co-founder of Twitter, Evan Williams, has also expressed disillusionment with the internet, especially in regard to its 'role in Mr Trump's populist rise', which he is reported to have said is 'a very bad thing' (Howard and Gorwa, 2017: 8). In Williams' view, 'the internet is obviously "broken" because it rewards extremes' and he admitted that he 'was wrong thinking that the world would be a better place if there was a platform for everyone to freely speak and exchange ideas' (ibid.: 8). Other internet and social media sceptics have also documented the problems of digital media, especially the dominance of big technology companies such as Google, Facebook and Amazon (Chapter 5). In light of its evident problems, some scholars have called for 'reimagining' the internet from the perspective of those who are currently marginal, so as to create a more democratic and egalitarian society (e.g. Srinivasan and Fish, 2017).

Promotion of the idea of the digital network

While there have been growing concerns about and critiques of digitalization in general, especially regarding the sharing, and potential threats to the security, of personal information via hacking, internet theft and cyber attacks, the promotion of the idea that the digital network is a public good has some powerful backers. These include, notably, the World Economic Forum, which hosts widely publicized annual meetings and is involved in various digital technology initiatives related to its stated mission of 'improving the state of the world' and advancing its goal of being 'The International Organization for Public–Private Cooperation' (World Economic Forum, 2016). The self-described non-partisan World Economic Forum brings together world leaders from different sectors, including governments, non-government organizations and universities, with the aim of addressing pressing social issues and problems such as food security, energy security, gender inequalities and health inequalities. Because the Forum is so well regarded and influential at the global level among leaders representing governments and influential groups, its vision of the future of digital technologies in health deserves serious consideration.

Among the Forum's many 'System Initiatives', digitalization figures prominently. These include, notably, the promotion of the 'digital economy and society', among which health is one of the six industries identified. As outlined on its webpage, digital technologies are ascribed a 'central role' in the future transformation of healthcare, which is needed 'to deliver continued improvements to the world's health' (World Economic Forum, n.d.). The Forum outlines a number of 'pressures facing healthcare systems', including the 'Economic cost burden' (with figures cited showing a growth in spending relative to GDP for various countries, especially Northern America and Western Europe); 'Ageing populations' (a trend evident in richer countries for some time, but increasingly evident in emerging economies); 'Increased incidence of chronic disease', and the 'Unsustainable cost of healthcare' (chronic diseases contribute to the overwhelming proportion of costs, with 'just 5% of patients driv[ing] almost half (49%) of cost') (ibid.). The Forum offers a portrayal of 'the healthcare system of the future', whereby digital technologies would 'revolutionize diagnosis and treatment' and effect 'a shift in focus to prevention and management'. In this vision, citizens would become less reliant on healthcare services and take a greater responsibility for managing their own health and care. 'Self-care and monitoring of vital signs' would provide the means to continuously track an individual's health. And, 'If needed, a virtual care consultation could be arranged, so that citizens could receive medical advice without leaving their homes.' In the event that individuals need medical care, 'the treatment plan would be personalized for each individual, maximizing the chances of a successful outcome' (ibid.).

The description then offers a future 'virtual care' scenario, which 'connects clinicians, patients, family members and health professionals in real time to provide health services, promote professional collaboration, support self-management and coordinate care.' This is followed by references to health and cost savings for patients and insurers, and the benefits for 'the younger generation, who are used to the convenience of apps such as Uber [and] put value in services that offer them the chance to get personalized medical advice without having to travel to a clinic.' It sees a 'future of health' where 'the pervasive and seamless use of apps and con-nected devices could transform both the patient's experience and the healthcare industry itself.' Examples cited in its detailed future scenario include the continuous monitoring of health, retail clinics, connected homes whereby individuals' health information can be 'enriched with insights to help simplify decisions and actions', and 'intelligent machines' that enable 'transparent, real-time updates on people's relevant data [which will] allow virtual health teams to refine treatment and improve outcomes for their patients' (ibid.). Finally, the Forum identifies four 'Digital themes' that are expected to be 'especially important as the industry moves towards a fully digital healthcare system over the next decade'; namely 'Smart care' ('Patient outcomes will be improved and the cost of healthcare reduced, by using precision medicine, robots and medical printing'); 'Care anywhere' ('Healthcare will move closer to the home through advances in the connected home and virtual care, which will also help broaden access, especially in maturing economies'); 'Empowered care' ('Through the development of "'living services'", empowered care initiatives will enable citizens to take a more active role in managing their own well-being and healthcare'); and 'Intelligent health enterprises' ('Data-driven solutions will enable healthcare workers and their enterprises to maximize their efficiency and allow patient health to be monitored more effectively in real time') (ibid.). The 'recommendations for business and other stakeholders' is evidently a sales pitch, highlighting the potential to bridge 'the gap between the digital and the physical worlds', connectivity, and 'better health outcomes at lower cost, coupled with convenience and a better consumer experience'. Some final comments in its recommendations section include the promise:

> Today, delivering consumer health outcomes offers a distinct competitive advantage; in a few years, it will become a catalyst for transformation. Beyond that, it will be nothing less than a strategy for survival.
>
> (ibid.)

These sentiments, which are common in the policy statements and reports of governments and supranational bodies such as the World Economic Forum, reveal a techno-utopian vision; that is, belief that technology *will* provide the path to a better, more democratic future. As can be seen in the above description, citizen/consumer empowerment figures prominently, as in the references to citizens taking 'a more active role in managing their own well-being and healthcare' and 'delivering consumer health outcomes'. It is a significant promise, and one that is unlikely to be fulfilled since, as noted, the internet that provides the platform for such a future has already been colonized by big data analytics companies, along with smaller operations, that aim to profit from the communicative opportunities provided by an electronically networked world.

The scenario painted by the World Economic Forum is but one of numerous optimistic portrayals of the role of digital technologies in future health, medicine and healthcare (Chapter 2). This particular version, like many others, reflects a technologically determinist perspective on digitalization: technologies are seen as the sole or single factor determining social arrangements and outcomes, and are objectified and abstracted from their socio-cultural and politico-economic contexts. In this case, digital technologies are seen as external tools that will assist humans to shape their world, it is presumed for the better. Other technologically determinist visions foretell a future where digital technologies *merge* with humans to create a new hybridity, the cyborg, which has been much discussed and popularized by Donna Haraway (1991, 1999). The history of the idea of the cyborg, like that of the internet, is tied up with military ambitions—in this case, the US Air Force-sponsored space program. However, according to Andy Pickering, 'a whole range of cyborg sciences were born in World War Two' which began to unsettle the boundary between the human and the non-human, of which the electronic computer was paradigmatic (Pickering, 2002: 19). The term 'cyborg', which involves the fusing of cybernetic and organism, was introduced by Manfred Clynes for a NASA conference exploring the modification of human life in space, and then discussed in a paper subsequently co-authored in 1960 with Nathan Kline, a psychiatrist and expert in psychotropic drugs (Gray, 2002: 18). The authors envisaged that humans could be modified with implants and drugs to enable them to exist in space without space suits. It is interesting to observe that, while human modification for space travel has yet to occur, at least as imagined by Clynes and Kline, aspects of the cyborg vision have arguably materialized via the 'always wired' connections that citizens have established with mobile devices such as smartphones, tablets and laptops (Chapter 3).

The question of how this connection has impacted or is likely to impact on the concept of the human—and whether we are entering a 'post-human' world—has been the subject of numerous discussions among policymakers, academics and sections of the media, especially in regard to the 'Fourth Industrial Revolution'.

The Fourth Industrial Revolution

According to Klaus Schwab, founder and Executive Chairman of the World Economic Forum, hybridization, or the conjoining of humans and machines, will characterize the Fourth Industrial Revolution. The topic for discussion at the 2016 Forum Annual Meeting in Davos, Switzerland, the Fourth Industrial Revolution captures the momentous change foreseen in technological development and the spread of ideas around the world, occasioned by the fusion of technologies including quantum computing, nanotechnologies and renewables, and their interactions with the physical, digital and biological spheres. As Schwab argues, it is this fusion that will make the Fourth Industrial Revolution 'fundamentally different from previous revolutions' (Schwab, 2017: 8). As Schwab predicts in the introduction of his book on this topic,

> The premise … is that technology and digitalization will revolutionise everything, making the overused and often ill-used adage 'this time is different' apt. Simply put, major technological innovations are on the brink of fuelling momentous change throughout the world—inevitably so.
>
> (ibid.: 9)

As Schwab goes on to argue, it is beginning to be recognized that society is on the verge of 'radical systemic change' requiring constant adaptation and a growing polarization between 'those who embrace change versus those who resist it' (ibid.: 97). Schwab seems to be suggesting here a future digital divide comprising the adapters/adopters and the resisters, respectively, which other writers also foresee with increasing digitalization. (In Chapter 5 I discuss some contemporary examples of resistance to digital technologies.) In his book, Schwab describes a number of 'technology shifts' and 'tipping points' when technological developments are likely to occur or fully mature. These include technologies already in development, such as the wearable internet, the Internet of Things, 3D printing and manufacture, and driverless cars. According to Schwab, there are different drivers and aspects to the Fourth Industrial Revolution that distinguish it from the earlier three revolutions; namely, the first, 'from about 1760 to around 1840', the age of mechanical production involving the construction of railroads and the invention of the steam engine; the second, commencing in the late nineteenth century and into the early twentieth century, the age of mass production; and the third, beginning in the 1960s, the computer or digital revolution, which encompasses the invention of semi-conductors, the construction of mainframe computers (1960s), personal computers (1970s and 1980s) and the internet (1990s) (ibid.: 6–7). In Schwab's view, the scale and scope of the Fourth Industrial Revolution will be momentous since it will involve automation and robotization, and 'a growing harmonization and integration of so many different disciplines and discoveries' (ibid.: 10). His predictions extend to health and medicine, with the suggestion that knowledge of genetics derived from 'increasing amounts of data will make precision medicine possible, enabling the development of highly targeted therapies to improve treatment outcomes' (ibid.: 21–22). In addition, 3D manufacturing; new devices, including neurotechnologies, that 'monitor our activity levels and blood chemistry, and how all this links to wellbeing, mental health and productivity at home and at work'; and 'designer babies ... who possess particular traits or who are resistant to a specific disease' are some of the health applications envisaged (ibid.: 22–23).

In some respects, Schwab's predictions are not new, since the idea of precision medicine or personalized medicine, whereby practices and products are oriented to the individual patient based upon their genetic and risk profile, and of designer babies, have been part of the scientific and popular cultural imagination for some decades. The idea of personalized medicine gained some momentum in the lead-up to, and especially since, the public announcement of the completion of the mapping of the humane genome in 2000. Aldous Huxley depicted designer babies in his classic science fictional novel *Brave New World*, published in 1932. In that book, Huxley describes a world where science is used to improve the quality of life and achieve universal happiness (Huxley, 1955 [1932]: 17). The idea of the manufactured life portrayed in this book has indeed already become a reality with in vitro fertilization, and informs the imagination of regenerative medicine using stem cell-based treatment to regenerate diseased and disabled bodies. Further, the apparent growing public acceptability of, and pressure for, public funding of pre-implantation genetic diagnosis, to screen embryos for hundreds of genetic abnormalities and thus accomplish what is described by Browne (2017) as 'the ultimate in preventive treatment', suggests that the idea of designer babies is perhaps closer than many people imagine. Schwab, however, offers a degree of specificity that predictions often lack. For example, drawing on data from a 2015 survey involving '800 executives and experts from the information and communications technology sector', he identifies tipping points that are expected to occur by 2025. These are 'moments when specific technological shifts hit mainstream society—that will shape our future digital and hyper-connected world' (Schwab, 2017: 25–26). The tipping points upon which the survey received very high agreement included '10% of people wearing clothes connected to the internet', '1 trillion sensors connected to the internet', 'The first robotic pharmacist in the US', and '10% of reading glasses connected to the internet' (ibid.: 26).

What is noteworthy about Schwab's predictions and other similar scenarios is that, although they present a complex picture of the anticipated interactions between humans, machines and the biophysical environment, and the likely outcomes—which are presented as mostly positive for society and individuals—they are based on the premise that technologies are the fundamental drivers of change. Like all predictions, they project past events and actions into the future, revealing a linear view of technological 'progress'. In the same way that road authorities plan roads based on past vehicle use, the scenario suggests that developments will inevitably play out in ways consistent with past trends, and that policies and actions will need to be aligned in ways that prepare citizens for the imagined future scenario. What is left out of the analysis is consideration of the workings of politics and power, and a role for citizens to fashion alternative futures (Chapters 2 and 5). Such scenarios present a rather pessimistic view of human agency and possibilities, suggesting that citizens have few options apart from adapting to an unfolding future. Citizens are seen as empowered by such developments, but have limited role in influencing outcomes. The scenarios serve to normalize current politico-economic and social arrangements including, as mentioned, the colonization of the internet ('cyber-colonization') by powerful commercial interests that stand to profit from the opportunities offered by the evolving data economy.

Singularity

The futurist Ray Kurzweil (who was employed by Google in 2012 to be its Director of Engineering) and the scientist and science fiction writer Vernor Vinge have described a similar technologically determined future, and specifically a dramatic shift in thinking associated with expected developments, namely 'singularity'. Singularity—a phrase taken from mathematics, and popularized by Vinge and Kurzweil—'describes a point which we are incapable of deciphering its exact properties' (Tzezana, 2017). Both writers believe that singularity will be achieved through super-human AI. As Tzezana (ibid.) argues, as AI operates to constantly improve itself, when it reaches the stage of being a 'super-human artificial intelligence' it will be able to create a superior version of itself, leading to 'an *intelligence explosion*' that 'will leave old poor us – simple, biological machines that we are – far behind.' Kurzweil believes humans are quickly approaching singularity, what he calls 'the law of accelerating returns', involving an exponential growth in technological capacities and the production of information in the future. Indeed, he predicts that the year 2045 will see the most dramatic breakthrough in human history, 'the kind that could, in just a few years, overturn the institutes and pillars of society and completely change the way we view ourselves as human beings' (ibid.). The idea that machines could become smarter than humans, who may be made redundant, is a long-standing idea and has been popularized in science fictional portrayals such as HAL, the sentient computer that controls the spacecraft and interacts with the crew in the Arthur C. Clarke's movie *2001: A Space Odyssey*. However, according to some techno-optimists, science fiction is fast becoming science fact, and events that were unimagined even a decade ago are now within the realms of possibility, or have even been developed or are in development. This includes implantable technologies (e.g. devices for sensing disease, and for automatically releasing medicines); wearable internet (e.g. Apple Watch, clothing with embedded chips that connect the item and those wearing it to the internet); the Internet of Things (connecting literally anything to the internet); the connected home; smart cities (defined by data-driven services, intelligent lighting and smart trash collection); driverless cars; 3D printing and consumer products; and neurotechnologies (Schwab, 2017: 120–172).

Interest in AI and machine learning, and concerns about their impacts, have become heightened in recent years, especially in the wake of stagnating economies and the failure of governments to stimulate 'growth' and create full-time employment and meaningful employment in the aftermath of the global financial crisis. Machine learning, whereby computers analyse large amounts of data and, in effect, write their own program on the basis of the statistical relationships that are discovered, is seen to have huge potential in health and medicine, and in other fields (Ford, 2016: 91–92). In fact, as Ford indicates, machine learning is already very advanced and is routinely used to capture vast amounts of data on individuals, finding applications in areas such as email spam filters, Amazon's book recommendations, Google's online language translation, and potential dates on Match. com. However, as Ford observes, it could also be used to develop software to automate much of the work that is currently being performed. Ford's contention is that this is already occurring, and with increasing frequency, transforming and/or replacing workers not just in the manufacturing sector and areas involving routine, predictable activities (e.g. supermarket and warehouse shelving), but also much white-collar work such as law, higher education, and health and medicine. Ford suggests that this is leading to a crisis in economies: such growth is premised upon consumption, and as workers are replaced by robots, consumption levels are falling, which is reinforcing social inequality and stagnation, while corporate profits continue to soar—a trend already evident in many economies (ibid.: chapter 10).

In short, as is common in many if not most areas of technological development, responses to AI and machine learning involve a mixture of utopian and dystopian visions. It is not the business of sociologists to engage in unfounded predictions of future technological scenarios. However, using sociological concepts and insights, including knowledge of previous technological developments, scholars can suggest likely technological paths. As I argue, if one is to understand how technologies are likely to evolve and to assess their potential impacts, one needs to look to previous developments and predictions, and appreciate how they have shaped the present, including the formation of path dependency (where historical precedents establish the path for later events) and technological lock-in (where policy commitment to certain innovations makes it difficult to shift technological priorities). In short, in contrast to Schwab's (2017) sentiment that 'this time is different', I argue that one should one adopt the more cautious approach of Ford (2016) and ask instead, Is this time different? And, if so, how?

Outline of the remaining chapters

Chapter 2 focuses on the networking of the self associated with growing digitalization in healthcare. Digital technologies are seen to provide the future means for transacting health and healthcare, exploiting data derived directly from citizens themselves or other sources. The chapter begins by exploring some early prognoses for the electronic age, namely the work of Marshall McLuhan and Erich Fromm, that seem to have foreshadowed recent developments in digitalization. These writers, however, portrayed technologically determinist visions of future society where citizens are largely passive, whereas recent developments in digital health are *premised* upon citizen's *active* engagements with technologies and the practices that they enable. The kind of society and economy that is emerging is better conveyed by the 'network society', developed by Manuel Castells (2010 [1996]) to describe the transformations of society and self wrought by the 'information technology revolution'. Chapter 2 introduces the concept of *bio-digital citizenship* to capture the intertwining of bio-based and digitally based identities, knowledge and practices, and related responsibilities characterizing contemporary digitally mediated healthcare. In the chapter I explore the technologies and techniques that serve to engender this new citizenship, which is manifest in areas such as digital patient activism and citizens' online searches for health information. I suggest that while citizens do have agency, which is expressed in diverse ways, the options for action are profoundly shaped by the architecture of choice that is established by powerful technology companies and other interests that seek to extract value and profit from citizens' data.

Chapter 3 examines the changing conceptions and practices of medicine associated with digitalization, AI, machine learning and related developments. Digital technologies are seen to hold the potential to transform medicine through big data analytics involving the use of computers to combine and analyse data from genomics, medical histories and other sources to enable a predictive, personalized (or precision) medicine. Consequently, this is a field that is attracting considerable investment in the US, the UK, Australia and other countries. The chapter critically examines the claims attached to personalized/precision medicine, which I view as part of a long history of personalization discourse in health and medicine that became more prominent in the wake of the public announcement of the mapping of the human genome in 2000. I look back to some earlier precedents, claims and arguments about personalized medicine, with particular reference to national biobank initiatives, after which I discuss some national precision medicine research initiatives and early-stage precision medicine programs in a number of countries. Google and IBM are hoping to capitalize on precision medicine, especially via cloud platforms, leveraging the promise and optimism regarding the applications of AI and machine learning in healthcare. As I note, genomics research and precision medicine rely on citizens' consent, which health authorities, technology companies, pharmaceutical companies and governments have sought to engender via various strategies, which I discuss with specific reference to Google's DeepMind Technologies.

Chapter 4 considers the dimensions and implications of the emergent digital healthcare economy. Digital technologies promise to transform healthcare systems, including strategies of personal risk management, modes of treatment and practices of care. The hospital itself is being reimagined, while care is envisaged to be increasingly digitally mediated and more self-centred and home-based, enabled by the use of personal voice assistants and new monitoring devices, along with cloud computing. Digital technologies have particular appeal in facilitating the care of the elderly in a context of rapidly ageing populations. The basic infrastructure for the envisaged future healthcare economy is being established, with electronic health record systems implemented in a number of countries in recent years, using automatic opt-in processes to encourage compliance, while citizens are incentivized to use wearable devices to monitor their health and/or share data. The chapter examines some of the major stakeholders in this emerging healthcare economy, including governments, insurance companies, pharmaceutical companies, advertisers, IT specialists, clinicians, and ordinary citizens themselves who are promised the benefits, efficiencies and convenience of a fully networked, seamless, big data-based healthcare system. The Quantified Self movement reflects the broader trend of technological colonization and quantification evident in healthcare and other areas of life. As I note, in the effort to recruit citizens to the world of apps and wearables, companies and governments have employed approaches or techniques such as user-centred design, behavioural psychology, concepts of nudge, and an appeal to convenience, personalization and empowerment. There are potentially profound socio-political and personal implications of the digital healthcare economy, including security and privacy issues raised by the general use of technologies such as cloud computing and personal care assistants; and yet, as I note, these issues have hardly figured in debates and policies on digital health.

Chapter 5 concludes with an overall assessment of the promises and perils of digital health. As noted, in policy statements and academic writings, digital health is defined in various ways or left undefined, but is mostly imbued with promise and optimism. It is claimed that related initiatives will make healthcare systems more efficient and effective, lead to improved health outcomes, empower citizens, and lay the foundation for wealth creation. However, on the basis of the evidence and arguments presented in the preceding chapters, and knowledge of the factors that shape health, in Chapter 5 I question whether digital health (however defined) will deliver much of what is promised, although related initiatives are likely to have far-reaching implications. I draw on various evidence to support my claims, including the unforeseen adverse consequences of technological initiatives thus far, noted with the electronic health record systems in the US, the UK and Australia; the adoption of restricted, biomedical conceptions of health; the fallacy of empowerment in a context dominated by powerful technology and pharmaceutical companies and advertisers employing algorithm-driven personalized advertising; and an emergent healthcare economy characterized by data and digital divides. I liken digital technology use to a Faustian bargain, where citizens are likely to surrender something of far greater value—their personal data—than what they obtain from its use. The dangers I describe are various and significant. However, while citizens' engagements with digital health may represent the ultimate Faustian pact—the trading of the most intimate aspects of one's self—there is evidence of growing citizen resistance to digitalization and datafication, and calls for companies to be accountable for their algorithms. This resistance and these calls, I suggest, underline the potential for citizens to mobilize to create alternative futures—societies oriented to fulfilling human needs, rather than techno-utopian visions that will do little to address the basic conditions affecting health in its widest sense.

2

'DIGITAL HEALTH' AND NETWORKING OF THE SELF

Digitalization, many commentators argue, *will* change everything. The idea that humans are on the verge of accelerating or exponential change, involving a growing convergence of different technologies and of technologies and humans, is not new and finds resonance in the predictions of futurists and the portrayals of science fictional writers. This includes the concept of artificial intelligence (AI) that, it has been suggested, will make humans dispensable, at least in some areas of activity, or fundamentally change our conception of the human. Such predictions provide the basis for business ventures, with futurist writers such as Ray Kurzweil (Chapter 1) and entrepreneurs such as Elon Musk capitalizing on anticipated developments, confident in their assurance that the portrayed futures are inevitable and should be embraced, and indeed celebrated. Whole cities and institutions, such as universities, likewise subscribe to this digitally enabled or enhanced future and have begun to prepare accordingly. In Australia, the concepts Melbourne 4.0 and University 4.0 at Latrobe University, also in Melbourne, are premised upon the kinds of radical change envisaged in Schwab's (2017) book *The Fourth Industrial Revolution*, discussed in Chapter 1. Similarly, Germany's Industry 4.0 idea, the Australian Prime Minister's Industry 4.0 Taskforce, India's 100 Smart Cities project, China's Made in China 2025, and Google's DeepMind assume the inevitability and desirability of AI-enabled economies and the growing application of the tools of information technology (e.g. the Internet of Things) to production in the near future.

It is in the sphere of health, medicine and healthcare, however, that many foresee digitalization as having its most far reaching—and it is assumed, mostly positive—impacts. Developments such as 'precision' (or 'personalized') medicine, designer beings, regenerative medicine, telehealth, 3D printing, and wearable and implantable technologies are expected to radically transform how the body, health, illness, risk and healthcare are understood and how citizens conduct and manage their own lives. It has been argued, for example, that individuals will be able to be constantly monitored by AI for susceptibility to risk and disease, have access to or benefit from access to robots, and connect to diverse sources of information on health, treatments and care (Ford, 2016). The idea of being able to use big data to determine who is susceptible to illness, to track the progression of disease, and to monitor healthcare remotely is already informing policies as well as visions of the future institutions of healthcare, with suggestions that the concept of the hospital itself will be reinvented (Margo, 2017). I examine some of these initiatives in detail in Chapters 3 and 4. Portrayals of this future healthcare convey many benefits for individual citizens and for society as a whole. While one may doubt that 'digital health' will deliver much of what is promised, for reasons that I explain later (Chapter 5) it is nevertheless evident that digitalization is already profoundly shaping citizens' self-conceptions, commitments and interactions.

This chapter focuses on the networking of the self that is associated with growing digitalization in healthcare. As I argue, digital technologies are seen to provide the foundation for new ways of *transacting* 'health' and 'healthcare', whereby economic and social value is derived from citizens' active involvement in practices of prevention, treatment and care. In Chapter 1 I introduced the concept of bio-digital citizenship to capture the interweaving of bio-based and digitally based identities, knowledge and practices, and related responsibilities that characterize digitally mediated healthcare. In a number of countries, digital health is being promoted as the means to enable citizens to gain access to 'tailored' treatments and care, and to provide more 'choice' and thus enhanced health, while reducing inefficiencies in healthcare systems (e.g. National Health Service, 2017; US Food and Drug Administration, n.d.). 'Choice, personalization and customization' have been guiding ideals of neoliberal healthcare, and digital technologies are widely promoted as the tools for their fulfilment. Despite many citizens' concerns about security and privacy, and consequent resistance to some initiatives (e.g. electronic health records; see Chapter 5), new digital health initiatives are under development or are being implemented on the premise that the economic, social and personal benefits will greatly outweigh the risks or disadvantages.

To begin, it is fruitful to step back from contemporary debates about digitalization and its impacts, including on conceptions of self, to briefly review some early, seemingly prescient prognoses of the future of technologically mediated communications. Current debates about digital health, and the impacts of digitalization on society and the economy more generally, seem to replay, and in some respects confirm, early predictions and concerns about technological developments, especially mechanization, automation and the emergent electronic media, articulated by the influential scholars Marshall McLuhan and Erich Fromm in the 1960s. While these scholars were not writing about health, medicine and healthcare specifically, their arguments seem prophetic in regard to technological developments of the kind that are emerging in this domain, such as the growing applications of AI and big data analytics, and individual citizens' engagements with digital media. Can we learn anything from this work? Are their predictions being realized?

Early prognoses for the electronic age

McLuhan is best known for his phrase 'the medium is the massage', a phrase that, according to the popular account, arose as a result of a spelling error on his proposed book of 1967, 'The medium is the message', but which he felt conveyed well the content of his book. In McLuhan's view, the medium of communication itself rather than the content was profoundly shaping social life and the ways in which people interact and respond with their environment. In his opening comments he observed,

> The medium, or process, of our time—electric technology—is reshaping and restructuring patterns of social interdependence and every aspect of our personal life. It is forcing us to reconsider and re-evaluate practically every thought, every action, and every institution formerly taken for granted
>
> (McLuhan and Fiore, 1967: 9).

As McLuhan elaborated, the new means of electronic communications enabled growing surveillance and intrusions on privacy, the reconfiguration of the relations between time and space (the rise of the idea of the global village), disruptions of established jobs and patterns of work, and the redesigning of whole cities (ibid.: 12–24). On the impact of television, he wrote, 'The main cause for disappointment in and for criticism of television is the failure on the part of its critics to view it as a totally new technology which demands different sensory responses' (ibid.: 128). Seen in the context of the growing influence of television and radio, and the growing use of computers in banking and other areas of life, McLuhan was observing the beginnings of what has now become largely taken for granted with the rise of the internet and social media. That is, people are now constantly 'connected' to electronic communication devices such as smartphones and iPads, interacting in novel ways via online forums and social media, and forging new alliances and forms of sociability, such as patient support groups. Individuals' sense of self and responsibility, and empathy for and trust in others, indeed would seem to be profoundly impacted by digital media. McLuhan, however, was not the only writer in the 1960s documenting trends such as these.

Erich Fromm, a member of the Frankfurt School of critical theory, who was writing around the same time, warned of the dehumanization accompanying increasing mechanization and automation in 'the present technological society'. Fromm observed a 'radical break between the first phase of industrialization and the second Industrial Revolution, in which society itself becomes a vast machine, of which man is a living particle' (Fromm, 2010 [1968]: 41). He noted,

> Cybernation is creating the possibility of a new kind of economic and social organization. A relatively small number of mammoth enterprises has become the center of the economic machine and will rule it completely in the not-to-distant future.
>
> (ibid.: 37)

Fromm's comments here seem highly prophetic, given the rise of the powerful global monopolies such as Google, Amazon, Facebook, IBM and Apple, and the hyper-connected world which they have produced and largely control. Fromm saw mechanization and automation as heralding a totally organized and controlled 'megamachine', a term borrowed from the historian Lewis Mumford (ibid.: 4). On the basis of then evident trends, he foresaw that it was inevitable that the envisaged 'technetronic society' would eventuate 'unless a sufficient number of people see the danger and redirect our course' (ibid.: 43). In his view, there were a number of 'guiding principles' underpinning 'the present technological system', which included the imperative that 'something *ought* to be done because it is technically *possible* to do it', and the striving for '*maximal efficiency and output*', involving the reduction of individuals to 'quantifiable units whose personalities can be expressed on punch cards' (ibid.: 43; emphases in original). The potential effect of this on future society was profound, in that it reduced humans to mere consumers and 'cog[s] in the production machine', who would likely become unquestioning, passive and perpetually bored.

With what now appears to be a nod to the forthcoming age of the internet and social media and its compulsions (porn, cybersex) and obsessions ('internet addiction'), Fromm comments on 'the effect of this type of organization on man'; namely, alienation, passive compulsive consumption, and conformity, which he sees to be 'the only way to avoid intolerable anxiety' (ibid.: 48–49). Fromm also noted the 'growing split of cerebral-intellectual function from affective emotional experience; the split between thought and feeling, mind from the heart, truth from passion' (ibid.: 5). This is manifest in the 'deep emotional attraction to the mechanical … to the man-made' and to the idea of constructing computers that think like humans. Fromm sees this as 'a flight from life and from humane experience into the mechanical and purely cerebral' (ibid.: 53–54).

In short, both McLuhan and Fromm recognized that the then emergent electronic media were profoundly shaping not only social institutions and social relations, but also citizens' subjectivities, including affective attachments to other humans and the non-human world. Recent popular science fictional portrayals, such as Spike Jonze's 2014 film *Her*, where a lonely man falls in love with his computer's operating system; and Dave Eggers' (2013) book *The Circle*, which recounts the groupthink associated with a future digital utopia (or dystopia, depending on one's viewpoint), would seem to capture these human-to-machine attachments. With recent observations that many citizens are obsessed with, or addicted to, their electronic machines (smartphones, iPads) (Alter, 2017) to the extent that they have lost the art of conversation (Turkle, 2015), McLuhan's and Fromm's predictions seem highly prescient from today's vantage point. However, I suggest that, while compelling, their portrayals of emerging societies were technologically determinist and portrayed citizens as mostly lacking agency. While developments in electronic media, and especially citizens' rapidly growing use of personal computers and access to the internet and social media, may be seen to confirm some of McLuhan's and Fromm's broad predictions, digitalization is shaping thinking and actions in ways that are far from uniform, with longer-term impacts that are uncertain. These writers' depictions underplay the potential for citizens to creatively engage with technologies and to subvert or resist them, and to forge alternative futures. Indeed, digitalization in healthcare and other spheres is *premised* upon citizens' agency. As I will explain, this activeness is taking various forms in the online environment, including research, fundraising, constructing new knowledge and/or combining lay and expert knowledge, and forming alliances with other citizens and with credentialled experts to build community profiles and effect change, especially in policies regarding research and new treatments. Further, this activeness may involve disregarding or resisting accredited experts and expertise. This bio-digital citizenship reflects the operations of a form of power that is increasingly de-centred rather than state-centred, and involves a refashioning of social institutions and relations in line with an imagined future medicine and healthcare. It is manifest in the establishment of new networks and modes of networking, the global mobility of people and ideas (e.g. as manifest in health tourism), and growing efforts to collect, analyse and trade data.

The network society

The idea that digitalization has inaugurated a new kind of society and economy—a 'network society'—was foreshadowed by Manuel Castells (2010 [1996]), who was writing much later than McLuhan and Fromm, in the mid-1990s against the backdrop of the newly developed World Wide Web and what he described as the 'information technology revolution'. Castells documented the ways in which information technology was transforming concepts of the self and identity politics (the rise of virtual communities), work and employment, the character and operation of economies, concepts of time, the workings of media, and the criminal economy—and in the process generating social, economic and technological inequalities. In Castells' view, 'the potential integration of text, images, and sounds in the same system, interacting from multiple points, in chosen time (real or delayed) along a global network, in conditions of open and affordable access, does fundamentally change the character of communication'—and hence culture (ibid.: 356–357). Castells takes issue with those earlier commentators, such as members of the Frankfurt School, who portrayed audiences as hapless, passive consumers and the media as all-powerful. The concept of the mass media, promulgated by those writers, he argues, has become redundant with messages and sources becoming more diverse, and targeted audiences choosing their messages and becoming 'segmented by ideologies, values, tastes, and lifestyles' (ibid.: 368). As Castells acknowledges, and as recent developments in digital media use confirm, citizens often use technologies to produce their own knowledge, to forge new bodies and identities and modes of action, and to challenge authorities and selectively use or ignore credentialled expertise. Even before the internet, Castells observes, citizens 'taped their own events, from vacations to family celebrations, thus producing their own images beyond the photo album' (ibid.: 366). Expressed in the terms familiar to scholars of science and technology studies, digital technologies and users are 'co-constructed', with technological objects being designed and produced with assumed users and uses in mind, and the users (comprising many types of lay and expert actors) engaging with and using technologies in diverse ways (Oudshoorn and Pinch, 2003).

That technologies and users are co-constructed is evident in the contemporary digitally oriented market of health and medical information, treatments and other interventions. On one hand, digital technologies are promoted by various authorities as the means for citizens to become 'empowered' through their enhanced connections with healthcare, and efforts have been made to engender citizens' 'digital literacy' to enable the self-management of health and risk, as part of a broader, neoliberal project of 'responsibilization' (O'Malley, 2009; see Chapter 1) On the other hand, citizens from communities of diverse backgrounds, ideologies and values are using the internet and social media—increasingly via smartphones and other mobile devices—to create their own preferred messages and, in some cases, challenging credentialled experts in their efforts to achieve their goals.

In the so-called Web 2.0 era, patients and their families are both consumers *and* producers of knowledge about health, illness, risk and care (Petersen et al., 2015). As I will explain, these 'prosumers' may curate online forums, engage in crowd funding, sponsor or undertake their own research, and lobby for access to treatments that are clinically unproven or have been approved for only certain conditions. Many are using the internet to connect with providers promising access to therapies or procedures that may be difficult or impossible to procure in the consumer's home country because they have not gained regulatory approval, such as stem cell treatments (see the section below on the case of stem cell therapies). Citizens' growing use of digital media, particularly smartphones and other mobile devices, also provides opportunities for new businesses to create or expand their markets by advertising their products directly to consumers over the internet (so-called direct-to-consumer advertising). With healthcare products, this enables providers to bypass accredited gatekeepers such as patients' clinicians, who in the pre-digital era would have played a major (often the sole) role in advising patients and prescribing treatments.

All advertising, in whatever form it takes, promises a changed identity, whether improved health status, or a longed-for bodily transformation, or personal fulfilment, and also membership of a community. Digital media offer advertisers an especially potent means to connect with consumers as they create a simulated world in the sense described by Baudrillard (1998 [1970]); that is, one involving imitation, deception and 'sham objects' (Ritzer, 1998: 12–13). Baudrillard saw advertising as being 'perhaps the most remarkable mass medium of our age' in that, while it speaks to a particular object and addresses each individual, it establishes a consensus between the individual and other consumers, and with other signified objects (Baudrillard (1998 [1970]: 125). Advertising, he noted, is a 'prophetic language, in so far as it promotes not learning or understanding, but hope'; it 'turns the object into an event' (ibid.: 127). While advertising through its history has been founded on promise and hope, the rise of the internet and social media has taken this to a new level by promising that citizens may readily create new identities and gain unlimited access to information. Such promise has been found to play a prominent role in technological development and in shaping investment decisions and market behaviours, including consumers' engagement with technologies (Petersen and Krisjansen, 2015; Petersen, 2018).

Technologies for networking of the self

Facebook

For many citizens, Facebook is a common source of information and means for connecting with friends, family and others. For patients and carers seeking information on health and treatments, it is often a crucial resource. In the US, a survey undertaken by Pew Research Center found that 68 percent of all adults are Facebook users (Greenwood et al., 2016). Globally, Facebook is the most popular social network with over 1 billion registered accounts, and is expected to grow as mobile device usage and mobile social networks gain popularity (Statistica, 2018a), notwithstanding growing critiques (including by some early Facebook employees and executives) of its operations, such as its newsfeed, which restricts information and enables the spread of 'fake news' (Seetharaman, 2018: 23) (Chapter 5). Facebook's success is due to its designers successfully exploiting a basic human need for social acceptance and to copy and compare one's self with others (Lanchester, 2017: 5). Facebook and other social media such as Twitter have come to provide significant platforms for the building of new communities and sociality, enabling citizens to become advocates on particular issues of concern to them, or to advocate on behalf of others and influence public discourse to an extent that was not possible in the pre-digital age. Facebook also provides the means by which advertisers can target specific audiences for products and services by leveraging Facebook's data about its audience of approximately 2.2 billion active monthly users (in 2018) (Statistica, 2018a).

The smartphone

The advent of the smartphone has been a crucial element in the 'networking of the self' (Greenfield, 2017) that has been a precondition for citizens' active participation in their own healthcare and in the anticipated future precision medicine (Chapter 3). As Greenfield notes, the genius of the smartphone is its replacement of various other items (diaries, watches, maps) and tasks previously needed to fulfil daily activities, making it an incomparable tool of convenience that has been quickly integrated into our daily lives. Access to a smartphone varies according to age, ethnicity, income and educational level, but by 2017, 77 percent of Americans owned such a phone (Smith, 2017). Further, 62 percent of smartphone owners in the US have used their phone in the previous year to search for information about a health condiotion (Smith, 2015). High levels of ownership are also high in the UK population (with a 95 percent penetration among those 16–24) (Statistica, 2018b); and in Australia with 84 percent ownership in the population (Deloitte, 2016: 7). However, the smartphone market has become saturated, especially in developed countries, notwithstanding the vibrant replacement market (ibid.: 10). It is interesting to note that the most successful technology producers are moving away from their focus on phones towards connected devices such as fridges and speakers, with the next perceived market opportunity being the sale of AI-based platforms (e.g. personal assistants) and the resulting opportunity to sell and advertise (Thomas, 2018: 19; Chapter 4)

Individuals' adoption of smartphones and health apps is consistent with the personalized, timely healthcare imagined by proponents of precision medicine (Chapter 3)
and digitally connected care (Chapter 4). The smartphone led the shift in internet traffic
away from desktop computers to mobile devices, beginning around 2012, that is seen as
decisive in the monetization of digital information (Lanchester, 2017: 7). Investors in
digital health, and especially the big technology companies such as Google, Apple,
Samsung and IBM, see the smartphone and health apps as fundamentally changing
medical care, by enabling medical diagnosis and treatment and self-care to be undertaken virtually anywhere by anyone. A recent article, titled 'Doctor in your pocket',
outlines what the smartphone and its accessories offers current and future medicine, and
predicts that 'Soon, there will be little difference from a technical standpoint between a
general practitioner's office and a fully equipped smartphone. On the contrary: it is
already the case that patients are sometimes better served by a mobile phone' (Müller,
2017: 36). The vision of future medicine conveyed here is one where citizens themselves use technologies to take charge of their own diagnosis and assume an independent, self-determining role in health. The article describes a range of smartphone apps
that are already in use, including M-sense, which is 'revolutionizing migraine diagnostics'; and Neotiv, which is 'being developed to reliably diagnose Alzheimer's'
(ibid.: 36). Apps such as these promise convenience, ease of use, and personal control
over monitoring of the self and health. The website for Neotiv proclaims that
'tracking your memory is convenient and flexible'. It explains that 'The app allows
you to track how the most important functions of your memory change over time
using tests chosen by neuroscientists who work in memory research.' Further, it
notes 'This takes only a few minutes on your smart phone or tablet computer and
can easily become part of the way you monitor your health and well-being'
(Neotiv, 2017). It is suggested that smartphone-enabled medical care is likely to
impact not just on patients and doctors, but also on 'manufacturers of large medical
devices', which may no longer be necessary. The scenario foreseen is one where

> in a few years, patients won't just be able to decide which doctor to go to, but
> will also be able to choose between local doctors, online diagnoses and intel-
> ligent scanning devices—and they will perhaps even be able to undergo an
> examination in their own cars.
>
> (Müller, 2017: 36)

A number of other technologies are in development or foreseen, such as car-based
medical examinations (anticipating that self-driving cars will free up drivers' time),
patients undertaking a 'complete diagnosis produced by their car or by their smartphone', and more online consultations by clinics and health insurers (ibid.: 38).

The above depiction, which involves informed patients using technologies to
self-diagnose, to choose doctors, or even to devise their own treatment regime and
care plan, is increasingly common in depictions of future medicine and healthcare,
and is shaping investment and policy decisions. It conveys a vision of a more flexible, tailored, mobile, constantly monitored, 24/7 form of care, where traditional

healthcare institutions and credentialled experts matter much less than they once did. As I note in Chapter 3, wearable technologies are seen to provide the means to provide 'real-time' data on health that may be utilized in big data-driven medical decision-making. Newer developments in smartphones may enable as-yet unimagined possibilities for self-diagnosis and connection with sources and means for healthcare. In 2017, Apple iPhone celebrated its tenth anniversary and released a new model (iPhone X), which includes face recognition among its various features. More than a decade ago, in 2007, Google registered a patent for 'systems and methods for patient identification using mobile face recognition' (Google, 2007). Capturing a patient's image is seen to overcome problems with current means of identifying patients, which may involve errors and are overly reliant on patients themselves, who 'may not remember or may be unable to communicate the information'. Further, the technology is seen to assist storage and retrieval, and to ensure that such information is accurate and enables comparison with previously stored images (ibid.). As the patent description makes clear, Google foresees this technology as offering not only a failsafe way of identifying patients, but also a means of tracking them as they move through different points in the healthcare system, enabling healthcare professionals to access their medical data more readily and 'to compare the patient image to a plurality of stored images to identify a matching image' (ibid.). This portrayal is not unlike the idealized vision of the network society, characterized by Castells (2010), noted earlier. It is likely that Google will roll out this technology in years ahead after Apple has already tested the market with its iPhone face recognition technology, and it is likely that patients of the future will be expected to become active participants in collecting and contributing images to a database as a citizen duty. However, facial recognition technology is not without its problems in that it has been shown to be prone to misrecognition and present the risk of privacy transgression. (Chapter 5)

As Greenfield observes, designers of smartphones have 'learned to stimulate and leverage' citizens' desire for communion and affirmation (Greenfield, 2017: 28–29). This includes affirmation of oneself as a 'healthy self' through demonstration of commitment to 'healthy lifestyles' and engagement in individualized practices of risk management and care (Petersen, 2015: 7–9). The smartphone enables a level of personalization and self-care not possible with desktop computers, since their tracking function harvests a wealth of information on individuals *as they move through time and space*, including on their physical location and real-time behaviours (including purchasing decisions), which can then be used by different parties acting in their own interests and used to tailor advertisements directly to the individual (Greenfield, 2017: 24–27). In the process, individuals have traded their privacy for convenience (ibid.: 26). The widespread use of smartphones has profoundly impacted social relations, at least for those in more affluent parts of the world who have access to this technology, enabling people to connect with others and transact business across often vast distances and on a 24/7 basis. No longer constrained by time or geography, the smartphone has contributed to the 'time–space compression' that has been under way since the mid-1960s with the move from Fordism (manifest in the production line) to flexible accumulation (evidenced in 'just-in-time' production) (Harvey, 1989: chapter 17). That is, the limits to capital accumulation imposed by distance and time have been significantly reduced, with businesses and consumers being able to undertake often instantaneous transactions.

For both businesses and state authorities, encouraging citizens to think in econ-omistic, calculative terms, and to use smartphones and apps to monitor and quan-tify their own health and to connect with providers of treatments and care, has considerable appeal given the potential savings and economic efficiencies to be had. Many governments subscribe to the 'digital economy' and are keen to encourage citizens' use of such technologies as part of the broader project of encouraging digital literacy. A common strategy used to nurture digital literacy has been 'gamification', based on behavioural theory that incorporates into technologies elements of game playing (e.g. competition, point scoring) to encourage citizens to engage with them. Queensland's Digital Health Strategic Vision, released in 2017, for example, includes references to 'Gamification and incentives', whereby 'real-time analytics, wearable devices, mobile applications and other tools' that 'allow consumers to continuously monitor their health' are combined with gamification 'to further enhance personal wellness outcomes and increase participation by individuals in their own healthcare' (Queensland Government, 2017: 36) As the vision statement explains, 'Gamification is triggering behavioural changes in people by motivating, rewarding and incentivizing people to follow the steps necessary to achieve their own health goals' (ibid.: 36). One 2014 review of the use of gamification in health apps concluded, 'the use of gamification in health and fitness apps has become immensely popular, as evidenced by the number of apps found in the Apple App Store containing at least some components of gamification' (Lister et al., 2014). Apple's iPhone has been designed as an aesthetically pleasing and multifunctional device that, when used with its apps, provides a highly convenient and seductive—and, some argue, addictive—technology that has proved to be a huge success (Alter, 2017; Turkle, 2015). The iPhone is largely responsible for Apple's rise to become the world's biggest company (Davidson, 2017: 45).

While Apple and other technology companies are looking to profit from e-health, this is not limited to smartphone applications. In September 2017, Apple announced that it was collaborating with Stanford University and telemedicine company Amer-ican Well 'to test whether its watch can detect heart problems' (Farr, 2017). An article reporting the collaboration noted that 'the effort would make its device a "must have" for millions of people worldwide'. It also noted that the Apple Watch had been used in studies to detect heart rhythm abnormalities, and the benefits were delivering practitioners 'real-time access to raw data from its heart rate sensor' (ibid.). The networking of the self and the multi-tasking that mobile devices enable arguably realize the idea of the cyborg, first envisaged in the 1960s (see Chapter 1). Among their various impacts, smartphones have contributed to the erosion of the distinction between public and private, with personal information—including about health status, once considered sacrosanct—readily shared with others through tweets, Facebook, online blogs and other forums. Patient forums such as PatientsLikeMe,

CureTogether and Smart Patients, for example, reveal the blurring of the distinction between personal and public, with some citizens evidently prepared to share personal medical information for 'the public good' as part of a perceived duty of citizenship.

Reflecting this sharing ethos, PatientsLikeMe, promotes on its website a technology called DigitalMe[TM], with the byline 'We're more than our disease. Together, we are the answer' (PatientsLikeMe, n.d.a). The technology is advertised on the basis that individuals can join together to share and combine information about their 'experiential, environmental, biological and medical information to create a digital version of you'—making an appeal to citizens' assumed desire for communion and altruism. The website description notes, 'What if you could join with a select group of other patients like you to advance personalized health and be the catalyst for meaningful change in healthcare? You can. It's called DigitalMe[TM].' (ibid.) As the DigitalMe[TM] website explains, 'The technology is not yet widely available, but we want to invest and partner with you, to make this more affordable and available to everyone in the future. It will not cost you a thing. That is how much we believe in this idea, and in you.' (ibid.) Behind this espoused altruistic goal lies a commercial imperative. PatientsLikeMe sells the information that patients share to 'partners' which, as it declares on its website, are companies that develop or sell products to patients, including 'drugs, devices, equipment, insurance, and medical services' (PatientsLikeMe, n.d.b) The partners listed on its website are AstraZeneca, Takeda and M2Gen—the former two being global biotechnology and pharmaceutical companies, the latter a health bioinformatics group with an espoused commitment to the development and delivery of precision medicine and to 'studying patients through their lifetime' in collaboration with 'the nation's [US] leading cancer centres' (PatientsLikeMe, n.d.c). The appeal to sharing personal medical data and other information as citizens' responsibility has resonance in neoliberal societies, where individuals are expected to contribute to advancing social objectives. However, such 'sharing' gives rise to a host of security and surveillance issues and goes beyond matters of health, putting one at risk of malware attacks, identity theft and other harms; in short, the 'doctor in your pocket' may also serve as the 'spy in your pocket' (e.g. Lucas, 2015: 154–172). By sharing such data, citizens are also contributing to the commodification of health by selling information about themselves that can be used to develop products and services that are then sold back to them.

The evidence indicates that many citizens already undertake the kinds of self-subjection, self-objectification and self-mastery required to participate actively in the emergent digital health economy; namely, an active, constant engagement with digital technologies, a preparedness to use these technologies to monitor and measure their own health and risk, and an evident willingness to contribute to data collection and sharing ventures. It would appear that a large segment of the population are prepared to potentially compromise their privacy and safety for convenience and/or other perceived benefits of their connections. This networking of the self is clearly manifest in the phenomenon of digital patient activism and citizens' online search for health and medical information, to which I now turn.

Digital patient activism

There are many examples of patient activism (or advocacy), including endeavours by individual citizens, or groups of citizens, to effect change of some kind (e.g. in research priorities, regulatory policies, and access to new, clinically unproven treatments). Activist groups may be limited to those who suffer specific conditions, perhaps predominantly affecting people of a particular gender, sexuality or ethnicity (e.g. breast cancer, prostate cancer, HIV/AIDS); or may be more broadly based, involving citizens drawn from different condition-specific and socially diverse communities who lobby for changes to policies or funding regarding a particular kind of treatment, such as stem cell therapy (e.g. Hoffman et al., 2011). However, regardless of their goals, most patient activist groups have integrated digital media into their operations to some extent. They may use a range of digitally based strategies, singly or in combination, including internet-based crowd source funding or other community fund-raising activities, blogging, social media communications, and news media—often in combination with offline public demonstrations (e.g. town hall meetings, street marches) (e.g. Pickard and Yang, 2017). Further, patient activists sometimes work collaboratively with health professionals to advance their interests, and may forge links with pharmaceutical companies, especially in the effort to develop new treatments. Recent studies have revealed that a large proportion of patient support/advocacy groups receive financial support (sometimes substantial) from drug, device and biotechnology companies, whose interests may not, and in all likelihood *do not*, align with those of the groups' members (McCoy et al., 2017; Moynihan and Bero, 2017; Rose et al., 2017). Some of these companies advise (and thus potentially influence) patients in their quest to gain access to treatments that have yet to be clinically proven, for example via 'compassionate access' (e.g. Janssen, 2017).

On its Australian website, the pharmaceutical company Janssen claims it supports many patient groups, representing those with various conditions, and has funded conferences (HealtheVoices) involving online health activists and representatives of patient groups to 'share insights' and to 'educate attendees', and has conducted a survey on online conduct with regard to health, especially chronic health conditions (Arlington, 2017). As this website explains:

> At Janssen, we put patients first. It's this commitment that drives us to deliver better patient access, education and outcomes. Central to this vision is a close collaboration with healthcare consumer organisations and patient groups.
>
> (Janssen, 2017)

The website also includes resources for those living with different conditions, along with tips on managing conditions. Such 'collaboration' and demonstrated concern for patient needs and welfare, including the hosting of events, allows pharmaceutical companies to bring patients and their families into their confidence, and provide the companies with the opportunity to learn more about patients' needs, how patients use digital media, and the kinds of information they seek, thus positioning them to better target them in the advertising of drugs and other treatments. Big pharmaceutical companies potentially profit from patients and carers accessing treatments that they may not otherwise be aware of, or that they can only access on the grounds of compassionate access (see below). Google's DeepMind Health, which I examine in Chapter 3, is also forging close links with patient communities, and has hosted a series of 'patient and public involvement workshops' to advance this goal. The growing role of drug, device and biotechnology companies in funding patient support/advocacy groups reflects the converging interests of business and patient groups (and sometimes governments) that has accompanied the commodification of health and responsibilization in healthcare.

In Chapter 3, I explore in more detail how these forms of citizen/patient activism interact with emerging institutions and practices of healthcare. For now, however, recent examples of citizen/patient activism reported in news media include parents who lobbied for their sick children to gain compassionate access to treatments offered by the Stamina Foundation in Italy in 2013 (Abbott, 2013); the UK case of Charlie Gard, whose case gained international coverage in 2017 following his parents' decision to appeal a High Court decision to withdraw his life support (BBC News, 2017); and an Australian patient who used her media profile, gained through a television program of her quest to receive stem cell treatment in Russia in 2014, to promote this treatment and the provider through her own curated Facebook blog (Petersen et al., 2015). In these efforts, patients are often combining expert knowledge and experiential knowledge to undertake what has been dubbed evidence-based activism (Rabeharisoa et al., 2014). This kind of activism is increasingly common as patients seek to inform themselves about scientific developments and the latest 'breakthroughs', and make their own judgements about the veracity of claims, in some cases accumulating more knowledge about particular conditions and their treatment than credentialled experts. Moreover, citizens are using their collective power to lobby for changes to policies so as to enable access to unapproved treatments—thereby unsettling established notions of trust based on a relatively clear and stable demarcation between expert and non-expert, credible and implausible.

'Compassionate access' to treatments

Individual patients and patient groups often seek to bring treatments to market through their own research ventures or via compassionate access (alternatively known as 'preapproval access' or 'expanded access'), in some cases working closely with medical practitioners, regulators and businesses to further this goal. A notable case is the Friends of the NYU Working Group on Compassionate Use and Pre-Approval Access, established in 2014. This advocacy group distributes email newsletters including items on policies and legislative initiatives, relevant news and articles, and upcoming events, and works closely with academic clinicians at the New York University School of Medicine (via NYU Langone Health, Department of Population Health), along with bioethicists, regulators (e.g. the Food and Drug

Administration), and other various experts, to advance its goals. The Working Group hosts a website, which outlines the aims and activities of the group and includes a link to disparate resources, publications and interviews of potential interest to users. As explained on its website, the Working Group was 'founded in 2014 to explore the ethical issues surrounding access to investigational products before they've received U.S. FDA approval, including: the fairness and transparency of access decisions, the role of social media, and legislative efforts to sidestep regulation of pre-approval access' (NYU School of Medicine, 2018). The site also explains that the Working Group works with patients to 'de-mystify pre-approval access and create community-specific resources', publishes articles in peer-reviewed journals and mainstream publications for patients and other stakeholders, and serves as a 'go-to resource for issues related to pre-approval access' (ibid.). While the area of compassionate access reflects the extensive links between patient groups, medical experts, regulators and business (even if indirectly), it is but one example of how the aspirations and hopes of individual patients and their communities have become entwined with the interests of researchers and various other experts, government and industry.

Seeking health information online

For many if not most citizens, regardless of whether they self-identify as activists (or advocates), or are overtly involved in related pursuits, their first port of call for information on health, tests or treatments will be the internet (Fox, 2014; Jacobs et al., 2017; Wong et al., 2014). The internet also offers sources of information on enhancements (e.g. botox treatments, facelifts, labiaplasty, penile enlargement) or other procedures for modifying one's body (e.g. limb lengthening, genital reassignment), or reproductive treatments, including surrogacy services. Many products are advertised for their promised lifestyle benefits or for their potential to transform bodies and identities in line with culturally prescribed ideals of health, fitness, body shape and size, beauty, vitality and happiness. These include weight-loss products, bodily modifications requiring surgery, complementary and alternative medicines, and the growing array of products advertised as anti-ageing treatments (Petersen, 2018). The online advertising of products labelled as anti-ageing treatments—including cosmetic products and 'cosmeceuticals', 'neutraceuticals', 'superfoods', hormone treatments and regenerative therapies—has steadily grown since the mid-1990s, with products becoming increasingly visible and accessible during this period (MacGregor et al., 2017). While citizens may also gain such information offline, from friends, family and other third parties, for many, information derived from digital media is likely to be the sole or main source, or used to complement information originally acquired from these other sources (Petersen et al., in preparation).

However, while the internet appears to open a world of unlimited options, those going online will be confronted with a glut of information that may confuse rather than inform (Lynch, 2016). Information on genetic tests is a case in point. In 2018, it was estimated that there are 75,000 genetic tests available, with about ten new tests entering the market each day, and they are the ones that doctors can order, not the ones marketed directly to consumers via the internet. However, only 10,000 of these tests have been assessed to be unique, working in ways distinct from others (Phillips et al., 2018). How do citizens assess their value? Which tests should they rely on for healthcare decisions? As Lynch argues, when citizens go online, 'Google-knowing' is likely to 'swamp other ways of knowing', and citizens are inclined to select and choose those sources that validate their existing opinions (so-called confirmation bias) and serve to reinforce existing disagreements and prejudices. Lynch refers to the ways in which rumours may spread via 'information cascades', whereby initial posts or expressions of opinion can form a sequence, which can begin to 'overweigh or alter later opinions' (Lynch, 2016: 32). In Lynch's view, this is a phenomenon to which the internet and social media are especially susceptible (ibid.: 32). Further, as Kartik Hosanagar (2016) observes, many citizens seem to be 'trapped in filter bubbles created by the personalization algorithms owned by Facebook, Twitter and Google'. While many people believed that Google would democratize information and create the global village imagined by McLuhan, Hosanagar (ibid.) believes it has had the opposite effect. He notes, 'Social newsfeeds on Facebook and Twitter and algorithms at Google perform the curation function that was previously performed by news editors.' This curation function also pertains to information on health and medicine. Those searching online for information on health and treatments will likely be unaware that advertisers will use the keywords employed in their searches to filter and personalize the information that they receive, and thus narrow the options that are presented to them. Further, in undertaking their searches, users are likely to be led to websites hosted in other countries. Since the internet is geographically unbounded, internet users may cross borders in search of information and treatments, which they frequently do, thereby participating in the market of health tourism (or medical tourism).

Health tourism

The internet has without doubt been a major factor contributing to the rise of health tourism. This constitutes a highly diverse market, or rather many niche markets, encompassing a diverse range of products and services, including medical and dental treatments, surrogacy services, organ transplant operations, stem cell treatments, and spa and wellness tourism, which present numerous physical and financial risks to patients and to healthcare systems (Turner, 2012). With consumers able to search for treatments and services online, and providers anywhere in the world able to market their offerings via direct-to-consumer advertising, the healthcare marketplace is less and less restricted by geographical borders and national or jurisdictional regulations. The health and wellness travel industry is global in its reach and is supported by many governments that seek to prosper from the 'bio-economy'—one founded on a promissory discourse that serves to create value from what *may* be delivered in the future (Petersen and Krisjansen, 2015). It is an industry that thrives in a context of the online marketing of personalized treatments and services, often sold on the basis of the host country's purported high competitive advantage in 'human capital', technology, level of care and/or price structure, with many provider clinics and hospitals located in countries where wages are low relative to the countries from which their clients come (Bookman and Bookman, 2007: ch. 5). In some cases, they also offer the prospect of packaged holidays so that patients receiving treatments may recover in an 'exotic' location. While it is difficult to ascertain the extent to which citizens' travel decisions are shaped by such advertising, their endurance and their use of established techniques, such as the inclusion of patient testimonials and 'question-and-answer' webpages, suggests that advertisers have found them to be successful in attracting customers.

The case of stem cell treatments

For many individuals, the search for information on conditions, tests, treatments and other interventions is underpinned by sentiments of hope, and—in the case of those with serious, life-limiting conditions where conventional treatment options may be limited—the need to 'do something' when 'doing nothing is no option' (Petersen et al., 2017: ch. 2). This is where direct-to-consumer advertising plays a crucial role: in linking providers with often-desperate patients in search of hope. In interviews undertaken as part of our four-year (2012–15) Australian Research Council-funded project on 'stem cell tourism', patients have been found to explore various avenues in search of information and advice, both professional and lay, offline and online (ibid.). However, clinical proof of the efficacy and safety of stem cell treatments for most conditions is lacking (ibid.: 4–6). Stem cell science is a field with considerable promise but with a painfully slow pathway from research to treatment, producing few therapies apart from bone marrow-based stem cell transplants to build a blood or immune system for the treatment of certain conditions, such as leukemia and lymphoma, or corneal or skin grafting (Daley, 2012). Many patients and their families, however, believe that stem treatments for other conditions exist, 'evidence' of which they can readily find online.

In interviews, patients and carers often conveyed feeling abandoned by health professionals, who they said offer limited treatment options and thus 'no hope' (Petersen et al., 2017: 40–44). In using the internet to research stem cell treatments, citizens will be confronted with mostly positive evaluations of their effectiveness in treating a vast number of conditions, including cerebral palsy, multiple sclerosis, cystic fibrosis and Alzheimer's disease. Advertisements for stem cell treatments, some of which figure prominently on a Google search due to the workings of search engine optimization, use familiar clever framing devices to achieve these positive portrayals. This includes patient testimonials that recount successful treatment outcomes—often provided by providers themselves. Whether these patient testimonials are representative of patients' experiences at particular clinics, and whether the claimed treatments in fact involved stem cells and, if so, what kind, is mostly not stated on providers' websites.

An analysis of online advertisements found that they include little scientifically credible evidence and rely heavily on testimonials offering stories of hope, along with reassurances of competence and of concern for patient welfare (Petersen and Seear, 2011). Such advertisements leave much unstated, including the risks and costs of undertaking treatment, details of clinical procedures and the science itself (e.g. the provenance and manner of storage of cells), and the additional costs associated with accommodation and travel for patients and their carers (ibid.: 342). Further, some patients have been found to use Facebook to advocate for treatments and, on occasion, recommend specific clinics, in effect serving as de facto marketers for providers (Petersen et al., 2017: 11, 40, 42, 162, 191). If they have an established public profile, as a celebrity or gained via news coverage or other media, as is common in the field of stem cell treatments, they may leverage this profile to draw attention to the benefits of treatments (Petersen et al., 2015).

Patients' accounts reveal that the financial costs of undertaking stem cell treatments can amount to tens of thousands of dollars, especially when travel, accommodation and carers' expenses are included; further treatments are often involved (Petersen et al., 2017: 45). Adverse outcomes, including deaths, have been noted in the scientific literature (e.g. Cyranoski, 2010; Tuffs, 2010; Pepper, 2012), yet the potential for such outcomes is never noted on clinics' websites.

Recognizing that citizens may seek information on purported stem cell treatments, and in some cases may be prepared to travel overseas to procure them, scientific bodies and health authorities have established various online health resources for patients, interested citizens and their families. These are typically presented as educational resources oriented to those wishing to learn about the state of medical research on particular conditions and treatments (Petersen, et al. 2017: 208), so that patients and/or their families may make 'informed' decisions before embarking on treatments. However, it is difficult to determine to what extent patients and carers consult the latter sources and, if so, whether they influence their decisions. The model of information provision is based on a rational actor model that assumes that, given the 'correct' package of information, citizens will weigh up the options and make an 'informed choice'. This denies the role played by emotions in the operations of markets, and especially those for treatments or other interventions that promise to relieve suffering and/or extend lives.

The digital architecture of 'choice'

In seeking to make sense of citizens' engagements with digital media, one needs to understand the broader context within which only some information and certain options are presented as valid: the 'architecture of choice'. In the online world, 'choice architects', notably big technology companies, seek to monitor and nudge behaviours in ways that they judge to be potentially profitable. These companies make their money largely through advertising and the use of search engine optimization using data derived from citizens' online searches and trackable behaviours. They understand that individual decision-making is emotionally based and they have devised techniques for exploiting citizens' fears, desires and insecurities in order to extract data used to generate profit. They would also seem to exploit their ignorance about how their data is harvested and used in their algorithms.

In 2016, Google made nearly 90 percent of its revenue through advertising via its own Google network websites (Statistica, 2018c). Since its birth in 1996, Google has been transformed from a search engine into an advertising machine and is increasingly moving into cloud computing. According to US venture capital firm Kleiner Perkins, in 2016 Google and Facebook accounted for 85 percent of the share of internet advertising growth in the US (Meeker, 2017: 15), a trend that is thought to be similar in other developing economy markets such as Australia (McDuling and Mason, 2017). In its public statements, Google declares that it aims to be an 'all knowing entity' and to become 'the primary repository of all things digital about you' (Remerowski, 2014). Google's omnipotent aspiration is of concern to many citizens worried about privacy and autonomy, as reflected in the European Union's 'right to be forgotten' law, which aims to protect privacy by requiring search engines to remove links to certain personal information (Douglas, 2016). Google collects information on digital users that it then sells to providers of products and services, potentially including treatments that may be clinically unproven. Information that is 'not forgotten' can be extracted for future purposes, including for marketing, without the knowledge and consent of users. Google has a vested interest in an *expanding* consumer market, including for new treatments and other products that are sold directly to consumers via the internet. In 2018 it was reported that the Australian Competition and Consumer Commission was investigating claims that Google 'harvests huge amounts of data from Android phones, including detailed location information' (Davies, 2018). It was alleged that not only did this data transfer raise further privacy concerns for the 10 million Android users in Australia, but also that they were 'reportedly paying their telco providers to send the data' (ibid.). Given the role of smartphones in the networking of the self, it has become increasingly difficult for citizens to avoid the reach of Google and other interests that seek to collect and monetize their data (Chapter 3).

A point often overlooked by commentators on digital technologies is that, in the online world, 'digital' refers not just to technological artefacts (the internet, mobile devices) but also to data and information that is collected, stored, analysed and conveyed via those artefacts. According to proponents of big data analysis, information or data that had not been ascribed value is transformed by digital technologies into a format that has useful, unique value (Mayer-Schönberger and Cukier, 2013: 77–79). Thus, increasingly, big data is being collected and analysed, often in real time, to enable the prediction of adverse health events and those who are at risk of becoming ill. Big data has found application, for example, in tracking the spread of the flu virus by looking for 'correlations between the frequency of certain search queries' and the spread of the flu or disease over time and place (ibid.: 1–3). Research teams are currently exploring means for forecasting the arrival of flu by drawing on data from various sources, including official notification systems, social media sources and Google Flu Trends, which aggregates search queries (Margo, 2018). While it has been argued that big data analytics will deliver many health benefits for citizens, its use of algorithms involves abstracting information from its social contexts, which may result in deleterious outcomes for individuals and communities. Difficult-to-measure qualitative information that gives meaning to data, such as that regarding individuals' personal circumstances, is largely ignored (O'Neil, 2016). Such data may be used for various purposes, including to determine health standards (e.g. body mass index for measuring weight), which may lead to stigmatization and discrimination against those who are found to be 'non-normal' (e.g. exclusion from certain kinds of healthcare); to establish criteria for investment in health initiatives, which may lead to a skewing of priorities towards those that are cost-effective rather than beneficial for health; or to decide insurance premiums, which may lead to certain groups being inadvertently punished because they happen to be at greater risk of illness or injury (ibid.).

As Cathy O'Neil argues, algorithmic models include human biases that reinforce discrimination against certain groups—generally those who are already socio-economically disadvantaged. Google, Facebook and other big internet companies routinely utilize and modify algorithms to enable them to better sort and categorize information on consumers and to decide how best to steer behaviours (ibid.). Algorithms are being adapted according to accumulated data on consumers' technology preferences. For example, in 2016 Google announced that it was 'boosting the effects of [its] mobile-friendly algorithm', developed the previous year (Schwartz, 2016). Those who do not use mobile devices or do not have mobile connectivity, but otherwise have access to the internet, for example, may find that they do not receive the same information or equivalent quality information to those who do own mobile devices. In research undertaken in 2013 involving a survey of Facebook's algorithm, it was found that 62 percent of people were unaware that the company tinkered with the newsfeed, but rather 'believed that the system instantly shared everything they posted with all of their friends' (O'Neil, 2016: 183). Further, citizens may not be aware that big data companies may manipulate their emotions. In 2012, without permission Facebook used data on 680,000 of its users to investigate whether updates on newsfeeds could affect their mood. Facebook used linguistic software to doctor newsfeeds and then studied users' subsequent behaviour to assess the impact on users' moods. They found evidence that 'the doctored new feeds had indeed altered their moods', as measured by their subsequent positive or negative posts (ibid.: 183–184). While such conduct may not be routine, it does highlight the potential for manipulations that may occur online and that may be used by advertisers to market products and by others with nefarious intentions (Chapter 5).

Conclusions

As explained, there is a long history of efforts to predict the future implications of technological developments, including electronic communications. These include the work of wellknown scholars such as Marshall McLuhan and Erich Fromm, whose contributions were briefly discussed at the beginning of the chapter. These scholars' predictions about the impacts of the then emerging electronic technologies seem prescient from today's perspective in terms of their foretelling of a future that now appears to be unfolding, at least in broad outline and in certain respects. However, as argued, these writers present a technologically determinist vision of media, which are conceived as singular and all-powerful, allowing little scope for human agency, including creative engagement with technologies, including subversion and resistance. While, as explained, the big data companies such as Google, Facebook, Apple and Amazon have colonized the internet and endeavour to monetize data through the use of algorithms and thereby shape the architecture of choice within which individual citizens make decisions and construct their identities, individuals *do* have agency and may express this in multiple ways, some of which may not align with what companies and various authorities may wish. But exactly how much agency do citizens have? And are they able to express it in ways that disrupt dominant relations of power? I will return to these questions at various points in the following chapters, and especially in Chapter 5, where I provide an overall assessment of digital health and its claims. In the next chapter I focus on medicine, a field that some see as being profoundly transformed by digital technologies, and especially the big data-driven algorithms that are beginning to find application.

agency

3

THE EMERGENT ALGORITHMIC MEDICINE

Digital technologies are finding rapid application in medicine and healthcare, as in other spheres of social life. There are great expectations that digital technologies will allow citizens to 'connect' with experts in new ways, and to collect, store, analyse and share the proliferating amount of data on health and illness. Digital technologies are also seen to offer new tools for educating practitioners, communicating advice, and administering treatment and care. As noted, many governments anticipate that digital technologies will usher in a future 'personalized', 'predictive' medicine that will offer treatments that are more timely, efficient and cost-effective, and safer, than what is currently offered. The analysis of big data offers the prospect of extracting value from a mass of otherwise valueless information, to identify those at risk of disease, to offer more targeted treatments to those who are ill and to better assist those who need care. This big data may take, and is taking, many forms including genetic, environmental and lifestyle information; however, as I explain, in medicine, biological and, especially, genetic information, and increasingly personal bio-physical data contributed by individuals themselves, is seen to hold particular value. It is anticipated that machine learning—a form of artificial intelligence (AI) whereby computers 'learn' as they are exposed to new data—will generate new insights about disease that will inform decisions about investments (e.g. in drug trials) and clinical interventions that will both enhance economic efficiency and advance health.

This chapter examines how the conceptions and practices of medicine and healthcare are changing in this context. It examines how discourses of promise, hope and expectation attached to technologies, and specifically digital technologies, shape how the future of medicine and healthcare is imagined and how this, in turn, impacts on policy and investment decisions and the conduct of those who have, or are expected to have, a stake in the imagined future of medicine and healthcare. Increasingly, policies and programs in healthcare are oriented towards a new future medicine, which may be called algorithmic medicine, drawing on big data analysis assisted through the use of AI, including machine learning, along with data generated by citizens themselves, who increasingly are expected to connect with health and medicine via websites, apps and wearable technologies. 'Digital health' presupposes and demands specific selves, social relations and forms of citizenship, and distinct ways of thinking about and enacting medicine, risk management and care. The establishment of this new digital health economy presupposes that people will play an active role in collecting, interpreting and acting on data about themselves as well as participating in big data projects. It is here, I suggest, that digital technologies, especially the internet and social media, play a crucial role, especially in engendering the self-monitoring of health and risk and the self-management of illness and care. This chapter identifies some of the major stakeholders and winners and losers from this emergent digital health economy. To begin, to help understand what is distinctive about the envisaged future medicine and its practices, it is valuable to first consider how medicine currently is and has been practised.

The different medicines

While commentators often refer to 'medicine' as though it comprises a singular, stable entity, through history and across societies and cultures there have been and continue to co-exist diverse forms of practice labelled as such. These include allopathic medicine, complementary and alternative medicine, Ayurvedic medicine, genomic medicine and molecular medicine. These different medicines entail competing theories about the body, its functioning and 'disease'; about the defining elements of health (or 'wellbeing') and how to measure and assess variations from its presumed 'normal' state; about manifestations of this 'disease', both objective (as signs, symptoms, cases) and subjective (e.g. as 'illness'); about the role played by biophysical, environmental and lifestyle factors in establishing, maintaining and compromising ideal 'health', and about what constitutes a remedy, treatment or cure; and about the ascribed administering authorities and the relationship between these authorities and subjects of treatment/cure or care.

Conceptions of health, body, disease, illness, medicine, healthcare and treatment are constructed and sustained or enacted through social practices, including those involving the active involvement of citizens. Moreover, as Mol (2007) observes, disease, illness and so on are 'multiple' objects or phenomena, whose status is achieved, negotiated and contested in different contexts. In contemporary Western societies, however, a particular kind of medicine, namely 'biomedicine', and related conceptions of health and normality, have become hegemonic—colonizing, supplanting or marginalizing other forms of medicine and healthcare. These encompass those that rely on local and traditional knowledge, such as indigenous and religious-based healing practices, rather than advanced, expensive technologies and associated expertise. In many contemporary societies, 'healthcare' has, to a large extent, become synonymous with high-tech biomedicine and the applications of the knowledge of specific forms of expertise.

This biomedical dominance—or rather imperialism, given its global reach and profound politico-economic and socio-cultural impacts—is enabled by many factors, some of which I will describe later in this chapter and those that follow. However, its origins can be traced back to the beginnings of the Western scientific age, the sixteenth century, and the development of a mechanistic view of the body (the body-as-machine) (Capra, 1983). From this period, the Cartesian mind/body dualism has prevailed, with the body and its workings viewed largely in isolation from psychosocial, physical and social environmental factors, and with the use of scientific knowledge and scientifically trained experts to 'correct' malfunctions. The focus on the body as an abstraction has led to the neglect of the power relations of gender, race, class and sexuality and how these shape 'health', and how healthcare is conceived and practised. However, through most of Western history the male body has provided the standard against which the female body has been seen as an inverted, inferior form (Laqueur, 1990)—a bias that has continued up to the present in the teaching of human anatomy (Petersen, 1998).

Historians and philosophers of medicine see the eighteenth century as inaugurating a major shift in conceptions of the body, health, disease and medicine that have provided the foundation for the much anticipated personalized medicine—or what is increasingly referred to as 'precision' medicine. As Foucault, for example, explains, up until the eighteenth century, 'medicine related more to health than normality', which referred to 'qualities of vigour, suppleness and fluidity, which were lost in illness and which it was the task of medicine to restore' (Foucault, 1975: 35). By the eighteenth century, however, medicine was becoming more classificatory and concerned with 'pathological anatomy' (ibid.: ch. 8), while health was 'becoming the object of calculation', and understood by reference to disease 'whose absence was generally held to be the equivalent of health' (Canguilhem, 2012: 44, 48). By the nineteenth century, medicine 'was regulated more in accordance with normality than with health', with concepts and prescriptions being defined in 'relation to a standard of functioning and organic structure' which was previously of only marginal and theoretical interest to doctors (Foucault, 1975: 35). The 'normal' and the 'pathological' henceforth began to be perceived as fundamentally different states, while disease or pathology defined as a deviation from normal bodily functioning. The nineteenth century saw the rise of the germ theory of disease, which profoundly shaped preventive and treatment practices, such as the use of diagnostic categories and methods of diagnosis based on the categorization of illness signs and symptoms. During this period, the hospital was refashioned to accommodate the social relations and technologies premised on an increasingly disease-focused, clinical medicine (ibid.: ch. 4). The contemporary hospital is, in many respects, a product of this period; however, as noted in Chapter 2, this institution itself is expected to undergo profound transformation in coming years.

The coming 'personalized' medicine

When commentators speak of a new, future personalized or precision medicine, they generally refer to specific changes in medical practice associated with the expected advancement and convergence of technologies arising from various fields of science, especially genetics and genomics (whole-genome sequencing), data science, and information and communication (IT) sciences. As noted, data on individual biophysical functioning is increasingly seen as crucial to realizing precision medicine. However, use of the term personalized medicine (or precision medicine) is inconsistent, varying somewhat between jurisdictions and other contexts of use, likely reflecting ambiguity about exactly what is expected to be achieved and with what degree of certainty, as well as proponents' concerns about publics' unrealistic expectations about unique, individualized treatments in the wake of early hyping of the field. In some contexts, other terms are used: 'customized medicine, 'stratified medicine', or 'P4 medicine' (P4 being shorthand for predictive, preventive, personalized and participatory)—each having their own particular nuances.

In a 2017 Australian Government report, precision medicine is defined as 'the application of clinical and laboratory data, including genetic data, gathered in aggregate across a population of healthy and ill people, to better guide the management of an individual patient' (Australian Government, 2017a: 86) In another report, *The Future of Precision Medicine in Australia*, also published in 2017, by the Australian Council of Learned Academies, personalized or precision medicine is defined as 'The ability to analyse disease in terms of an individual's makeup, when compared with and studied alongside aggregated clinical and laboratory data from healthy and diseased populations'; further, that 'precision medicine allows health and disease to be viewed at an increasingly fine-grained resolution, attuned to the complexities of both the biology of each individual and variation within the population' (ACOLA, 2017: 2). Elsewhere in that report it is stated that precision medicine is 'an umbrella category encompassing medical and scientific techniques that work at a molecular level to identify and address disease-related variation' (ibid.: 14).

These definitions are broad and potentially confusing, but convey the considerable ambitions underlying the vision of future medicine, in terms of the intent to cross-link and analyse different kinds of data at the level of both populations and genomes, and the promise of more individualized treatments. The analysis of 'big data' is central to this envisaged future medicine. The idea that these different kinds of data derived from different sources may be combined to create treatments that are tailored or customized to those who share a particular genetic profile has gained momentum during the first two decades of the twenty-first century. There have been growing expectations that new developments in IT will enable the collection, storage and analysis of the big data that will ultimately make this personalization possible. Digitalization is seen to provide the means by which medicine will be able to offer a more refined disease classification, so that treatments can be more targeted to genetically similar sub-populations and delivered to the patient in real time. However, it is noteworthy that in many recent government reports and programs, such as those by the US National Academy of Sciences, the term personalized has been largely replaced with precision, as the former is seen to be potentially 'misread as implying treatment crafted individually for each patient'; although, interestingly, precision, too, is seen as potentially misleading in that it 'suggests a degree of certainty that is unlikely to be reflected in the realities of precision medicine' (Hunter, 2016 citing ACOLA, 2017: 14). The politics behind the growing adoption of the latter terminology is itself intriguing, especially given observations made by sociologists and others years ago in regard to the definitional problems and practical limitations of personalized medicine (Hedgecoe, 2004; Petersen, 2006, 2011: 30–32). While both terms are arguably misleading and politically loaded, for the sake of clarity in the following discussion I adopt 'precision' in line with the current terminological preference.

As I discuss later, the promise of precision medicine goes beyond the delivery of tailored treatments. It offers the prospect of fulfilling broader health and politico-economic and nation-building objectives. In the above Australian Government report, genomics and precision medicine are seen to play a role in early diagnosis of rare and chronic diseases, especially cancer; in prevention ('enabling targeted public health campaigns, more specific cohort screening, increased awareness of individual susceptibility, and self management of lifestyle and prevention activities'); and 'better and safer treatments' through 'facilitating individual drug and treatment matching' (Australian Government 2017a: 86) In this report, which received much media coverage, it was announced that genomics and precision medicine would become a 'national mission' and help make Australia 'the healthiest country on earth' (ibid.: 86). The ACOLA report notes that 'precision medicine and the technologies that support it are poised to reshape healthcare, invigorate biotechnology and ripple out to fields such as agriculture, environmental science, defense and beyond' (ACOLA, 2017: 2).

In 2016, the Australian Health Ministers' Advisory Council 'agreed that a whole-of-government National Health Genomics Policy Framework was required to "capitalize on emerging genomic knowledge by better integrating genomics into the Australian health system"' (Australian Government, 2017b citing ACOLA, 2017: 18). Under this framework, a number of strategic priorities have been identified, including 'delivering high quality care for people through a person-centred approach to integrating genomics into healthcare'; 'building a skilled workforce that is literate in genomics', and 'ensuring sustainable and strategic investment in cost-effective genomics' (Department of Health, 2018a). The USA's Precision Medicine Initiative and Genomics England have articulated similarly ambitious aspirations and are seeking to mainstream genomics into healthcare via targeted investment, the establishment of related infrastructure and the training of personnel (National Human Genome Research Institute, 2018; Genomics England, 2018). Clearly, high expectations attach to this field and while technological developments, especially in big data computational analysis (big data analytics), have undoubtedly heightened these expectations, optimism for the kind of medicine that is envisaged has a long history, much longer than many recent discussions suggest.

'Personalization' in the history of biomedicine

The concept of personalization in medicine can be traced back to Hippocrates around 2,400 years ago. However, the idea of a personalized medicine involving precise diagnosis and treatment only gained a foothold in Western medicine in the nineteenth century with efforts to diagnose and distinguish diseases at the cellular level, although at that time categories of disease were broad and treatments limited (Abrahams, 2011). The idea of personalized medicine began to gain serious traction in the early 2000s, with the announcement of the 'mapping' (sequencing) of the human genome in 2000, and numerous news articles reporting 'breakthroughs' that implied changes were imminent. The announcement that the human genome had been mapped (a metaphor commonly used at this time) was seen by many to have laid the foundation for a post-genomic future, where attention shifted to under-standing how genes function and how to apply such knowledge to the develop-ment of new tests, treatments and interventions. From the early to mid-2000s, news articles heralding new medical 'breakthroughs' began to make increasing reference to treatments being tailored to individual patients, or 'patients' genes', or 'genetic make-up' (Petersen, 2001, 2002). The idea that one could tailor treatment to a person's genetic make-up has strongly resonated with policymakers, scientists and clinicians, suggesting as it does that medicine may become more cost-efficient, predictive, effective and safer. This predictive medicine, it is argued, will enable conditions to be treated, or lifestyle changes undertaken, before they become chronic and require expensive high-tech interventions and hospital care.

With growing anxieties about the ability of healthcare systems to cope with the expected growing health demands and financial costs of rapidly ageing populations, many governments have looked to technologies that may help prevent conditions or assist people as they age (Chapter 4). At the same time, biotechnology and pharmaceutical companies have sought to capitalize on these anxieties through marketing new tests, treatments and devices (Petersen, 2018). The language of personalization is consistent with the individualistic and consumerist ethos of con-temporary neoliberalism, implicitly ascribing responsibility for health (and, in effect, blame for ill health) to individuals who are expected to care for themselves through the personal exercise of 'choice' in the market of healthcare products and services, increasingly available online. Personalization is a term used in a growing number of areas, in healthcare and beyond, and increasingly informs the language and practices of marketing ('personalized marketing'), whereby data analysis and digital technol-ogies are used to deliver individualized messages and products to consumers. However, the drive to develop a medicine that is personalized in the sense of paying cognisance to the individual's genetic profile is also underpinned by an economic rationale linked to the efficacy and safety of current medical practices.

One of the enduring concerns in medicine has been patients' variable adverse drug reactions that limit the effectiveness of treatment and may result in illness or death, and it is here that precision medicine is seen to play a significant role in the future. The variability of drug responses is thought to be due to a number of factors, including the person's age, weight, sex, ethnicity, environmental influences (such as diet, alcohol consumption and cigarette smoking), the nature of the disease, interac-tions with other drugs, the dose of the medicine and whether it is taken as prescribed, the time of the day the response is observed, and a possible genetic variation, among other factors (Royal Society, 2005: 6–7). In its 2005 report *Personalised Medicines*, the Royal Society noted that 'a 20- to 30-fold variation is commonly seen in the response to drugs'. Further, it observed, 'The contribution of genetic factors must be considered, with the factors listed above, on a case-by-case basis' and 'Each factor is like [sic] to contribute differently to each drug response' (ibid.: 7).

This presents a more complicated, qualified picture of the role of genetics in disease than is portrayed in more recent depictions of the future of personalized medicine. Further, as some geneticists have acknowledged, many genetic-related conditions involve a complex interaction of genes, and genes and environments, which will make accurate prediction of genetic diseases difficult if not impossible (Holtzman and Marteau, 2000). Nevertheless, the promise of personalized treatments has underpinned the development of a whole field of research, pharmacogenetics, devoted to studying 'how people's genetic make-up affects their responses to medicines.' (Royal Society, 2005: 1) Writing in 2005, the Royal Society saw the introduction of pharmacogenetic testing in healthcare as having 'the potential to reduce costs through improved interventions, greater efficacy, less inappropriate prescribing and fewer ADRs [adverse drug reactions]', although it acknowledged that 'it is not clear whether or not the tests will increase or decrease overall health costs' (ibid.: 34).

A cautious optimism

Despite the complexity of genetic-related conditions, and the multiple influences on individuals' drug reactions, in its summary statement the Royal Society was generally positive about the future of pharmacogenetics and the potential for personalized medicine, albeit offering a qualified conclusion:

> Pharmacogenetics is unlikely to revolutionise or personalise medical practice in the immediate future. Rather, as related research identifies sub-groups of common diseases based on different genetic or environmental causes [...] it should become possible to introduce genetic testing to predict people's response to at least some drugs.
>
> (ibid.: 1)

These measured comments do not convey the expectation of the imminent wholesale transformation of healthcare that has been suggested in many media reports and scientific portrayals of personalized/precision medicine. Rather, the Royal Society called for more research, noting that 'Studies of pharmacogenetic variability will require the analysis of large repositories of clinical data during and after a clinical trial', as well as education of health professionals, which is seen to have lagged behind scientific and technical developments (ibid.: 1). As recently as 2017, medical authorities continued to offer qualified assessments of precision medicine, with Australia's National Health and Medical Research Council, for example, cautioning against 'desperate patients investing hope' in genetic tests, with a spokesperson for the Council commenting that for 'a majority of patients', such testing 'is a way off' (Walker, 2017).

At least one pharmaceutical industry representative has expressed concerns about the use of the terminology of personalization in medicine. The head of GlaxoSmithKline's genetic research unit, Lon Cardon, has stated that 'the terms pharmacogenetics and personalized medicine should not be used' and that 'the idea that treatment will eventually be personalized is simply not possible' (Cardon, 2009, citing Lock and Nguyen, 2010). Nevertheless, despite these critical or cautionary comments, heightened optimism for the concept of precision medicine endures. Recent evidence of this was evident in the level of coverage given to the claimed breakthrough involving the development of a new blood test, called CancerSEEK, that may be able to detect eight common cancers via DNA and proteins released into the blood (Cohen et al., 2018). In some coverage, this 'breakthrough' was presented as something of a game-changer, allowing a number of cancers to be screened at once and at the same time as a routine blood test, although it has been suggested that the test may still be some years away from clinical application (Gibbs, 2018).

The significance of public consent

An often-overlooked issue in debates about precision medicine is that, if it is to become established as envisaged, it will be necessary to achieve public legitimacy and consent for the collection of large repositories of data and the testing of populations. As the Royal Society observed (2005: 1), public support is crucial for realizing the potential of scientific and technological advances, and a public dialogue commissioned as part of its study found that 'there were major concerns, including issues of consent and confidentiality in the handling of biological samples, and whether the Government and the healthcare system could successfully deliver genetic technology in the future'. Community concerns about the collection of biological samples appears to have endured— at least in the UK. In 2017 the House of Commons Science and Technology Committee, in its report *Genomics and Genome Editing in the NHS*, highlighted public concerns about sharing genomic data, especially with insurance companies, and emphasized the need to 'raise public awareness of genomic medicine, and the data sharing needed to enable it, ahead of the introduction of the planned Genomic Medicine Service'. (House of Commons Science and Technology Committee, 2017: 4.75)

While obtaining consent from those participating in the UK's fundamental genome research venture, The 100,000 Genomes Project (which I discuss in more detail later) 'had not been problematic […] such observations relate to cohorts of patients with specific diseases and who received substantial guidance through the consent process, which our witnesses agreed would be too demanding for routine genomic sequencing' (ibid.: 4.71). Obtaining consent among the wider public could not be assumed, especially given low levels of public understanding of genomics and concerns about the sharing of data. The Committee cited evidence that 82 percent of the general public in the UK 'had either never heard of the term "genomics" or had little understanding of it' (ibid.). It also presented evidence revealing the public's particular concerns about insurance companies accessing their data, which could result in premiums being struck on the basis of the results. This factor, along with the limited funding for the training of NHS staff via the Genomics Education Programme, it was argued, hampered the development of genomic medicine in the UK.

Recently, securing public consent for the sharing of personal information has become even more crucial with reports on the data breach by Cambridge Analytica, whereby the personal details of up to 87 million people may have been harvested from Facebook in the effort to influence the 2016 US elections (Siegal, 2018). This followed an earlier incident in 2017 whereby the US consumer credit reporting agency Equifax announced a 'cybersecurity incident' whereby credit card numbers and other personal information were hacked by approximately 143 million US consumers and UK and Canadian residents (Equifax, 2017). Ironically, one of the services offered by Equifax is credit monitoring and fraud detection. In its press release, Equifax describes itself as 'a global information solutions company that uses trusted unique data, innovative analytics, technology and industry expertise to power organizations and individuals around the world by transforming knowledge into insights that help make more informed business and personal decisions' (Equifax, 2017). As has become evident, it is (or until relatively recently, has been) easy for researchers to harvest information from people's Facebook pages. In 2018, it was reported that in 2014 Swedish and Polish researchers used a program called 'scraper' to 'log every comment and interaction from 160 public Facebook pages for nearly two years', and that 'By May 2016, they had amassed enough information to track how 368 million Facebook members behaved on the social network' (Frenkel, 2018). The report also noted that 'It is one of the largest known sets of user data ever assembled from Facebook', citing one of the researchers, who said 'We were concerned how easy it was to collect this' (ibid.).

Public concerns have long been expressed about the collection of biological samples for population-wide biobanks, especially the ability or capacity of authorities to deliver what is promised and ensure that contributed data is not misused, or used for unauthorized purposes, or used in a selective way. Some scientists, policymakers and non-government organizations have voiced similar concerns, especially the implications of personal data being interpreted or used in a manner that may compromise its usefulness or actually cause harm, which was evident during the establishment of UK Biobank (Petersen, 2005). In commenting on UK Biobank, Ian Gibson, Chair of the House of Commons Select Committee on Science and Technology (2001–05), commented in a Parliamentary Petition that,

> Sampling adults and using their genetic information via-à-vis their patchy recollections of past behaviour and exposure to environmental risks will make it difficult to disentangle genetic and environmental factors, which will have important implications for the findings of Biobank.
>
> (Gibson, 2002)

As Gibson went on to note, this would lead to an over-emphasis on the genetic influences on disease processes, since this would be the only hard data that could be relied upon, leading to a 'bias' in results which would 'have important consequences for public health policies'. Despite such concerns, public debates about personalized medicine have been limited, with key decisions, for example about biobanking involving large-scale (population-wide) repositories of genetic, medical and lifestyle information, occurring behind closed doors and limited to a relatively few decision-makers (GeneWatch, 2010). UK Biobank was established at an initial cost of £61.5 million as a resource to enable pharmaceutical companies and other commercial interests to undertake research on 'gene susceptibility for common diseases and adverse drug reactions, using biological material materials links to electronic medical records' (ibid.: 44).

According to GeneWatch, a UK-based activist group that focuses on genetic technologies, in the establishment of UK Biobank, the Medical Research Council 'did not follow the MRC's usual research assessment processes' (ibid.: 79). GeneWatch described the various commercial and government pressures to establish UK Biobank in terms of 'return on investment', with the Government's commitment to the knowledge-based bio-economy being prominent among these (ibid.: 79–96). The idea of a 'genomic revolution', it noted, 'was promoted by a small circle of government advisors', and 'the Government has invested billions of pounds of NHS money in the idea of "early health", which includes using people's genetic make-up (their genomes) and information stored in their medical records to try to predict which diseases they will get and treat them while they are still healthy' (ibid.: 95). The project was established despite many doctors' and scientists' concerns that 'early health' will unlikely benefit the population (ibid.: 96). National biobanks have, in many cases, been established with little or no public consultation; and where this has been undertaken, it has been of a limited form involving, for example, surveys or one-off stakeholder-driven focus groups (Petersen, 2005; Gottweis and Petersen, 2008).

One solution that has been suggested in regards to concerns about the security of personal information that has been contributed to precision medicine initiatives has been to adopt blockchain technology, which involves a distributed database, rather than a central database that may be attractive to hackers. According to proponents of this technology, blockchain is a superior means of ensuring security, since all computers in the network must approve an exchange before it can be verified and recorded (Schumacher, 2018). In short, with blockchain the contents of messages are encrypted so that only authorized users have access to information. As Schumacher explains, 'if someone were to try to dishonestly change an entry on one computer, those changes would be rejected by the many computers used in the verification process because the data wouldn't match up' (ibid.). However, while the idea of distributed databases sounds appealing, some advocates have a vested interest in the technology. A distributed database does not resolve the fundamental issue of the failure of the custodians of such collections to achieve public consent and legitimacy for their practices. Biobanking in the UK, Iceland, Australia and many other countries has a poor record of public engagement. In many cases, decisions about these repositories of personal medical and lifestyle information have been made by authorities in the absence of meaningful public deliberation on fundamental issues, such as consent for the use of data in the future, third-party access to information, benefit sharing, changes in ownership terms should there be changes in the company storing the data, and so on.

National precision medicine research initiatives

Underpinned by optimism regarding the potential of precision medicine, national governments, including the UK, the USA and Australia, have begun to invest heavily in population-wide genome sequencing or related research initiatives. As we shall see, big companies such as Google and IBM also see opportunities for monetizing genomic data. Genomics and precision medicine have been promoted as the foundation for future healthcare and the means for developing national bio-economies. The advancement of the precision medicine agenda, however, involves cross-national collaborations and networks, comprising researchers, healthcare organizations, life science companies, patient advocate groups, data scientists and IT specialists. Project media releases, overviews and mission statements reveal the bold visions that underlie recent personal medicine initiatives.

In October 2017, it was announced that Australia, through Australian Genomics, would join an international alliance of three 'national genomic medicine initiatives', including Genomics England and the USA's All of US program. It was reported that these three national initiatives were selected by the Global Alliance for Genomics and Health (GA4GH) as 'driver projects'. (Australian Genomics Health Alliance, 2018) On its website, GA4GH is described as 'an international non-profit alliance formed in 2013 to accelerate the potential of research and medicine to advance human health'. Further, it is noted that the venture brings together '500+ leading organizations working in healthcare, research, patient advocacy, life science, and information technology […] to create framework and standards to enable the responsible, voluntary, and secure sharing of genomic data. (Global Alliance for Genomics and Health, 2018) The media release announcing that Australian Genomics would be a 'key driver project' for GA4GH noted that 'These [national driver projects] will pilot GA4GH data sharing frameworks and standards in real-world healthcare settings, and share their experiences and knowledge in integrating genomics into clinical practice' (Australian Genomics Health Alliance, 2018).

Although the announcement of the above initiative did not use the term big data, it made clear that it was envisaged that the alliance would enable genomic sequencing to achieve the scale required for big data analysis and would serve to expedite the realization of the genomic medical vision. Data exchange is seen as essential to fulfilling this genomics vision; for example, 'GA4GH believes researchers and clinicians have an opportunity and a responsibility to exchange this wealth of data as part of a global "health learning system" to collaboratively investigate, and diagnose, genetic disorders' (ibid.). The announcement referred to researchers' and clinicians' responsibilities in regards to 'this wealth of data' and to the 'global "health learning system"', which suggests an altruistic endeavour underpinned by nationally shared goals, belying the considerable national and cross-national politico-economic interests and investments in this imagined future medicine, and the issues at stake in the potential to patent medicines and claim intellectual property over related technologies (ibid.).

The UK 'driver project', the 100,000 Genomes Project launched in 2012, aims to sequence 100,000 genomes from approximately 70,000 people—those with rare diseases and their families, and patients with cancer. In 2015, the USA's National Institutes of Health launched its Precision Medicine Initiative (All of US), which aims to gather data from at least 1 million people. The latter is a $US1.5 billion decade-long venture that will require citizens to share data on their biology, lifestyle and environment (JASON, 2017: 37–38). Data will be collected continuously over a 10-year period, and there are future plans to collect all electronic health data along with data recorded via wireless sensor technologies, including mobile and wearable devices, along with geospatial and environmental data (ibid.: 36). (On the enthusiasm for wearable devices, see Chapter 4.) A major purpose of the research program will be to make data available to participants, researchers and the public, which raises privacy concerns (ibid.: 37). However, the Precision Medicine Initiative has recognized that de-identification cannot guarantee that the privacy of participants will be guaranteed (ibid.: 37).

Both the US and UK programs, it should be noted, are heavily marketed on the basis of their 'public benefit', as well as the individual benefits to those who participate. For example, the 100,000 Genomes Project notes on its website that 'Researchers will study how best to use genomics in healthcare and how best to interpret the data to help patients', and that 'We also aim to kick-start a UK genomics industry' (Genomics England, 2017). On the website of All of US, it is stated that, 'Among the scientific opportunities […] is the ability to empower study participants with data and information to improve their own health.' It also notes that 'The program will set the foundation for new ways of engaging research participants, sharing health data and information, and employing technology advances to mine the information for comprehensive results' (National Institutes of Health, 2017). However, according to at least some of those associated with the project, optimism for the venture during its mid-development phase appeared to be overblown.

In mid-2016, at the approximate half-way point through the 100,000 Genomes Project, a study of the views of those associated with or employed by the parent company, Genomics England, such as staff members, board members, ethics advisory committee members and representatives from the Department of Health, revealed respondents' disquiet about the overly optimistic 'geno-hype' and 'overpromise' attached to this venture. Concerns expressed included the financial constraints, the complexities of building the infrastructure, and the difficulties encountered in recruiting participants and effecting the organizational and cultural changes required to apply findings in clinical practice in the NHS (Samuel and Farsides, 2017). However, as the authors note, while at the time of the study it was too early to conclude that the project may have been 'overpromised', 'the promissory discourses attached to it have become a part and a drive of the project itself', enabling the venture to gain momentum and for Genomics England to use its resources in its efforts to effect change at the level of clinical delivery (ibid.: 350).

Such global biomedical research alliances in the field of genetics and genomics, involving optimistic visions of research translation for the public benefit, and established for 'information sharing' among scientists, research institutions, and sometimes policymakers and funders, are not new. In the field of biobanks, for example, the international Public Population Project in Genomics (P3G) Consortium, involving the participation of many experts working in the field of genomics in more than 40 countries, was incorporated in 2004. Such ventures can be considered to be large infrastructure projects that involve a unique set of risks—financial, socio-cultural and personal—that go beyond those generally associated with national or regional infrastructure development (e.g. airports, bridges, roads). These ventures need to be sustained over an often extensive (decades-long) period, and involve complex negotiations across borders and academic fields and with diverse actors, including research participants, who, in this field, commonly hold concerns about privacy and commercialization of knowledge and may, in some cases, be distrustful of experts and authorities (Gottweis and Petersen, 2008: 10–11).

While reports on genomic medicine frequently refer to 'responsible' practices (e.g. in regards to the sharing of data) and adherence to ethical and governance protocols, in practice the development of such ambitious ventures generally allows little scope or time for broad deliberation on issues to which they give rise. Little acknowledgement is made of the distinct set of risks and quandaries posed by the collection and analysis of big data, especially involving genomic/genetic data, that is both shared and personal, and is ascribed particular significance in health and medicine and in different communities. The unaddressed question is: how will authorities effectively govern a field involving personal data and high diverse expertise that in many cases is located across national jurisdictions? Mirroring the situation evident in regenerative medicine and other bioscience fields, scientists in this field increasingly are becoming entrepreneurs, straddling the worlds of university and business, while science is becoming increasingly commercialized and expected to contribute to the creation of economic value (Mirowski, 2011). It can be seen in this program of research how diverse expertise—statistical, genetic and digital—is being, or in the near future is expected to be, employed to advance the field—involving often close links between publicly funded institutions, including many universities, and the private sector, spanning the globe. In this context, what or who is to be regulated and by what means? The boundaries between public and private, and local and global, are becoming less and less clear, which creates difficulties for regulation, much of which was developed in the pre-digital era.

Recent initiatives: taking big data to clinical practice

Despite the many risks, quandaries and uncertainties, in recent years a number of small-scale, sometimes disease/condition-specific precision medicine initiatives have gained momentum, with some already marketing their services, or planning to do so in the near future. In Australia, these include the Zero Childhood Cancer program (2017), described as 'Australia's first precision medicine program for children with high-risk or relapsed cancer', and Sydney's Garvan Institute of Medical Research's (2017) Genomic Cancer Medicine Program. They also include the German company Shivon, reported to be seeking to raise investment via 'crypto-currency friendly private equity investors, as well as wealthy individuals and institutions' (Redrup, 2018), and Nebula Genomics, co-founded by Harvard geneticist George Church, which is using 'cryptocurrency as a behavioural incentive' for individuals to sell their data to researchers (Lovett, 2018).

Australia

Rare genetic conditions and childhood cancers have tended to be the focus of these early precision medicine initiatives, since those with rare conditions generally have few treatment options, and the younger one is, the greater the likelihood that the condition is genetically linked (Walker, 2017: 17). The Australian company Genome.One, a wholly owned subsidiary of the Garvan Institute of Medical Research, which was offering personal genome sequencing at the cost of approximately A\$6,400 in 2018, is described on its website as 'the first private clinical genomics service in Australia, offering specialist genetic counseling and genomic testing.' (Genome.One, 2018a) The emergence of such companies signals the movement of precision medicine into the world of direct-to-consumer advertising (Nicol et al., 2016: 293). Advertised services include the provision of diagnostic testing or specialist advice on medical conditions that have a suspected genetic basis; genetic and genomic testing for particular conditions such as those common in certain groups (e.g. Tay-Sachs disease in Ashkenazi Jews); for family planning; and 'wanting to learn about or access genomic testing as part of a personalized health assessment' (Genome.One, 2018a). A link on the Genome.One website notes that it is 'developing an increasing portfolio of services and tools to enable precision healthcare, including: convenient and efficient analytical platforms for evaluation of cohort sequencing data, flexible diagnostic and prognostic genetic testing solutions, sophisticated applications that capture and securely share clinical data and highly accessible software interfaces' (Genome.One, 2018b). In 2018, it was reported that Genome.One was seeking funding from investors to undertake a pilot investigation of integrating its genomic technology into GP practice software (Minion, 2018a). The article reported that 'working with vendors [the company] aims to make genomics seamlessly available via GP desktops'. Professor Dinger is quoted as saying that the software 'was being designed to sit side by side with medical records, so being able to interface directly on the desktop of the physician', and by doing this 'you can actually take information from the medical record, select out the key information that is needed to be able to identify what parts of the genome need to be interrogated, and discover if there is something relevant there' (ibid.).

There are a number of points to make in relation to the above companies. Firstly, it is interesting to observe how genomic/genetic data is already being commodified and monetized, and moving quickly to the marketplace. In public portrayals of Genome.One and its services, there is no evident recognition or concern about the substantial socio-ethical issues raised by such data and its use as the basis for personal decision-making; for example, the fact that genomic/genetic data is never just personal in that it can reveal much about a family, including susceptibilities to disease and issues of paternity. The German company Shivon and the Harvard company Nebula Genomics, as noted, are using cryptocurrencies either to raise funds for their ventures or to incentivize citizens to sell their data to researchers. In their public portrayals, both companies emphasize the potential for genomic data to 'empower' individuals, but seem to pay little attention to the substantial socio-ethical issues raised by the sharing of personal genomic data. It should be noted that Nebula Genomics is not alone in encouraging citizens to sell their health data. The health aggregation platform Health Wizz provides channels for individuals to sell their health records to researchers and pharmaceutical companies, arguing that 'even if the consumer doesn't sell their data a third party may—and probably already has' (Lovett, 2018) (see Chapter 4).

In the case of Genome.One, the company claims to offer a legitimate, comprehensive set of testing options, underpinned by relevant counselling and clinical support. On its website it notes 'Our team of experienced genetic health professionals are available for face-to-face consultations at our rooms in Darlinghurst, Sydney, as well as telephone or telehealth consultations' (Genome.One, 2018a). Such comments are presumably designed to reassure those who are unfamiliar with genomic sequencing, or who are cautious, of the provider's professionalism and attentiveness to the consumer's needs and convenience. However, news reports on the company offer a picture of its development and plans that suggest the need for a more cautious appraisal of its value and implications. For example, the Chief Executive is cited in one report as saying that he 'intends to expand the service to a trusted network of GPs, which will help lower the price' and that 'We still need to provide genetic counselling, so there is a workforce implication in terms of how fast it can be scaled' (Redrup, 2017: 25). This suggests that the infrastructure is much less well developed than is conveyed by the company's public representations. The article also notes that Genome.One had formed a partnership with 'one of the largest US health providers, Sanford Health', which is 'utilising Genome.One's software which takes clinical notes and turns them into a standardised vocabulary, meaning that information can be analysed and used in machine learning algorithms and in research and diagnostics' (ibid.).

Given the information available on Genome.One's website, consumers are unlikely to be aware that their personal information is being aggregated and shared in the way described, which may be contrary to what they desire. Further, while the costs of genomic sequencing have reduced significantly in recent years, the cost (variously A\$1,000–5,000) would still be prohibitively expensive for many people. As Redrup observes, 'it is only really available to the wealthy, except where a pre-existing medical condition requires it', although, as the article also reports, Chief Executive Marcel Dinger believes that 'there would be a progressive mainstreaming of genomics, so that it would eventually be available to the masses' (ibid.: 25) Finally, whether costs will be covered by national or private health insurance schemes is questionable. Genome sequencing is not covered by Australia's Medicare, although some state governments (Victoria and New South Wales) recently allocated funding for the 'genomic testing of children and adults with rare conditions' and for genomic sequencing research, respectively (ibid.: 25). As noted above, the costs of genomic sequencing are likely to exclude many citizens to begin with, and those who do use this service would contribute significant out-of-pocket expenses unless, of course, future governments decide to cover costs, which would likely be hugely expensive—or unless individuals have private insurers who will.

UK

In 2017 the UK Government announced a five-year plan to 'systematically open up genome-based personal medicine for cancer patients through the National Health Service, replacing haphazard testing conducted via regional and local labs operating as a "cottage industry"' (Walker, 2017). Such initiatives have gained impetus from recent developments in computing technology that have reduced the costs of whole-genome sequencing, which are seen to make genetic testing on a large scale feasible (ibid.). For example, whereas in 2012 whole genome sequencing was considered prohibitively expensive, 'upwards of $50,000 a sequence', by 2017 testing could be undertaken at less than $1,000 and performed at the rate of 200 per month (ibid.). Some scientists see the advent of relatively cheap sequencing as the tipping point in the advancement of precision medicine. The argument is that currently many drug trials go down blind alleys and may harm participants. However, as sequencing becomes cheaper and routine, AI and machine learning can be used to mine the accumulated big data to identify people who already have a disease or bodily change due to a genetic variation, which can then inform decisions about which drug trials to pursue (Margo, 2017). Margo's article, focusing on the work of Peter Donnelly, an Oxford University statistician and chief executive of Genomics plc, describes how the linking of each individual's disease history via their medical records and wearable technology would create 'a tsunami of data'. Donnelly is cited as saying: 'The real analytical challenge would be making sense of it and extracting key insights that would help develop better drugs and improve treatment. So we formed a science-led company to bring together the data and develop the tools' (ibid.: 45).

Note that Donnelly is not a biomedical scientist, but rather 'regards himself as a geneticist with a quantitative background' who, with colleagues at Oxford, 'developed a method of combining computationally-intensive statistical approaches with insights from population genetics models to extract as much information as possible from the large datasets now being routinely generated' (ibid.). His comments on the 'analytic challenge […] of making sense of […] and extracting key insights' required to develop improved drugs and treatment are thus significant. Seth Stephens-Davidowitz, an advocate for research using big data who worked as a data scientist for Google, has referred to the pitfalls of identifying too much data and many variables in studies, which may lead to spurious statistical associations. As he comments, this 'curse of dimensionality' is a 'major issue with Big Data, since newer subsets frequently give us exponentially more variables than traditional data sources—every search term, every category of tweet, etc.' (Stephens-Davidowitz,

2017: 247). As he observes, 'if you test enough things, just by random chance, one of them will be statistically significant' (ibid.: 248). Stephens-Davidowitz cites examples of where this curse of dimensionality can mislead, including in studies that have purportedly found genes linked to high IQs (ibid.: 248–250). In relation to the latter, he concludes, 'The human genome, scientists now know, differs in millions of ways. There are, quite simply, too many genes to test' (ibid.: 250). However, the overriding danger of reliance on data from genomic sequencing is the tendency to attribute particular significance to DNA, to the neglect of the multitude of other factors likely to affect health status, and for an over-reliance on machines to determine the significance of associations. Genome sequencing is based on the assumption that it is possible to produce objective, incontestable 'proof' of our health by screening out biases implicit in human judgements.

Estonia

The optimism surrounding genomic medicine is perhaps nowhere more apparent than Estonia, where the Government announced in 2018 that it would offer 100,000 people free genetic testing as part of an initiative involving collaborations between the Ministry of Social Affairs, the National Institute for Health Development and the Estonian Genome Centre at the University of Tartu (HIMSS Insights, 2018). This initiative will involve translating citizens' personalized reports into everyday medical practice via an e-Health portal. Estonia has a long history of biobanking via the Estonian Genome Project, which has been seen as a 'bridge to Europe' and a means for advancing national political identity in the wake of the post-Soviet era (Eensaar, 2008). As part of its nation-building endeavours, Estonia has embraced new technologies, including digital technologies, and has developed telecommunications and electronics industries. A report announcing the genomic medicine initiative noted that Estonia had already established 'many encrypted digital solutions incorporated into government functions that link the nation's various databases via end-to-end encrypted pathways' (HIMSS Insights, 2018)—a description that evidently reflects government sensitivity to the kinds of security issues raised earlier in regards to centralized databases, which are prone to hacking. The website of the Ministry of Social Affairs states that, as part of its personalized medicine initiative, the Ministry intended to undertake two clinical pilot projects, one focusing on 'Personal prevention and early detection of breast cancer', the other on 'Prevention of cardiovascular disease, statin treatment (cholesterol lowering treatment) determination and implementation of personal indications' (Republic of Estonia Ministry of Social Affairs, 2018). The Estonian example illustrates how genomic medicine initiatives closely align with national politico-economic objectives, especially nation building. While this nation-building ambition, especially through technology-driven wealth creation, is not unique to Estonia, this national example clearly exemplifies the role that governments often play in these big data-driven ventures, in investment decisions in particular areas of medicine and healthcare. However, as I explain in the following paragraphs, big companies are also major actors in the development of genomics medicine.

Google Genomics

Google is one among a number of big technology companies—notably IBM (see below)—that are keen to exploit the opportunities presented by genomic medicine. It has advertised its Cloud Platform as enabling life science companies to 'securely store, process, explore, and share large, complex datasets' (Google Genomics, n.d.a). The claimed benefits of using Google Cloud include speedy completion of large genomic research programs; the ability to process 'as many genomes and experiments as you like in parallel'; the potential to scale projects regardless of their size; the capacity to share tools and data with one's group or collaborators or with the broader community 'if and when you choose'; security of data 'that can meet or exceed the requirements of HIPAA [Health Insurance Portability and Accountability Act] and protected health information'; and data sharing. Google Genomics is evidently keen to assist its users to maximize the transactional value of their research endeavours: 'With GCP [Google Cloud Platform] you can better monetize the access and usage of your genomics data by hosting it in a storage bucket where operations, network and retrieval costs are easily billed to your clients' (ibid.).

To promote its service, Google has produced a 'white paper', *Genomic Data is Going Google*, lending gravitas to a document that is essentially an advertising blurb promoting the value of Google Genomics to researchers (Google Genomics, n.d. b). Google would no doubt be aware that a majority of healthcare and life science organizations are already active in genomic medicine initiatives, or plan to be in the next few years, but that many faced the difficulty of having insufficient technical structures to realise their objective (Siwicki, 2018a). The 'white paper' emphasizes the move in biology from a qualitative to a quantitative science, and the fact that DNA sequencing has made this a 'data-rich field for the first time'. It is here that Google, it is argued, provides unparalleled benefits in providing the 'scalable technologies' that will enable genomic medical research to be undertaken. As it notes, 'Cloud computing provides a useful, elastic resource for manipulating enormous datasets without the time or cost of moving that data from place to place' (Google Genomics, n.d.b).

Critiques of genome hype and quantification

Underlying the idea of precision medicine and associated big data analytics are implicit and problematic conceptions about the kinds of knowledge and understanding that are valuable in terms of advancing health and creating economic wealth and social benefit. This is knowledge that is based on a molecular understanding of the body and health, employing quantitative and computational methods, oriented to creating ever-finer categorizations of disease. Renée Fox (2003) describes the so-called biological revolution, in which molecular and cell biology, with its genetic focus, became ascendant in the wake of Crick and Watson's (1953) research findings on the double helix structure of DNA, unleashing 'a veritable explosion of information and knowledge' epitomized in the Human

Genome Project. However, as Margaret Lock and Vinh-Kim Nguyen (2010: 308) argue, the 'genomic hope' that has surrounded the Human Genome Project and related gene mapping endeavours 'ignores local biologies; local, regional and global politics; environmental variables; the reality of social arrangements and worsening poverty; and it makes the assumption that technological innovation, in and of itself, is always for the good'. These are themes that I elaborate on later, in offering my overall assessment of digital health and its economy (Chapter 5).

Artificial intelligence and machine learning

With suggestions that precision medicine will rely more and more on computational analysis, there is the potential that subjective, 'intuitive' (and thus difficult to quantify) forms of knowledge and experience that the practitioner brings to practice, established over an extensive period of training, are being supplanted by the purportedly objective knowledge produced by AI. In his book *The Digital Doctor*, the physician Robert Wachter documents the profound impact of information technologies on medical practice in the US. In his view, technologies have had mixed results, sometimes improving the delivery of healthcare, at other times adversely affecting health outcomes through an over-reliance on machines, especially AI (Wachter, 2017) (Chapter 5). The imagined future of medicine, with a greater role for AI and machine learning, involves a more restricted role for *qualitative, contextual* information that provides meaning to the 'metrics' that are collected and used to assess health status and treatments, and other phenomena. While it is argued that the use of algorithms eliminates human biases through introducing mathematical 'impartiality', in many cases they reproduce biases and faulty assumptions (the 'garbage in, garbage out' principle) since they ultimately rely on human instructions. The utility of AI for diagnostics, clinical decisions or other applications is limited by the quality and accessibility of information, and this is questionable in a number of jurisdictions.

A 2017 report undertaken for the US Department of Health and Human Services flagged a number of issues regarding the quality and accessibility of data used in AI: privacy issues, which make the collection and sharing of data 'cumbersome compared to other types of data'; the expense of collecting data (e.g. derived from longitudinal studies and clinical trials) which means that 'it tends to be tightly guarded once it is collected'; the lack of interoperability of electronic health records that can impede even simple computational methods; and 'the inability to capture relevant social and environmental information in existing systems' that 'leaves a key set of variables out of data streams for individual health' (JASON, 2017: 7). This report also drew attention to the 'imbalance in the effort to capture the diverse data needed for the application of AI techniques to precision medicine, with information on environmental toxicology and exposure particularly suffering' (ibid.: 3–4). It made a number of recommendations to address this deficit, including the collection of environmental exposure data: 'build[ing] toxin screening (e.g. dioxin, lead) into routine blood panels', collecting information on diet and environmental toxins via health questionnaires, and 'develop [ing] protocols and IT capabilities to collect and integrate the diverse data' (ibid.: 4).

The limitations and biased character of the data used to inform AI may have far-reaching socio-political and ethical implications. O'Neil (2016) has documented the various ways in which algorithms in their operations discriminate against certain groups, especially women, ethnic minorities, and socio-economically disadvantaged groups—in such areas as academic selection, hiring and firing decisions, credit ratings, and health insurance. Replacing or augmenting human decision-making with algorithmic decision-making carries various other risks, including threats to privacy, opaque decisions, and the drawing of spurious correlations (Mittlestadt et al., 2016). Because algorithms are increasingly used to infer characteristics such as personality, gender and language use on social media, there are significant implications for personal privacy (Koene, 2017). As Koene observes, algorithmic categorization reduces human diversity to discrete social and psychological 'classes'. This can be seen in a study he cites where algorithms were used to determine whether a person is gay or straight, based upon 35,326 facial images taken from public profiles on a US dating website. As the authors of the study concluded, 'given that companies are increasingly using computer vision algorithms to detect people's innate traits, our findings expose a threat to the privacy and safety of gay men and women' (Kosinski and Wang, 2017).

Enrolling citizens in big data projects

Recent trends suggest that in the future medicine and healthcare will rely more and more on information derived from big data analytics, AI and machine learning, whereby a computer 'dives' into data on the basis of limited instructions to find patterns of its own (including in the burgeoning research literature) and then connects these with particular outcomes (e.g. disease). It is also likely to shape decisions about, and the provision of, care in coming years, a theme that I explore in Chapter 4. The other crucial aspect of the story of future big data-based medicine that has not been touched on thus far, however, is the enrolment of citizens in the project of collecting and contributing their own data via wearable and implantable devices. In an upbeat assessment of the future of precision medicine, John Mattick, Executive Director of the Garvan Institute of Medical Research writes,

> Given the benefits of genomic sequencing for individual health, it's assumed most people will consent, and have the results incorporated into their personal medical records. Amalgamation of this information with clinical records will provide rich data that can be mined for biomedical discovery.
>
> (Mattick, 2018)

Mattick predicts that medicine will be at the forefront of a data-driven industry that will change medical practice and health outcomes, with significant implications for national economies. (Mattick, 2018) The underlying assumption in this depiction of big data medicine is that if enough citizens can be connected and encouraged to contribute to (the assumed) public good in this way, the collective impact will be considerable, producing data of value that is more than the sum of the parts.

Engendering citizen consent

As I have noted, the realization of the promise of precision medicine presupposes public consent for what is proposed: the collection, storage and analysis of big data sets, and large-scale (population-wide) testing for genetic conditions or susceptibility to risk or adverse drug reactions. Further, it presupposes that citizens will participate in related programs and projects. While surveys and other means of assessing public views have revealed that citizens hold concerns about population-wide data sets, including about privacy and commercialization of personal genomic/genetic data, many people evidently do decide to contribute to big data projects, although they are not always described as such. This includes the UK Biobank, which by 2017 had enrolled more than 500,000 volunteer participants (UK Biobank, 2017), and the 100,000 Genomes Project which has sequenced more than 75,500 genomes of the 100,000 target as of August 2018 (Genomics England, 2018). Further, according to a survey published in 2016, undertaken by the US National Institutes of Health in regards to its All of US program, a high proportion (54 percent) of people 'would definitely or probably participate [in this program] if asked' (Kaufman et al., 2016).

Despite many citizens' evident willingness to participate in such projects, one can question whether participants can ever be adequately informed about and fully understand the aims and implications of large-scale, prospective ventures such as these. The latter include as yet unresolved regulatory problems, such as the protection of personal privacy in regards to one's 'genetic secrets'; questionable consumer protection from the growing private industry marketing genetic tests directly to consumers via the internet; and the healthcare costs incurred by worried individuals undergoing costly, and potentially unwarranted, tests and treatments (Nicol et al., 2016). Consent for such ventures cannot be taken for granted since, as recognized by scientists, health professionals, digitally reliant businesses and governing authorities, public sentiment may change quickly, especially if there is adverse publicity regarding the collection, storage or sharing of personal information. Evidently recognizing 'the risks' to ventures posed by distrustful or resistive publics, authorities have endeavoured to ensure that optimism for the envisaged future medicine is generated and sustained and that citizens play an active role in its realization.

To lay the groundwork for precision medicine, health authorities, technology companies, pharmaceutical companies and governments have pursued various strategies, including educating citizens about projects and encouraging them to become 'digitally literate' and to participate in efforts to collect and share personal information, including about their health status, activities and lifestyles. As mentioned in Chapter 2, pharmaceutical companies work closely with patient organizations, support them financially, and seek to educate individuals and their families through conferences and other forums. There has been growing investment in programs (e.g. formal education, public engagement) to support these endeavours, and various incentives to encourage citizens' use of technologies and participation in the project of advancing health. With increasing use of personalized algorithms, some businesses and authorities have begun to use the insights of the behavioural sciences and neurosciences to learn more about how people think and process information, so that technologies can be designed to better appeal to citizens.

Google's DeepMind Health

Google, as one of the largest internet companies, has an evident interest in engendering citizens' online connections with health, given the significant potential to generate profit from the presumed forthcoming avalanche of new personalized drugs, devices and other interventions. Google's ambitious, if not grandiose, vision underpinning its investments in healthcare in general, and precision medicine in particular, can be seen in its self-representations of its AI-oriented venture, DeepMind Health. Google's substantial investment in this venture reflects its belief in the potential of AI to create value from big data, including that concerning and contributed by citizens. The high aspirations for the venture have been articulated by one of its co-founders, Demis Hassabis, as the Apollo program of artificial intelligence, aimed at 'solving intelligence and then using that to solve everything else' (Simonite, 2016). 'Hassabis wants to create what he calls general artificial intelligence, something that, like a human, can learn to take on just about any task. He envisions it doing things as diverse as advancing medicine by formulating and testing scientific theories, and bounding around in agile robot bodies' (ibid.). DeepMind was founded in 2010 as a start-up company by Hassabis, Mustafa Suleyman and Shane Legg in London, was bought out by Google in 2014 for £400 million, and has since attracted funding from venture capitalists and entrepreneurs such as Scott Banister and Elon Musk—such are the anticipated financial prospects for AI in healthcare.

In 2016, DeepMind Health was launched by one of the co-founders of Deep-Mind, Mustafa Suleyman, who remained as part of the team. This initiative reflects the heightened optimism attached to technologies and neuroscience to uncover the workings of the mind, thus extracting value from what is perceived as this new frontier of science. On its website, DeepMind Health makes a considerable effort to emphasize its public-minded motives, including attention to upholding the ethical principle of right to privacy, while downplaying its commercial aspirations. It seeks to sell a vision of future healthcare that many citizens will likely find troubling, given that this vision relies on Google, a commercial operation that profits from the collection and analysis of big data, and its assurances that it will operate in the public's best interests. One of Google's stated aspirations is to 'build a brain' using its extensive data and computing power, under the stewardship of the futurist Ray Kurzweil, one of Google's directors of engineering and author of *How To Create a Mind* (Kurzweil, 2012) (Chapter 1).

As noted in Chapter 2, Google has an omnipotent ambition that is of concern to many citizens. Consequently, the DeepMind team have sought to manage how the venture is publicly represented. For example, its website offers detailed explanations of processes and links to supportive authorities and evidence. The benefits are conveyed by its stated aim to 'make a practical difference to patients, nurses and doctors and support the NHS system we know and respect'. Further, it is noted that DeepMind Health seeks to become 'a self-sustaining initiative, through hospitals choosing to pay us for our software if they think they can have a positive impact on clinical outcomes and experience'. Evidently anticipating concerns about the commercial aspects of the venture, the website assures visitors that 'We aren't looking to maximise profit, but rather to achieve sustainability so we can continue to grow our team, work with more hospitals and help more patients' (DeepMind Health, n.d.a). On the same webpage, it articulates 'Our relationship with Google', noting that DeepMind would continue as an independent operation and that 'we would put our technology at the service of other groups like the NHS in line with our social mission'. It goes on:

> Most importantly, NHS patient data will only ever be used to help improve hospital care. No NHS data will ever be connected to Google accounts or services, and it won't ever be used for any commercial purposes like advertising or insurance. Doing so would be illegal
>
> (ibid.).

Such comments reveal acute awareness of growing public concerns about Google and its operations, and of the potential for the exploitation and commodification of personal information. In these expressed concerns about illegality and the need to conform with ethical culture and work, DeepMind Health endeavours to convey its trustworthiness. To reinforce this portrayal and its concern for the public interest, a weblink offers an invitation to patients, clinicians and NHS Trusts who would 'like to join our team'. Under 'Patients' (Suleyman and Snow, n.d.), visitors are taken to 'Our first formal patient and public involvement (PPI) strategy', which goes to some length in explaining its commitment and practices in this area. Visitors are also invited to 'upcoming patient and public events' and to 'site meetings in King's Cross, London' and to 'take part in online video conferencing calls'. The PPI strategy, co-authored by Mustafa Suleyman and Rosamund Snow, describes DeepMind Health's commitment to patient involvement and the basic principles that guide its approach to health service users: 'treat us with respect and value the ways our input adds to the team's expertise' (Suleyman and Snow, 2016). The PPI strategy document offers a number of 'key suggestions (for further discussion at consultation events)', the 'overarching principle' being 'at every level where clinicians have influence, ensure patients do too'. This includes setting aside resources to create an 'entirely patient-led AI project'; 'Appointing patient advisors alongside the clinical advisory team for existing projects'; and 'Create a patient panel' which could 'hold DeepMind Health to account from the patient point of view, help with networking to patient groups and other connections across the country, and provide "critical friend" perspectives' (ibid.).

The trend to develop AI

The extent of the immersion of DeepMind Health (a big data-driven business) within the NHS (a still largely publicly funded organization) is worrying, given the expected heavy reliance on AI for healthcare decisions in the future. Artificial intelligence is seen to have potentially both positive and negative impacts on healthcare, including on the character of healthcare work and employment levels, and how information is shared among hospitals, insurance companies and various providers (Ford, 2016 104–105, 153–159, 166–168). It has been predicted that AI may replace certain occupational categories or redefine the content of work, which may be beneficial for some groups in terms of allowing more tedious, time-consuming work to be handed over to computers; however, it may also make redundant those who have few skills, and raise privacy concerns and erode trust in data, among other issues (Schwab, 2017: 144–145). Despite concerns about AI, the claims of mass automation have been questioned on various grounds, including the technical limitations of machines, the inability to substitute for workers who perform multiple functions, and the creation of new jobs in ancillary sectors (Dellot and Wallace-Stephens, 2017). In any event, the emphasis on AI is consistent with the broader deregulatory trend in UK healthcare and many other national healthcare systems, and a growing reliance on the private sector to solve problems, especially through technological means.

On its webpage 'From tests to treatment', it is claimed that DeepMind Health's AI research will 'help NHS hospitals get patients from test to treatment as quickly and accurately as possible' (DeepMind Health, n.d.b). The site highlights the pressures that NHS staff currently endure and the 'avoidable life-changing conditions' that patients confront because their test results cannot be acted on in time, drawing attention to the 'outdated tools like pagers and cumbersome desktop systems' used to share and prioritize clinical information. It is in this context, it is claimed, that AI offers the prospect of providing 'the right specialist in time for them to help' (ibid.). It also refers to feedback from 'many clinicians and patients' (with links to supportive comments from various medical experts, medical charities and representatives of patient groups) that 'they think better IT can make an important difference'. Further, it is explained that

> In the future, we think AI tools will be able to learn how to analyse test results and scans to instantly recognize whether a patient might be at risk, and continually improve to get even better […] Public trust and privacy must be protected at all costs.
>
> (ibid.)

It is interesting to note the implicit promise being made here: greater economic efficiency achieved through 'time–space compression' and the fulfilment of the post-Fordist ideal of just-in-time production, that is, providing the right specialist at the right time. In 2017, DeepMind Health reported it had produced an app, called Streams ('which doesn't include any AI'), which 'directs clinicians to patients who are at risk of or who have developed a serious condition called acute kidney injury', which was claimed to have saved nurses time and potential deaths related to this injury; and 'a set of longer-term AI research projects' (Royal Free London, n.d.). As is explained, the ultimate aim of DeepMind Health's endeavours is to bring together these separate technologies 'so that patients and clinicians can benefit from AI-supported care wherever they are in hospital'.

In pursuit of its goals, DeepMind Health has formed collaborations with two NHS hospitals 'to combine their clinical expertise with our machine learning technology', with research 'centred on a technique called deep learning', which, as explained, involves interpreting visual information from de-personalized head and neck scans so as to 'identify potential issues within these scans, and how to recommend the right course of action to a clinician.' (DeepMind Health, n.d.c) Seemingly anticipating public concerns about privacy, especially evident in relation to personal health information, DeepMind Health offers an assurance that its research data will be 'de-personalized' and that 'this work will be subject to rigorous clinical scrutiny, and will be published in peer-reviewed academic journals' (DeepMind Health, n.d.d). Further, it notes that 'strict controls' on the use of data will also be 'governed by our hospital partners, and vetted by their information governance teams before being sent to DeepMind Health' (ibid.).

AI technology 'lock-in'

At the time of writing, details of exactly what DeepMind Health proposes could not be found in the public domain. However, the venture is part of a wider trend for technology companies and other interests to look to AI in medicine and healthcare more generally. As more investment in AI occurs, the higher the likelihood of 'technology lock-in', whereby a particular technological path becomes firmly established and it becomes easier and/or more cost effective to stay on course rather than shift direction. Google, Facebook and Microsoft are all investing heavily in AI and see huge potential profits from using the technology to exploit customer data in areas such as driverless cars and medicine. More recently, Apple has joined the AI 'race' (Regalado, 2017) (Chapter 4).

A notable venture in this regard is the Partnership on Artificial Intelligence to Benefit People and Society (Partnership on AI), launched in September 2016 by founding partners DeepMind, Amazon, Google, Facebook, IBM and Microsoft. Since that date it has assembled a large number of partners, including eBay, Intel, Sony, non-profit AI groups, civil liberties and human rights groups, UNICEF, think tanks and data research groups, among others (Partnership on AI, n.d.a). IBM Watson Health is a high-profile outcome of the effort to develop and apply AI in the field of medicine and healthcare. IBM Watson for Genomics is seen to have considerable potential in cancer care, in 'Bringing the promise of precision medicine to more cancer patients' by 'interpret[ing] genetic results faster and with greater accuracy than manual efforts' (IBM Watson Health, 2017a) The company's website emphasizes the personalized nature of the treatment (e.g. 'Your cancer, your treatment'), describing how Watson may help them:

> In addition to providing information regarding your tumor's genetic alterations, Watson for Genomics also draws evidence from a vast corpus of medical literature [...] A comparison that may typically take a team of medical experts weeks to prepare can now be completed in significantly less time.
>
> (IBM Watson Health, 2017b)

As this description reveals, advocates for AI in medicine say this technology has been invaluable in mining large bodies of literature and combining this data with medical data to offer a more timely, accurate and individualized treatment. The scale required for this mining, however, necessitates the harnessing of various expertise and financial investment, including in 'connecting' patients, who contribute the essential resource—biomedical data. Watson Health's website refers to its partnerships with Quest Diagnostics and Illumina, 'deep cancer expertise from over 20 leading healthcare institutions', and genome sequencing capabilities at Massachusetts Institute of Technology and Harvard University. Quest Diagnostics, which advertises various health diagnostic, clinical trials testing, health IT and wellness, and risk management services, offers a MyQuest^{TM} patient portal which claims to provide patients with 'insights into your personal health, get lab results directly to their mobile device and computer, and the ability to share information with physicians and other healthcare professionals and to 'learn how to take the right steps forward'. A link allows users to download a MyQuest^{TM} app, in Apple or Android versions (MyQuest Diagnostics, 2017)

The statements found on the websites of companies involved in AI reveal a strong belief in the future benefits of this technology, especially in 'empowering' patients and personalizing their treatments. However, the involvement of groups such as these also reveals the aim of AI enthusiasts to engender broad community consent for their envisaged future, including in medicine and healthcare. The byline of Partnership on AI is 'to benefit people and society', and on its 'Tenets' link it proclaims: 'We believe that artificial intelligence technologies hold great promise for raising the quality of people's lives and can be leveraged to help humanity address important global challenges such as climate change, food, inequality, health, and education' (Partnership on AI, n.d.b). These 'tenets' include statements of its commitment to 'ensure that AI technologies benefit and empower as many people as possible' and 'educate and listen to the public and actively engage stakeholders to seek their feedback on our focus, inform them of our work, and address their questions'. The Partnership on AI also outlines its commitment to 'research and dialogue on the ethical, social, economic, and legal implications of AI', ensuring the benefits of AI are maximized, and 'creat[ing] a culture of cooperation, trust, and openness among AI scientists and engineers to help us all better achieve these goals' (ibid.).

Deep learning

The clearest indication of Google's and other internet companies' commitment to AI is the investment in research in so-called deep learning, whereby artificial neural networks are 'trained' to recognize images or spoken words, undertake translation, and perform other tasks (Ford, 2016: 94–96). While the idea of the neural network has been in existence since the 1950s and the beginnings of AI research, and has long been used to recognize patterns, increasingly powerful computers and improvements in mathematical formulae have enabled computer scientists to model more layers of virtual neurons than ever before (Hof, 2013). Neural networks have been developed that have capacities in pattern recognition surpassing those of human experts who competed against the system (Ford, 2016: 44; Hof, 2013). The prediction is that as computers get bigger, and conceptual and software break-throughs occur, this ability will increase, with computers eventually outperforming humans in their capacity to recognize patterns. Google published 218 journal or conference papers on machine learning in 2016, twice as many as it had two years previously, which is attributed to the tripling in the number of machine learning researchers working for the company over that period (Regalado, 2017). As Regalado observes, commenting on this increase, 'Research is occurring in the hothouse atmosphere reminiscent of the early days of computer chips, or of the first biotech plants and drugs, times when notable academic firsts also laid the foundation stones of new industries.'

Conclusion

Promise, hope and expectation play a powerful role in shaping technology policies and practices in digital health, as they do in other fields. This is perhaps nowhere clearer than in the field of genomics and precision medicine, examined in this chapter. Recent developments in computational technologies and in biotechnol-ogy, especially genomic sequencing, are seen to herald the dawn of a new era, where the mining of big data enables customized treatments to be delivered more efficiently, effectively and safely, and when needed. However, despite the heigh-tened optimism surrounding this vision, what is promised by precision medicine is likely to be limited at best, in terms of mostly or only benefitting those with rare genetic conditions and childhood cancers, where genes are more likely to play a significant role.

The effort to realize this future medicine represents a substantial investment of money and human resources that is having uneven and inequitable effects—a point that I will explore in Chapter 5. Nevertheless, the promissory discourse that sur-rounds digital technologies, and especially AI and robotics, is shaping policies, institutions and practices in profound ways. Already, digital technology applications are unsettling established ways of 'doing' medicine. This includes the provision of diagnosis, treatment and care at a distance via telemedicine and tele-rehabilitation, computer-aided medical diagnostics, 3-D printing of body organs, and the use of virtual and augmented reality and virtual anatomy in the education of doctors and other health professionals. Such investment in a technologically mediated future raises a series of questions: what are the implications for the healthcare economy as a whole—including the roles and responsibilities of those who sustain it? Impor-tantly, where is *care* in this emergent future? In the next chapter I address these questions as part of my analysis of the emergent digital healthcare economy.

4

THE DIGITAL HEALTHCARE ECONOMY

If recent predictions can be believed, digital technologies will give rise to new healthcare economies that will 'transform' established institutions and practices, as well as personal experiences. The World Economic Forum, for example, depicts a future digitally enabled healthcare that will allow the continuous monitoring and self-tracking of individuals, and for more care to be undertaken in the home rather than in specialized institutions such as hospitals or aged care facilities (World Economic Forum, n.d.b). The 'virtual care' scenario portrayed by the Forum is one where clinicians, patients, their families and health professionals will be connected in real time to permit coordinated, 'personalized' support. The use of apps, monitors and other digital devices is seen to make this care seamless and to transform the experiences of patients and the healthcare industry itself. While the anticipated impacts of digitalization on the institutions and practices of medicine and healthcare have received most attention in public debates and policies, the approaches and practices of public health and health promotion are also expected to be transformed; for example, strategies of community-based and personal risk management. Indeed, if predictions are to be believed, the established boundaries between prevention, treatment and care will become much less clear than they once were. Care will be 'holistic' and comprehensive, in its idealized form entailing the ongoing monitoring and management of risk in all its aspects (biophysical, lifestyle, environmental) and of illness throughout life, as an ongoing rather then episodic process, and to be consumer-centred or patient-centred. Policymakers, clinicians and businesses see the impacts of digital technologies on future health, medicine and healthcare as being mostly positive: enabling citizens to live independent, autonomous lives and to play an active role in their own health and care, generating economic value through the development and sale of related technologies, and creating efficiencies in the sharing and use of data.

This chapter explores the dimensions and implications of this envisaged digital healthcare economy. The changes associated with the development of the new care economy promise to transform people's lives and relationships by enabling new, more efficient and effective ways of undertaking care. Focusing on some contexts where digital technologies are having, or are expected to have, major applications in coming years, including personal risk management strategies, and care of the ill, disabled and aged in hospitals, workplaces and at home, the chapter describes how care and caring work are configured within 'digital health', and considers the ramifications. While care is a core concept in medicine and healthcare, and invoked by policymakers and clinicians when justifying health-related policy decisions and practices, its meanings are rarely scrutinized in policy statements and the academic literature. This includes the growing literature on digital health policies and initiatives. Consequently, it is useful to begin by considering how care is currently conceived and related to technology, specifically in the domain of health and medicine.

The care–technology relationship

In modern health systems, care tends to be equated with the provision of biomedical tests, treatments and other technical interventions. Hospitals, as the institutional hubs of specialized expertise and technologies oriented to the delivery of these interventions, are central to this conception. However, in practice, medicine and hospitals operate in ways that are often far removed from professional and popular cultural representations of care. Back in 1974, Ivan Illich wrote about the personal harms inflicted by modern high-tech medical treatment and diagnosis. On one reading of history, the rise of bioethics and its cardinal principles (autonomy, beneficence, non-maleficence, justice) from the early 1970s was a response to the abuses inflicted by biomedicine via human experimentation (Fox and Swazey, 2008). Many writers have since documented the harms or potential harms associated with biomedical interventions, including treatments based on limited or biased evidence (e.g. Goldacre, 2012; Harris, 2016), and the overuse of diagnostic tests (e.g. Welch, 2011). The international Choosing Wisely initiative, launched in the US in 2012, has grown quickly in response to recognition of the potential adverse consequences, including financial costs associated with over-testing and over-treatment (Choosing Wisely, n.d). Implicitly, this initiative and other earlier initiatives pay cognizance to the dangers posed by technological interventions to what is considered by accepted social standards to constitute good care, regardless of whether concerns were initially sparked by budget blowouts, patient welfare or other considerations. They are, however, part of a much longer-standing discourse on the (fraught) relationship between 'care' and 'technology'.

As AnneMarie Mol and her colleagues observe, during the twentieth century it was frequently argued that care was *other* than technology:

> Care had to do with warmth and love while technology, by contrast, was cold and rational. Care was nourishing, technology was instrumental. Care overflowed and was impossible to calculate, technology was effective and efficient [...] Care (and caring relations) at home, technology (and instrumental relations) in the workplace.
> (Mol et al., 2010: 14)

In Mol and her colleagues' view, this idealized depiction of the care–technology distinction is belied by evidence of caring practices, which involve subtle skills, experience, attentiveness and 'adaptive tinkering' (ibid.: 14–15). Technologies are not as instrumental, cold and rational as they may be represented; nor do they have effects that are often attributed to them. Rather, their applications depend on care work, with tools and situations being adapted through a process of endless tinkering (ibid.: 14–15).

The work of Mol et al. is useful insofar as its highlights how the meanings and practices of care are emergent and context dependent, and 'co-constructed' with technology (e.g. Oudshoorn and Pinch, 2003). It serves as a caution against dualistic and technological determinist thinking; the view that technology is always necessarily opposed to and undermines care. It also suggests that there is scope for the subversion of technologies; for adapting them for uses other than those envisaged by the people who designed and produced them—a point to which I return later. However, it is important to acknowledge that, in medicine and healthcare, and more generally, care increasingly is commoditized, technologized and standardized—transformed into a consumable product—and its provision has generally been aligned with market priorities rather than human needs. Governments' adoption of neoliberal policies has led to many state-based services being outsourced to the private sector, and/or existing services being downsized or the burden of responsibility shifted onto families and the community sector—which means, in practice, women. The vast majority of caring work currently is undertaken by women and is generally poorly paid or unpaid. This work is mostly performed in the private sphere and is thus invisible and, while crucial to domestic and national economies, is not fully valued as emotional labour that generates surplus (Hochschild, 1983). While it is suggested that digital technology will free people from mundane tasks, enhance efficiencies, and assist in achieving improvements in health and wellbeing, descriptions of applications provide few details of how this will likely impact on the gender division of caring labour, or on those from different ethnic and linguistic backgrounds, social classes, abilities or regions.

Governments' focus on economic efficiency has also led to growing attention to the use of new technologies, such as AI and machine learning, to complement or replace human labour, including the labour of care. Companies, including manufacturers and providers of digital products and services, are already marketing devices and apps on the basis that they will enable or help patients to better manage their illness at home or in another setting. A growing trend is for digital technologies to replace or complement humans in virtually all areas of healthcare, including care in the home. Robots are increasingly being used in workplaces, including hospitals, in some cases as potential substitutes for human carers, especially where (as in Japan) there is a rapidly ageing population (Economist, 2017). Other areas of healthcare such as caring for the elderly are also adopting robots, or are expected to do so in the near future, for example for assistance with mobility (robotic walkers), dispensing medicines and assisting with routine tasks (e.g. providing a glass of water, retrieving misplaced items) (Ford, 2016: 161–163). While robots may be able to assist with undertaking these physical tasks, it is difficult to see how they could fulfil other needs, including for the empathy, intimacy and touch that characterize human interactions.

In the UK, the National Health Service has outsourced many services and looked to the private sector for the provision of care and treatment. However, this has created many problems. This includes lack of transparency around decision-making due to commercial confidentiality, an absence of control over pricing, discontinuity of care when unprofitable services are jettisoned; and (despite the claims of free marketeers) has led to inefficiencies (The Week, 2018). In Australia, while healthcare involves a mixture of public and private provision, with citizens subsidizing the public system via Medicare, market principles have increasingly shaped policies. Citizens are expected to shoulder the costs through private insurance and to minimize their reliance on the public healthcare system through greater attention to preventive and risk-management practices and self-care. The US, too, is strongly reliant on the private provision of healthcare, historically much more so than the UK and Australia, with medical care and other costs generally covered (by those who can afford it) by insurance, with a 'safety net' for those who are most vulnerable. However, in these countries, and others influenced by neoliberal policies, the individualization of risk management combined with the self-care ethos has become predominant.

In this context, digital technologies are seen by governments to hold considerable promise in 'empowering' citizens to become more responsible for their own risk management and care throughout their lives. Many governments and businesses also see economic opportunities in the 'digital revolution', with the latter seeking to generate profit through the development and sale of technologies, including robots, AI, self-tracking devices, monitors, and apps with multiple applications. In one estimation, the global mHealth market was worth $US10.5 billion in 2014 and is expected to grow 33.5 percent annually between 2015 and 2020 (Deloitte, 2015: 2). I will examine some of these technologies and how they are being applied, or expected to be applied, later in this chapter.

The converged experience of risk and disease

Related to these shifts in healthcare policy has been a general trend in medicine for experiences of risk and of disease to converge (Aronowitz, 2015). That is, medicine has shifted from its focus on episodic illness and curing or ameliorating diseases to a more risk-oriented, anticipatory approach calling for tests and treatments (e.g. preventive drugs) that demand behavioural change. In Aronowitz's view, this has fundamentally altered people's experience of illness. It has also underpinned a burgeoning market for products and services that promise to detect and manage risk or prevent and treat 'conditions' (e.g. 'pre-cancerous' lesions) that would previously have not been considered as such. The demand for risk-reducing interventions, Aronowitz argues, has been shaped by various factors, including direct marketing to consumers, the hyped claims of self-interested parties, and the problematic extrapolation of aggregate-level data to individual decisions (which, I suggest, will accelerate with the growing use of big data in healthcare, especially whole-genome sequencing) (ibid.: 6; Chapter 3) The introduction in Australia, the UK and a number of other countries of national cancer screening programs for breast cancer, bowel cancer and cervical cancer is a manifestation of this risk-and-prevention ethos. Such programs have undoubtedly contributed to citizens' heightened risk awareness and the creation of proliferating categories of the 'at risk' and 'pre-symptomatically ill'.

The growth of population screening, beginning with the Pap smear introduced in the 1940s, and then breast cancer screening and bowel cancer screening, has initiated a broad shift from the use of tests for purposes of diagnosis after an individual has exhibited symptoms of a disease to screening for susceptibility to risk. Revealingly, on its website Cancer UK describes screening as 'testing apparently healthy people for signs of disease' (Cancer Research UK, 2018), a phrase that neatly captures the shift in biomedicine's focus from treatment of the ill or diseased to the detection of those at risk and the pre-symptomatically ill. That is, people who currently do not feel unwell and do not display symptoms of disease may nevertheless harbour disease. Screening may result in them being classified as at risk of disease, calling for further investigation via tests, and then potentially treatments, which may be unnecessary and in fact may cause harm. In his book *Over-Diagnosed*, Gilbert Welch describes the 'enthusiasm for diagnosis' associated with cancer screening that has led to a focus on 'removing pre-cancerous abnormalities rather than trying to find early cancers' (Welch, 2011: 69), as well as the overuse of tests and scans in general to detect all manner of 'conditions', including incidental findings ('incidentalomas'), such as nodules that will never become cancer. These practices, he argues, constitute the phenomenon of over-diagnosis that is driving up healthcare costs and making otherwise healthy people feel ill. The phenomena of 'healthy anxiety' and the 'worried well' are recognized in the health literature and can be seen as a manifestation of a much wider 'healthism' first identified in the 1970s (Crawford, 1980), but are becoming more acute and widespread as risk and 'new prevention strategies of social administration' have become integral to political rule in many societies (Petersen, 2015: 79–86).

Digital health policies and programs, I suggest, are closely bound up with these changes in the economies of medicine and care. That is, they are seen as the means to increase efficiencies by reducing burgeoning healthcare costs—associated in particular with high-tech biomedicine and treating the degenerative diseases of ageing populations—and to enhance strategies of risk detection and management, prevention and care premised upon an active citizenship.

Envisioning 'connected care' in policy and the media

Recent government policy statements and news media reports provide insight into the 'consumer-centric' healthcare vision conveyed by digital health: one that is increasingly mediated by technologies that 'empower' individuals through their 'connections' with sources and experts that facilitate their self-management of risk and care. The language used in portrayals of digital health reveals a shift in the politics of citizenship, in that individuals increasingly are encouraged to think of themselves as consumers who exercise autonomous choice in the market, rather than as citizens with state-ascribed rights with assumed access to designated services and support.

Reflecting this shift are comments reported in a news item about a 'Future of Health' roundtable event organized by *The Australian Financial Review* and the Commonwealth Bank in 2018, which was attended by some leading healthcare companies such as Australia's Primary Health Care Limited and Israel's Clalit Health Services Digital. The event, of course, offers a business perspective, but it is one shared by many governments that look to market-led solutions to healthcare needs. The item noted 'That the digitally enabled consumer will continue to drive the revolution in healthcare as it changes from being a provider-centric system in Australia was the consensus among attendees' (Worthington, 2018). Malcolm Parmenter, Chief Executive of Primary Health Care, a business that is 'responsible for more than 8 million GP visits a year', was cited as saying that Australia had 'a very provider-centric healthcare'. His quoted comments reveal much about contemporary visions of the factors that shape healthcare:

> In Australia, you go to a general practice and you see that GP and it's a consultation [...] The reality is that if we're going to get a consumer-centric care .... We should be able to provide care where people want it, how they want it, when they want it.
>
> (ibid.)

Parmenter presents a view held by many contemporary policymakers and business leaders: that healthcare is or should be 'driven by demand'; that consumers will judge healthcare on the basis of experiences derived from other market transactions. Further, the final comment, 'We should be able to provide care where people want it, how they want it, when they want it' conveys the consumer-centred approach that many policymakers and businesses believe will, or should, determine priorities, irrespective of other considerations such as societal need. In this future consumer-centric scenario, governments are seen to play a facilitative rather than directive role, establishing the basic infrastructure and regulatory framework to enable new business entrants to drive innovation. Reflecting this view, Australia's Digital Health Strategy, approved by the Health Minister in August 2017, highlights the importance of 'accelerating innovation in the health system', which is to be achieved through initiatives such as forging partnerships between industry, health consumers and researchers; 'removing the barriers which prevent the development of new products and processes in the health system'; 'making investments that drive change'; and 'creating conditions for entrepreneurs to try new things' (Australian Digital Health Agency, 2018: 50). Elaborating on these goals, it is noted that 'The Agency will simplify, guide and support developers on how to bring new ideas to market, facilitate test environments, provide an open source hub of code tests, and provide support on how digital health national infrastructure services can support developers to deliver valued services for patients, carers, clinicians, researchers, administrators and technologists' (ibid.). Elsewhere in the report, it is noted that 'Government will be a platform for industry and innovators to foster an agile and self-improving health system that is sustainable' (ibid.: 7).

Electronic health records

A first step in advancing digitally enabled healthcare has been establishing the physical infrastructure—a personal electronic health records (EHR) system. In Australia, this takes the form of 'My Health Record', which employs an automatic opt-in participation process. In the US, the HITECH (Health Information Technology for Economic and Clinical Health) Act of 2009 has enabled the adoption of EHR and supporting technology. In that country, doctors have been incentivized to adopt EHR and, after 2015, incur a penalty of 1 percent of Medicare payments if they do not adopt EHR (HealthIT.gov, 2018). Within the decade to 2018, the US was seen to make massive strides in the development of EHR systems, with one well known medical scholar and writer, Robert Wachter, author of *The Digital Doctor*, cited in one recent article as saying that whereas '10 years ago fewer than one in 10 American hospitals had electronic health records […] today, fewer than one in 10 do not' (Monegain, 2018). While the idea of a 'wired healthcare system' gained momentum under the Obama administration, the first EHR systems in the US were installed in 1988; however, by 2008 only 17 percent of doctors' clinics had basic EHR systems, and only about one in ten hospitals (Wachter, 2017: 12). Under Obama, however, healthcare reform was a priority and the stimulus package developed to kick-start the economy in the wake of the global financial crisis provided the impetus to invest heavily (US$30 billion) in the program that became known as HITECH (ibid.: 16).

In March 2018, it was reported that the Trump Administration had made 'interoperability' in US healthcare a priority for the Federal Government (White House, 2018). The term interoperability refers to the ability for computer systems to 'talk to each other'; that is, to share information quickly and effectively. As Wachter explains, interoperability is fundamental to modern digitally connected economies, allowing people to use credit or debit cards to withdraw funds from banks and to transfer funds between banks. However, as Wachter observes, 'ensuring interoperability in the banking world is orders of magnitude easier than it is in healthcare' (Wachter, 2017: 13) In a White House press release, Jared Kushner, Senior Advisor to President Trump, was cited as saying: 'Interoperability is about our shared bottom line: saving lives […] There is overwhelming consensus:

America needs better access to patient data and interoperability now' (White House, 2018). The press release, which outlined 'key principles from the Administration's Strategy', reflected the consumer-centric vision underlying interoperability, with phrases such as 'You, the customer, should be in charge'; Americans being 'on the cusp of a technological healthcare revolution centered on patients'; 'more decision making in hands of customers'; and 'ensuring access to health information empowers patients by helping to reduce waste, fraud, and abuse through the system'.

As I explain, the UK has had a fraught experience with the implementation of EHR systems, but like other countries in recent years is making concerted efforts to introduce such records, often through top-down initiatives that appeal to the public benefit and 'patient empowerment'. Authorities recognize that incomplete EHR systems offer a major impediment to the envisaged comprehensive, 'always connected' healthcare system of the future. However, as authorities also acknowledge, citizens need to be encouraged to contribute their data. Public forums undertaken by Australian Digital Health Agency, involving panels comprising a range of expertise, have conveyed authorities' concerns with low levels of public participation in national electronic health records systems, where this is voluntary. In this regard, Australia's experience reflects that of the UK, despite the latter's well established and comprehensive National Health System, and generally high public support for the NHS.

Relatively poor public participation in national EHR is often ascribed to publics being lethargic, or unaware or ignorant of the benefits of such records—a view that was implicit in some public forums organized by Australian Digital Health Agency in 2017. These views reflect a deficit model of the public understanding of science, whereby citizens are effectively blamed for their failure to engage (in terms defined by decision-makers) with science or technologies (Irwin and Michael, 2003; Petersen and Bowman, 2013). In the UK, governments have encountered a distinctive set of problems in engendering public consent for a national EHR system. These are in part related to the scale and general approach of the initial attempt at a 'fully integrated care records systems across the NHS', namely the National Programme for Information Technology (NPfIT) NHS Care Records Service, launched in 2002 by the then Blair Government, which was ultimately judged to be 'top down, government driven' and lacking engagement with its multiple stakeholders, and was eventually abandoned in 2011 (Centre for Public Impact, 2017).

However, despite this assessment, authorities have persisted with endeavours to ensure that all UK citizens have an EHR (Summary Care Record), as evident from a briefing paper published in April 2016, which outlined a schedule for 'A paperless NHS' by 2020. The plan is that by 2020 'all care records will be digital, real-time and interoperable' (ibid.: 7). The briefing paper noted 'As of February 2016, 55.06 million people have had a Summary Care Record created'. (House of Commons, 2016: 3) The briefing paper also outlined plans for a national collection of anonymous data, 'Care.data', 'to enable population-level analysis of health trends' (ibid.: 3), but this was also eventually abandoned following widespread criticisms of the venture, especially regarding data sharing of sensitive patient records. However, it was proposed to replace this with 'an eight-point consent model [...] with separate opt-outs for patient data used for research and for data used for running the health service' (Evanstad, 2016). It is interesting to note how this initiative is being marketed in the wake of the failed National Programme for Information Technology project. The briefing paper emphasizes that citizens will be given 'full access to their care records' including GP records and 'will be able to view copies of that data through apps and digital platforms of their choice' (House of Commons, 2016: 5). Further, the briefing paper refers to the importance of building and sustaining public trust to 'ensure citizens are confident about sharing their data to improve care and health outcomes' and 'mak[ing] the quality of care transparent' by 'publish[ing] comparative information on all publicly funded health and care services, including the results of treatment and what patients and carers say' (ibid.)

The Australian Government's efforts to sell the idea of a national EHR system to the wider public has involved a similar emphasis on quality, transparency, ease of access and attention to users' perspectives. In Australia's National Digital Health Strategy, it is stated that 'The imminent rapid growth in the number of users of My Health Record will provide an opportunity to transform healthcare, allowing better integration of health information, better quality healthcare and financial savings to the health system' (Australian Digital Health Agency, n.d.c: 10–11). The reference to 'imminent rapid growth' refers to the adopted national opt-in strategy (presumed consent), announced in May 2017, whereby all Australians will be automatically included in My Health Record by the end of 2018 unless they exercise the 'opt-out participation model', that is, make it known that they do not wish to contribute. In May 2018, the Government announced that the *secondary use* of Australians' health data recorded in My Health Record would also involve an opt-out model. This approach is criticized by the Law Council of Australia, which is proposing the opposite: the use of opt-in for the use of secondary data to ensure that any use of such data is by consent, as required by legislation (Law Council of Australia, 2017). A document, *Framework to Guide the Secondary Use of My Health Record System Data*, has been published to establish the principles guiding this use (Department of Health, 2018b), including processes to ensure the protection of individuals' privacy. However, interestingly, in this report it is noted that while 'data linkage may provide important information about the effectiveness and safety of treatments', 'it also poses additional risk to individual privacy' (ibid.: 34). These include researchers wishing to 'link MHR [medical health record] system data to a database of clinical trial participants to investigate subsequent hospitalisations, morbidity and mortality'; as well as data being linked to other datasets such as hospitals, the Medical Benefits Scheme, the Pharmaceutical Benefits Scheme and registry data (ibid.). In some of the public forums hosted by Australian Digital Health Agency in the period before the announcement of the My Health Record system, the participating experts suggested that citizens' reluctance to participate was due in large measure to their lack of understanding of the potential benefits of the resource, which disregards the concerns that citizens may have, and have expressed in the past (e.g. in relation to some biobank projects) about the sharing of personal data, especially when commercial interests are involved. The adoption of the opt-in strategy is a means by which citizens are, in effect, *compelled* to participate and thus potentially to share their data.

Compulsion through the opt-in strategy used with My Health Record and the UK's Summary Care Records could be seen as an example of libertarian paternalism where, it is argued, citizens have 'freedom to choose' (in this case to opt out) but are 'nudged' in a direction that is presumed to improve their lives (Thaler and Sunstein, 2009: 5). However, as Thaler and Sunstein argue, in cases of presumed consent, as pertains with My Health Record, 'the harder it is to register your unwillingness to participate, the less libertarian the policy becomes' (ibid.: 187). Presumed consent is often used by governments, for example in organ donation programs, because it is known to have a much greater participation rate than instances where consent is explicit; that is, where individuals have to take active steps to register. In the case of My Health Record, if individuals are to opt out, they first have to be aware that their records have been included and then take the initiative to pursue this option. In this area, as in other areas of public policy, policymakers are using the same psychological techniques as those employed by Google and other digital companies in their advertising and in keeping users 'connected' with their devices (Chapter 2)

Evidently attuned to the sensitivities surrounding the idea of a national electronic patient records system, perhaps including the automatic opt-in process, the authors of Australia's National Digital Health Strategy emphasise the 'national achievements in digital health' thus far (Australian Digital Health Agency, n.d.c: 10–11), and the benefits and transformational changes that will derive from My Health Record for the care of those living with chronic illnesses, and for care of the aged and the mentally ill. The report describes the 'extensive "*Your health. Your say*" consultation process' that has been undertaken 'to ensure that the Strategy was informed by Australian consumers, carers, healthcare providers, community groups, professional bodies and many other key health stakeholders' (ibid.: 16). Further, it outlines plans to 'test' and prove the benefits of the digital technologies that will support 'new models of healthcare' 'in real-world environments [...] prior to being scaled up to the whole of the Australian health system' (ibid.: 38). It is envisaged that by 2022 six 'test beds' will be launched, each of two years' duration, focusing on Health Care Homes for chronic disease management, where patients voluntarily enrol with a medical practice designed to coordinate care for people with chronic conditions; telehealth; babies' and children's health; residential aged care; end-of-life care; and emergency care. It notes that these 'pioneering initiatives' will be 'co-produced between consumers, governments, providers and entrepreneurs' (ibid.).

It is interesting to note the references in the Strategy document to co-production and co-design—terms used in science and technology studies and some other academic fields (e.g. design studies)—which suggest a democratic process of inclusion. For example,

Given the Agency's ongoing commitments to co-production, the next step in implementation is to co-design a Framework for Action with the broader health and care sector to agree an implementation plan. This co-design is imperative to ensure that the national priorities of this Strategy complement existing investment in digital health initiatives

(ibid.: 15).

The report also articulates a set of guiding principles that will underpin the development of Australia's National Digital Health Strategy, including 'putting users at the centre', 'ensuring privacy and security', 'fostering agile collaboration', 'driving a culture of safety and quality', and 'improving equity of access' (ibid.: 19). It is interesting to note how the Agency defines its own role in digital health, as an enabler or facilitator rather than a direct overseer of innovations. As the report notes, 'The Strategy is not intended to govern everything digital in healthcare – rather, it is about laying a common digital health foundation, with which patients, carers and healthcare providers are engaged, and on which industry and researchers can innovate.' Further, 'The Agency will operate as a leader and facilitator, supporting and empowering health consumers, healthcare providers and industry (ibid.: 15).' Underlying this rhetoric lies a market rationality that, as noted, is also evident in the vision of genomic medicine (Chapter 3). The economic benefits of the Strategy are emphasized at various points, for example it is suggested that 'secure messaging' could deliver approximately '$2 billion over 4 years and more than $9 billion over 10 years' (ibid.: 24), while 'a mature test bed model will attract international interest, with economic benefits to the Australian community' (ibid.: 39).

As is clear from this report and others, it is envisaged that the EHR systems that are being established will provide the foundation for an anticipated far-reaching change in conceptions of care—impacting relationships between formal (paid) carers and lay citizens, and between informal (unpaid) carers at home, at work and in the community—while transforming economies. As I show in the following paragraphs, areas where digital technologies are seen to assist this care are highly diverse and proliferating.

Home and community care, including of the elderly

Policymakers and health professionals see considerable promise in the use of digital technologies, and specifically wearable devices, to enable assisted care or self-care in the home and community, especially in light of the rapid ageing of populations in many countries and the anticipated burgeoning costs of aged care. Commercial interests, including device manufacturers, the IT industry and health insurers, also see benefits in the widespread adoption of such technologies, either to generate profits through the sale of products and services, or to harvest and trade in health data, or to target populations on the basis of their risk profile. In many countries, the 'baby boomers' have been identified as a demographic particularly receptive to the adoption of assistive technologies of care, given their presumed independence and purchasing power, although they constitute but one of the different niches targeted by advertisers. Even a cursory reading of the business pages of daily newspapers and reports on health industry events, such as conferences organized by the Health Information and Management Systems Society (HIMSS), convey the high optimism surrounding digital health in general and the patient-centred approach in particular (Sanborn, 2018). The number of apps, wearable devices and monitors is already extensive, and the field is seen by businesses as having considerable potential for further growth. mHealth (mobile or digital health) apps and network devices are being designed to support the entire spectrum of the population—from the healthy to the sick—or, as the authors of a recent US report on artificial intelligence in health and healthcare describe it, 'from episodic Fitbit users to diabetics who use glucose monitors' (JASON, 2017: 21).

The JASON report lists some examples of health-monitoring tools that may be used on mobile devices, including a personal cardiogram (Personal EKG) that requires no wires or gels and 'claims to use AI-enabled detection of atrial fibrillation'; a smartphone app (CloudUPDRS) 'that can assess Parkinson's disease symptoms [using a] gyroscope found in many mobile devices to analyze and quantify tremors, patterns in gait, and performance in a "finger tapping" test'; and AsthmaMD, an asthma tracking and control hand-held flow meter that 'gauges lung performance by assessing peak flow during exhalation' (ibid.: 22). It is interesting to note the meshing of these monitoring devices with AI algorithms that allow surveillance from a distance and potentially contribute data to precision medicine-related research ventures. The description of the CloudUPDRS smartphone app, for example, notes that 'An AI algorithm differentiates between actual tremors and "bad data", such as a dropped phone or the wrong action in response to the app's question. This tool enables Parkinson's patients to perform in-home testing, providing valuable and quantitative feedback on how their personal lifestyle factors and medications may affect their symptoms' (ibid.). The report also notes that there is active research involving the design and testing of the usability of the apps and devices, the value of which will ultimately rely on their acceptability among users and the willingness of health professionals to incorporate mHealth into healthcare (2017: 21).

A number of clinical trials involving Fitbits are recruiting participants or have already been completed. A search of ClinicalTrials.gov in March 2018 found 78 studies involving Fitbit registered as 'recruiting', and 67 as 'completed'. These trials pertain to a wide range of applications, including for monitoring exercise levels, weight management, sleep patterns and clinical outcomes; however, those focusing on behavioural/lifestyle change figure prominently. Some listed projects include: 'Use of wearable activity tracker in elderly undergoing abdominal surgery' (recruiting); 'Individualized prediction of migraine attacks using a mobile phone App and Fitbit' (recruiting); 'Fitbit One and text messaging prompts to promote physical activity in overweight/obese adults' (completed); 'A wearable mHealth device to promote teenagers' physical activity' (completed). In May 2018, Fitbit announced that it was partnering with Google to integrate Fitbit data with EHR systems using Google's new Cloud Healthcare application programming interface (API) for 'bi-directional' information exchange (Muoio, 2018). The article noted that 'The wearables maker will use Google's API to more smoothly integrate its day-to-day user health metrics with a patient's EHR', and that the collaboration would allow it to leverage Google Health API's AI and machine learning expertise to undertake predictive analytic algorithms, while strengthening Fitbit's relationship with health plans and healthcare systems. In the article, the CEO of Fitbit, James Park, is cited as saying:

> Over the past decade, we have built an incredible foundation as the leading wearables brand, helping millions of people around the world make lasting behaviour changes that improve their health and wellness through fun and engaging experiences [...] Working with Google gives us an opportunity to transform how we scale our business
>
> (ibid.).

Given that Fitbit claims to have sold 76 million devices and 'built a community of more than 25 million active users' along with 'one of the world's largest health and fitness databases' (ibid.), the company is obviously well positioned to profit from both data mining and the predictive information that it expects to generate in the future. The collaboration with Google reflects the growing links with between the wearable device market and technology companies, and offers a powerful means for prospectors to mine and add value to otherwise valueless data.

The US report mentioned above comments that the American Medical Association (AMA) has noted the growing amount of research on mHealth applications used to monitor and communicate health status to professionals, and consequently 'adopted a set of principles to promote safe, effective mHealth applications' (JASON, 2017: 21). Further, it states, 'AMA is encouraging physicians and others to support and establish patient-physician relationships around the use of apps and associated devices, trackers, and sensors'—citing AMA survey evidence released in 2016 showing that 31 percent of physicians support the use of digital technologies to improve care, with approximately half believing that they will improve current practices, including enhancing patient safety, 'improved diagnostic ability, and physician-patient relationships' (ibid.). However, as the report notes, for mHealth to achieve its goals, the technologies will need to mesh with existing systems and practices to encompass issues such as liability, data privacy assurance, the ability to link with EHR, and billing and reimbursements—issues that are also pertinent to AI applications in health and healthcare such as testing for heart disease (ibid.). Given concerns voiced by the public about data sharing, privacy and the commercialization of personal information, these are not trivial issues, and it is difficult to see how they will be easily resolved without engendering public resistance—a point discussed in more detail in Chapter 5. Thus far, the approach of policymakers when justifying initiatives has been to emphasise the resulting benefits—for health, the economy, society and individuals—rather than to utilize population-wide deliberate mechanisms to ensure public consent and legitimacy.

For aged care, arguments for the use of such technologies are sometimes framed in terms of the value of 'ageing in place', which is defined in various ways, but commonly as 'the ability to live in one's own home and community safely, independently and comfortably, regardless of age, income or ability level' (Centers for Disease Control and Prevention, 2009). The concept 'ageing in place', which explicitly or implicitly informs many aged care policies, implies 'empowerment' for individuals who are able to exercise autonomy and control over their living arrangements, but its connotations vary somewhat across contexts. For example, when used in the context of private residential care, the term suggests a more constrained set of options than may exist in non-residential care, in that the individual may not need to move but is still obliged to remain in residential care with its prescribed standards of safety and support (e.g. BlueCross, 2018).

Apple has positioned itself as a major player in this new healthcare landscape, advertising a number of devices and apps on the basis that they will empower individuals by allowing them to monitor their own health, as well as enabling them to contribute to wider medical research endeavours. One assumes that this includes research that will advance precision medicine (Chapter 3). An Apple advertisement states that 'The Health app makes it easy to learn about your health and start reaching your goals' (Apple Inc., 2018). It claims to do this by 'consolidat[ing]' data from iPhone, Apple Watch and third-party apps already used, enabling an individual to 'view all your progress in one convenient place'. Further, 'it recommends other helpful apps to round out your collection—making it simpler to move your health forward'. The Health app, it is stated, will provide constant feedback on 'four categories: Activity, Sleep, Mindfulness and Nutrition'. It will show 'all your stats at a glance to help you stay on track'. The Health app promises to keep you motivated by showing you how much you move, and claims to combine activity from one's iPhone, such as steps and distance travelled, along with metrics from third-party fitness apps. Further, 'Apple Watch automatically records simple but meaningful kinds of movement, like how often you stand, how much you exercise and your all-day calorie burn' (ibid.). The advertisement makes extensive use of the language of personalization and empowerment: 'The Health app lets you keep all your health and fitness information under your control and in one place on your device'; and 'You decide which information is placed in Health and which apps can access your data through Health app' (ibid.). The Apple Store is also a repository of numerous health apps, either produced by Apple itself or by other companies and/or developed or sponsored by patient organisations, that one can readily download, occasionally free of charge. For example, the MindShift™ app, developed by the Anxiety Disorder Association of British Columbia (AnxietyBC), advertised as 'designed to help teens and young adults cope with anxiety' using 'step-by-step strategies based on psychological treatment', can be downloaded free of charge from the Apple Store (AnxietyBC®, 2018).

While advertisements such those by above by Apple use a language of personalization (as in 'you choose', 'your mind', 'how you feel') and the rhetoric of empowerment, their content does not convey exactly who the 'you' is who is being addressed. These advertisements are likely to be variously interpreted by different sections of the population, according to their opportunities to purchase the technologies and their propensity and ability to engage in the level of self-monitoring required for the kind of care envisaged. Advertisers nevertheless evidently recognize that such language resonates with some sections of the population, as seen in the phenomena of 'self-tracking' and 'self quantification'.

Self-tracking and the quantified self 'movement'

While the widespread use of wearable, self-tracking electronic devices is a relatively recent global development, the idea of wearable devices first emerged in the 1970s. However, early technologies were cumbersome, and efforts were made to reduce their size and weight and build circuitry directly into clothing (Mann, 1998). Steven Mann, who has been described by some as 'the father of wearable computing' for having developed an all-purpose wearable computer rather than a specific-purpose device (e.g. wristwatch), has advanced the use of cameras as 'quantimetric sensing instruments' (Mann et al., 2002). Mann developed the digital eyeglass as early as 1978, a forerunner of Google's (commercially failed) Glass, an application of which, the DrChrono app, has been heralded as a 'wearable health record' (Farr, 2014). The early 2000s saw a rapid rise of the phenomenon of self-quantification, whereby citizens integrate tracking and sensing technologies into aspects of their everyday biophysical lives, to measure such things as bodily input (e.g. food consumption, exercise levels) and biophysical states and functioning (e.g. heart rate, mood, arousal) (Petersen, 2015: 104–106). The idea behind self-tracking is that the feedback from the sensing technologies will allow individuals more insight into their biophysical lives and their surroundings, and encourage 'reflective learning' (Riphagen, 2013: 2).

The 'quantified self movement' has attracted some momentum and a corresponding level of academic scrutiny (e.g. Swan, 2013; Lupton, 2016; see also Health Sociology Review (2017) special issue on 'self-tracking, health and medicine'). Quantified Self, a California-based company started in 2008 by Gary Wolf and Kevin Kelly, has as its byline 'Self knowledge through numbers', and 'serves the Quantified Self user community worldwide by producing international meetings, conferences and expositions, community forums, web content and services, and a guide to self-tracking tools' (Quantified Self, 2017). However, this self-quantification is part of a much broader trend of technological colonization, and specifically digital colonization, where machines have become integrated into everyday affairs and individuals define and conduct themselves in accordance with technologically determined norms of health and normality. For example, recent years have seen the emergence of online communities of users of transcranial direct current stimulation devices, which can purportedly help 'treat' mental illness or enhance cognitive abilities.

The self-quantification trend, while interesting if not troubling in some respects, thus far has had limited impact. A survey undertaken by Gartner in 2016 revealed that many citizens find wearable devices unappealing and, of those who do wear them, many abandon them over time because people 'do not find them useful, they get bored with them or they break' (Gartner, 2017). One issue is that their constant use calls for a great deal of self-discipline and commitment, a fact increasingly recognized by business entrepreneurs. With this in mind, designers have drawn from the behavioural and neurological sciences to design devices and apps to affect the 'architecture of choice' (Thaler and Sunstein, 2009) so as to encourage citizens to actively engage with their technologies. 'Behavioural architects' seek to understand the techniques needed to capture people's attention and to increase the so-called conversion level: the number of internet users who make it to checkout. This includes the use of feedback mechanisms that encourage learning (Alter, 2017: 121–146) and single-purpose, easy-to-use devices that make purchasing goods and services more convenient, time efficient and/or cost-effective; for example, Amazon's Dash Button, to assist in the ordering of consumer goods (Greenfield, 2017: 36–38).

Companies that market digital platforms make strong appeals to 'consumer control' and convenience in their advertisements, and often use financial and other incentives to encourage the sharing of personal health data. The US-based company Health Wizz, founded in 2016, employs both techniques in its efforts to encourage citizens to share their health data (Chapter 3). Health Wizz is described in the company's 2017 press release as 'a decentralized mobile platform' that 'enables people to aggregate, organize, and share personal medical health records securely and efficiently'. Security is assured via a 'blockchain-powered technology solution to address the mounting Electronic Health Records (EHR) problem and give consumers control over their medical data' (Health Wizz, 2017). The press release goes on: 'Built with the belief that people must have the ability to access and manage their health information electronically, the Health Wizz secure, decentralized mobile platform enables people to aggregate, organize and share personal medical health records securely and efficiently' (ibid.). The Health Wizz website provides further insight into its vision of 'citizen empowerment':

> What we are about is that every individual on the planet carry a complete copy of their medical records and genetic information on their mobile phones. They have a longitudinal history of all their health data—from birth to present—in one place—on their phones.
>
> (Health Wizz, 2018)

As noted, this language of personalization and empowerment permeates both industry and government communications on digital health, and marketers and insurers are using insights derived from behavioural psychology and nudging techniques to align technological use with 'consumer preferences'—with the financial bottom line in mind. Those who stand to profit from the evolving economy of consumer-centred healthcare are many and various, including the pharmaceutical industry and the health insurance industry.

Pharma 3.0

As mentioned in Chapter 3, the pharmaceutical industry sees major opportunities in the digitalization in health, and has already made efforts to forge links with patient communities through sponsored conferences and other means, to learn more about their perspectives and needs. Sociologists have documented the expansion of the pharmaceutical industry's domain into diverse areas of life, whereby biophysical, behavioural and social conditions are treated, or deemed as treatable with pharmaceuticals (Abraham, 2010). Industry insiders and marketers are evidently aware of the impacts of this growing pharmaceutical influence on healthcare, a trend that has been dubbed 'Pharma 3.0' (Ernst & Young, 2018). The term has been used to signify various offerings that go beyond drugs, to encompass an expanded scope of technologies, disease categories, and 'stages in the cycle of care', as well as health outcomes and responses to the demands and expectations of patients who are increasingly using mobile technologies and social media (Bianchi, 2012; Ernst & Young, 2018).

According to one industry commentator, 'Pharma 3.0 can be described loosely as "Pharma + Web 2.0". That is, "social media" plays a big role' (Owen, 2012). As this writer goes on to say, social media has 'brought a voice to the end consumer' who 'has become more knowledgeable about their ailments, and more critical of the medicines they are taking'. This is where 'social media, and related technologies, come into play. Companies are starting to identify ways that they can not only "talk to the customer", but also "listen"' (ibid.). According to a marketing report, Pharma 3.0 offerings include, in addition to drugs, monitoring devices, smartphone apps, 'patient-oriented services', and education programs (Ernst & Young, 2018).

The enlargement of pharmaceutical influence to encompass risk management and prevention activities is leading to the development of new business models, skill sets and expertise, both to meet the changes associated with this new mode of healthcare and to respond to the entrance into the healthcare market of 'non-traditional players' (ibid.). For example, Australian telecommunications company Telstra has increasingly moved into the healthcare field, including developing apps for assisting in the management of medications, clinical care management and home care management. Telstra has interests in these areas through iCareHealth, which was acquired in 2014—adding to its growing healthcare portfolio. Among Telstra's various interests is a telehealth service, Telstra ReadyCare, which is a joint venture with Swiss company Medgate, offering GP consultations via phone or video consultations on a 24-hours-per-day basis. A number of other telecommunication companies—including major US concerns Verizon and AT&T—have also entered the field through the application of their expertise into areas such as telehealth and patient monitoring sensors, but have struggled to compete with Google and Apple (Wasserman, 2016).

Health insurers

Health insurance companies are major stakeholders in the evolving digital health market, and many have made efforts to nudge policyholders to use wearables and to share their data. Their interest in tracking health and risk is hardly surprising given the nature of their business, where their ability to accurately calculate risk and establish premiums is crucial to their profitability. A survey of 'more than 200 insurance executives' undertaken in 2015 reported 63 percent as saying that they 'expect wearable technologies to have a significant impact on their industry' and will be adopted broadly within their industry 'in the next three to five years', with a number already using them to 'engage customers, employees or partners' (Accenture, 2015). Some providers are providing new policyholders with a fitness band to track their health progress, which is rewarded by way of reduced premiums and reward systems such as discounted premiums and gift cards.

In Australia, one of the largest private health insurers, Medibank, offers policyholders who use Fitbit, Garman, Jawbone or Polar wearables the opportunity to accumulate points through a flybuys loyalty scheme (Information Age, 2015). One of the US's largest health insurers, Aetna, which claims to serve 'an estimated 46.3 million people with information and resources to help them make better informed decisions about their health care', announced in 2016 that it would 'make Apple Watch available to select employers and individual customers during open enrollment season […] and subsidize a significant portion of the Apple Watch cost, offering monthly payroll deductions to make covering the remaining cost easier' (Aetna, 2016) In addition, the company offered to provide 'Apple Watch at no cost to its own nearly 50,000 employees, who will participate in the company's wellness reimbursement program, to encourage them to live more productive, healthy lives' (ibid.). A link on Aetna's website takes one to 'Engaging employees with wearable fitness devices', which explains the benefits of such devices for 'worksite wellness programs'. When one scrolls down the page, it is evident that the site is advertising 'MyActiveHealth engagement platform' to employers (ActiveHealth Management, 2015). The site includes reference to various statistics on the growing wearable fitness device market, citing as one source a market research company, CCS Insight, which reported that 'By 2018 over 250 million smart wearables will be in use, 14 times more than in 2013' (CCS Insight, 2014), a message evidently oriented to underlining the significant market of users. ActiveHealth Management (2015) goes on to list 'a few of the devices and apps that can be integrated with the platform', namely Fitbit Charge HR^{TM} (for monitoring heart rate, activity, and sleep patterns and to time runs and 'other workouts'); Garmin Forerunner 920XT ('a GPS-enabled multisport watch that tracks heart rate, steps, sleep and calories burned all day'); Jawbone Up24 ('tracks calories, steps and sleep' and also 'features recipes for healthy dishes, drinks and snacks from an extensive database' and allows bar codes on packaged foods to be 'scanned to quickly see nutrition facts'); Misfit Shine ('tracks running, walking, swimming… calories burned and sleep patterns'); and MapMyFitness app ('can track workouts on any device anytime and anywhere' and 'keeps track of eating habits and provides a full view of the fitness journey'). Further, 'Workouts and accomplishments can be shared with friends through social media for some extra encouragement.'

Market researchers predict that wearables will have a socially transformative effect. In an extensive report, *The Wearable Future*, based on a population survey and interviews with business executives, wearable technology users and 'digital services leaders', PricewaterhouseCoopers sees a 'wearable future' ahead that will 'dramatically alter the landscape of society and business as we know it' (PwC, 2014: 4). The report comments that wearables are already being used in workplaces and that 'people are remarkably uncon-cerned about the net impact wearable technology could have on their security or autonomy' (ibid.), although it adds, 'Without question, consumers of all demographics are leery of the impact wearable technology will have on the privacy and security of their personal information' (ibid.: 6). The report extols the benefits of wearables, for example for employer-sponsored health and wellness programs that increase worker productivity, for 'speeding up the onboarding process through real-time feedback', for improving customer services and, in manufacturing, to 'help expedite production by creating hands-free guidance tools'. However, one of the biggest challenges, it notes, is the 'consistency of data', which can be 'very basic and a closed experience between a device and sup-porting app or mobile web experience'. Further, for wearables to be most valuable to users, 'data from the wearables experience will need to be integrated more broadly in an interoperable ecosystem, rather than acting standalone'. It goes on,

> And when this happens, Big Data is poised to get a whole lot bigger—and better. A critical inflection point for the wearable category will be its ability to account for environmental surroundings and take data in as seamlessly as it pushes data out.
>
> (ibid.: 4)

PwC also believes that wearables 'will continue to revolutionize the health care industries'. It notes that 'while consumers have not embraced wearable healthcare technologies in large numbers, they are intrigued'. It advises that companies should produce products that 'offer greater value for both users and their healthcare part-ners' so that they will be 'incentivized' to use them (ibid.: 4–5).

While marketers see wearables as presenting a major business opportunity, and encourage employers to promote their use among their employees, they are but part of a much larger digital health technology industry that includes AI, personal assistants, implants, monitors and telehealth devices. It is in the institutions of healthcare, especially hospitals, where the impact of digitalization is becoming most apparent and is expected to have far-reaching impacts in the years ahead. Indeed, with rapid and projected digitalization, the concept of the hospital itself is said to be in transition. Precision medicine is, as discussed in Chapter 3, a central element of the digital health imaginary. However, as I explain in the following paragraphs, there are other technologies on the horizon or being applied in healthcare that promise to transfigure concepts of health and healthcare—indeed, to move practice towards the anticipated virtual care scenario—but that are likely to have impacts very different from what is imagined (Chapters 1 and 2).

Personal voice assistants

While, as noted in Chapter 3, the smartphone has been the foundation for the 'networking of the self' (Greenfield, 2017), at the time of writing, major technol-ogy companies such as Amazon, Apple, Google, Samsung and Microsoft are com-peting for what it is claimed will be an increasingly dominant and lucrative sector of the digital health market: AI-based platforms, and specifically personal voice assistants. Some predict that 'ambient listening tools' such as personal voice assistants will eventually replace smartphones, just as the latter replaced laptops as our primary means of undertaking computing. As one business reporter wrote in early 2018, 'Companies are not just battling over who can get the plastic devices [smartphones and other mobile devices] into the house, but over who gets to have the sound of the voices of their personal assistants heard in the living room: Alexa, Bixby and Siri (Thomas, 2018: 19). The market for smartphones has risen rapidly and the level of ownership is high in some countries; however, as noted in Chapter 3, the market has become saturated and technology companies have been looking to the next potentially profitable 'frontier'. The rise of the personal voice assistant is seen to offer the next wave of technological innovation, which will be even more personalized than the experience offered by smartphone apps.

In early 2018, it was reported that Amazon's Alexa 'rose to the top of Apple's App store while Amazon's Echo Dot was its own best seller' (Siwicki, 2018b). Hospitals are either trialling, or in the early phases of using, these technologies. For example, in the US, Boston's Beth Israel Deaconess Medical Center is using voice assistants tasked with various 'skills' that are being used in patient rooms (ibid.). In this particular hospital, patients can ask Alexa to 'call a nurse' or ask questions about one's diet while under treatment. Other US hospitals are using Alexa in combination with Google Home to provide patients with information about wait times in emergency rooms and the urgent care centres that are near one's post (zip) code. Still other hospitals are using these technologies to 'create individualised care environments for [...] members and patients', including 'hands-free calling' to others who have Alexa, and using Google Calendar to access 'personal care assistant schedules', thus obviating the need to constantly ask others to check the usually written schedules (ibid.). In the UK, in March 2018, Public Health England announced that it had launched a new service for breastfeeding mothers via Amazon's Alexa. The report noted that 'Through Start4Life's "Breastfeeding friend", users can ask the cloud-based platform a variety of questions about breastfeeding and receive answers tailored to the age of the baby' (Crouch, 2018a). Start4Life is an NHS advice service for pregnancy, birthing and parenthood. According to the report, the service was launched after recognition that searches for online information support peak 'between 2am and 6am when help in-person is not available' (ibid.). This data, together with surveys, had justified the need for the service and that 'Using technology and keeping pace with developments can support both parents and healthcare professionals in ensuring evidence-based advice and support is accessible when needed' (ibid.).

Healthcare moving to the cloud

The growing use of AI technologies and machine learning, should they evolve as anticipated—to become more human-like and 'sentient'—when linked with cloud computing, presents the prospect of the realization of a fully networked society (Chapter 2). The big internet companies, including Google, Amazon and

Microsoft, see cloud technology as the way of the future and are planning to collect disparate information, currently held in hospitals, labs and other sites. In early 2018 Google announced that it was using a new application programming interface (API) to 'ingest all of the important health-care data types', using several hospital partners, including Stanford School of Medicine, for its 'early access program' (Farr, 2018a). Google claims that its stated goal for healthcare reflects the company's overall mission; namely, 'to organize the world's information and make it universally accessible and useful.' (Moore, 2018). Apple, on the other hand, asserts that its approach to cloud computing is different from its competitors' in allowing users to download their health records onto their phone and then to store it or share it with their doctor, caregiver or friend (Farr, 2018b). In a news report on the announcement, Apple's Chief Operating Officer Jeff Williams is cited as saying: 'We view the future as customers owning their own health data', and explaining that 'Apple doesn't see the data unless the consumer chooses to share it' (ibid.) As the report states:

> It all works when a user opens the iPhone's health app, navigates to the health record section, and, on the new tool, adds a health provider. From there, the user taps to connect to Apple's software system and data start streaming into the service.
>
> (ibid.)

It is explained that the information will include 'allergies, conditions, immunizations, lab tests, medications, procedures and vitals'. Further, 'The information is encrypted and protected through the user's iPhone password' (ibid.). Google is working with a number of medical records companies to 'make it easier for people to view that information on the iPhone' so that 'they can simply pull it up and suggest their doctor to take a look'. In the report, it is noted that 'its primary goal is to give users a better experience and not to sell more iOS devices' (ibid.).

The term 'cloud robotics' refers to 'the migration of much of the intelligence that animates mobile robots into powerful centralized computing hubs' (Ford, 2016: 21). As Ford explains, the sheer speed at which information can now be communicated means that much of the computation required by robots can be offloaded to huge data centres, while enabling individual robots to access network-wide resources. Individual robots may rely on a centralized machine intelligence, which can be available to other machines accessing the systems, thereby making it easier to scale machine learning across a large number of robots. Google announced support for cloud robotics back in 2011, and allows robots to be serviced by Android devices. In time, Ford argues, using these clouds, robots may reach a point where they develop capabilities making them ever more useful for everyday tasks, such as housekeeping chores (ibid.: 21–22).

In the healthcare field, IBM has developed its Health Cloud, which it markets as having multiple benefits—for providers, patients, businesses and researchers. On its website, IBM claims its Health Cloud will: 'Improve collaboration among patients, providers and payers to deliver more effective care'; 'Digest vast amounts of data to reveal personalized recommendations to the point of care'; and 'Improve business processes to drive efficiency and cost savings' (IBM, 2018). Cloud computing is seen to enable users to access the services offered by massive supercomputer-like networks of servers, which will massively reduce the amount of time previously taken to solve complex problems and save considerable costs through renting rather than buying servers in the cloud. The hosting of technologies such as IBM Watson Health (Chapter 3), deep learning neural networks and narrative writing engines, Ford argues, will 'become the building blocks that can be leveraged in countless new ways'. The result, he claims, will be to make groundbreaking AI technologies ubiquitous and accessible even to amateur coders (ibid.: 107). The move to cloud computing as the main or sole backup storage, however, poses security threats, such as distributed denial of service and related types of cyberattacks, although AI technologies are seen as playing a role in dealing with these threats (Deloitte, 2018: 13, 21–22).

Despite the enthusiasm among technology companies for cloud computing, and market projections for healthcare expenditure on cloud computing to triple between 2018 and 2020 (Synoptek, 2018), updating of the technology has been slow in healthcare systems (even when this is mandated), with issues of security and management being paramount, at least for some service providers. In the UK, for instance, the uptake of public cloud computing—which is accessible over a public network and its infrastructure shared by multiple organizations rather than being restricted to a single organization, as with a private cloud—has been slow, despite this being mandated for use by central government organizations in 2013. In one view, this may be due to a lack of clarity concerning 'how and what NHS services should be stored in the cloud' (Hughes, 2018a). A Freedom of Information request sent to every NHS Trust in England revealed that 61 percent of Trusts cited concerns about 'security' and 'compliance and data privacy' as 'the biggest barriers to cloud adoption' (Winder, 2018). In practice, this includes concerns about 'vulnerabilities in web applications' and 'poor implementation of available access controls', which leaves applications and data exposed to security attacks (ibid.). Relatively few (17 percent) of the 160 Trusts expected to see a return on investment by adopting public cloud services. Further, a survey of NHS Trusts revealed that fewer than a third (30 percent) had adopted any form of public cloud in their organizations, and of these approximately four in five (79 percent) indicated that they had 'no plans to migrate everything to the cloud' (Hughes, 2018a). Public fears about the increasing use of cloud computing are likely to grow in the UK in the wake of NHS Digital's plans to store patient data 'offshore' with third parties in Europe and the US (Knowles, 2018). Reportedly undertaken to reduce costs and allow more flexible data sharing, critics lambasted the proposal on the grounds that it bypassed UK cloud providers (the now-bankrupt Manchester-based DataCentred being cited) and increased the risks of personal data being shared with third parties of all kinds, including technology companies such as Amazon, Microsoft, Google, Salesforce and IBM, resulting in discriminatory practices, for example in relation to employment (ibid.).

The colonization and monetization of healthcare

As the above developments make clear, the domain of health and healthcare is rapidly being colonized, datafied and monetized by the big internet companies, which see potential to profit from the massive amount of information generated by patients themselves and from other sources. Significantly, in February 2018, Apple announced that it was opening on its Apple Park campus two 'AC Wellness health clinics' for its employees and families in Santa Clara County. At the same time, it was reportedly 'scaling back' its partnership with its current in-house provider, Cross-Over Health (Clover, 2018). As the article notes, Apple plans to use its medical clinics as a 'test bed' for its health services and products, such as blood glucose monitoring and the use of Apple Watch to predict irregular heart rhythms (Aouad and Beaver, 2018) At the time of writing, details about this venture are scant, and the AC Wellness website suggests it is still in the development phase ('Coming spring 2018'). However, using language that is now familiar with many digital health initiatives, this website explains that 'AC Wellness Network believes that having trusting, accessible relationships with our patients, enabled by technology, promotes high quality care and a unique patient experience' (AC Wellness, 2018a) The website's careers page offers a glimpse into the range of expertise that will be involved, including a primary care physician, a clinical exercise coach, an acute care physician, a care navigator (who 'sets the tone for the patient's experience, whether it's the patient's first phone call, or their first interaction with a team member entering the center'), a phlebotomist (for 'accessioning, receiving and specimen processing, report distribution'), and a medical assistant (who 'works within the care team to create a frictionless experience for patients of the Wellness Center') (AC Wellness, 2018b).

It is interesting to ponder the socio-ethical implications of Apple using its own medical clinics, used by its employees, as a 'test bed' for digital health initiatives. A number of questions arise: Does employees' involvement in research projects potentially jeopardize their employment, for example, if they are found to have a previously undiagnosed disease? Do they have the option *not* to participate in research? Given Apple's control of other kinds of big data, is there the potential for their employees' information to be used for other, non-health-related purposes? Apple, like other big companies, presents its research endeavours as benevolent and oriented to citizens' best interests. Its purported concern for the welfare of its employees, however, sits uncomfortably with its practices and its drive to garner newer sources of data to generate profit.

As Paul Taylor (2018) observes, in a recent article on the trade in medical records, 'When it comes to data, this is a buyer's market'. In referencing the NHS's increasing marketization and deals in regards to data sharing with business, including an agreement between (Google parent company) Alphabet's DeepMind and Royal Free NHS Trust in London (see Chapter 5), Taylor observes that there are many countries desperate for this business investment. An example he cites is the agreement signed by the Italian Government and IBM in March 2016, whereby the company invested US$150 million, of which US$60 million would be provided in state subsidies, 'in a new centre in Milan to develop data-driven applications'. The article citing this case notes that, in return, 'IBM expects to have access to the health data of the population of Lombardy, if not the whole of Italy', including demographic data along with such details as emergency room visits, outpatient prescriptions, historical medical diagnoses and other personal medical details (ibid.). Taylor notes that the Italian data protection authority and the European Commission had asked the Government for details of the arrangement, but had thus far been ignored.

Dave Eggers' book *The Circle* (2013) highlights the dangers that accompany the digital utopianism and datafication that permeate contemporary societies (Chapter 2). The vision portrayed in this scenario, where the world's most powerful internet company takes care of all the needs of its employees at the price of their own personal freedoms, is salient in this regard. With a diminished role of the state and a shift in conceptions of citizenship, where citizen entitlements (e.g. to participate in political affairs and to enjoy rights to health and welfare services) increasingly are supplanted by their responsibilities as consumers, one should be cautious about promissory claims. As noted in Chapter 1, even some of the founders of the internet and social media have become sceptical about digital media and have offered warnings about their pernicious aspects. With the increasing domination and monopolization of the digital economy by relatively few powerful companies, there is a danger that datafication and the actions that follow will supplant other ways of understanding and responding to health issues.

Conclusion

As the developments described in this chapter make clear, the basic infrastructure and many of the constituent elements of the digital healthcare economy (EHR, wearable technologies, cloud computing) are in place, or are in the process of being created. This economy is underpinned by promise and expectation of the realization of a widely anticipated fully networked, 'seamless' healthcare system involving the contributions of governments, businesses and other actors, including individual citizens themselves, who are encouraged to contribute their data and play an active role in monitoring and managing their health. Various strategies have been adopted to advance the digital healthcare economy, such as the automatic opt-in model for EHR and initiatives that make individuals' use of personal technologies (social media, wearables), and the connections that they enable, convenient, effortless and 'rewarding'. It is here that behavioural psychology and positive reinforcement, via the use of incentives or default options, find extensive application. However, the socio-political implications of related initiatives and innovations, including the use of technologies such as personal care assistants and cloud computing, that raise issues of security and privacy and promise to change the fundamental character of care—potentially in adverse ways—have hardly figured in public debates and policies on digital health. Given the various substantive claims and initiatives regarding digital health, including those described in this and earlier chapters, it is fitting to conclude in Chapter 5 by offering an assessment of this field's promises and perils.

5

'DIGITAL HEALTH', ITS PROMISES AND PERILS

> Health is the biggest industry in the world. It's the most important and it's about to go through a rapid transition from the last of the great cottage industries to the most important of the data-intensive industries on the planet. That's going to happen over the next twenty years.
>
> *John Mattick, outgoing head of Australia's Garvan Institute (Minion, 2018b)*

As I complete this book, the optimism surrounding 'digital health', and the potential of big data-related innovations to transform healthcare systems and individual lives, is unabated. A constant stream of news items on new digital technologies and applications in the areas of medical research, health records systems, clinical practice, and risk management and prevention, lend the impression that the predictions for a 'personalized', fully networked healthcare system will very soon be fulfilled. The above comments of John Mattick, who until early 2018 led Australia's Garvin Institute, one of the country's leading organizations in the field of genomic medicine that uses big data and bioinformatics in its research, reflects a widely held view in this regard (Chapter 3). In the article in which the above comments appear, Mattick is cited as saying that 'changes here [in Australia] will be swift, dramatic and inevitable' (ibid.). The preceding chapters have considered the role of promissory discourse and optimism in shaping practices in medicine and healthcare through investments in technologies and associated systems, expertise and institutions. As I argued in Chapter 1, discourses of promise and hope, and associated expectation, play a crucial role in the development of new technologies, in mobilizing actions, including investment decisions that help shape futures. Belief that the fourth industrial revolution is inexorable and that economies, societies and individuals *will* need to adapt (Chapter 2) implies that there is little scope for imagining alternative futures and for considering how technologies may be resisted or technological paths disrupted.

However, as research in the field of science and technology studies reveals—and as my own investigation of the representations and development of various technologies over a period of more than twenty years confirms—innovations tend to develop in unexpected ways and have unforeseen consequences. Initial promises and expectations often fail to be fulfilled, yet they often shape actions in profound ways. As noted in Chapter 1, the 'hype cycle' is a well recognized pattern in technology development and has provided the basis for a whole field of business of technology research and advice. The disillusionment that often follows a period of heightened optimism attached to technologies can have a detrimental impact on science by undermining public confidence and trust in experts and expertise. In medical research and practice, as well as other fields where optimism is high (e.g. business investment, crime control), researchers and supporters of particular initiatives have sometimes attempted to develop strategies to manage hopes and expectations, to ensure that they are not higher than warranted by the accepted standards of evidence. An exemplary case is that of stem cell science (Chapter 2), where scientists and regulators have sought to temper publics' hopes and expectations for treatments that have yet to be clinically proven and may consequently cause harm (Petersen et al., 2017), with little evident appreciation of the mechanisms that shape these hopes and expectations.

Digital health, it is claimed by proponents, will make healthcare systems and practices more effective, efficient and 'seamless' and thereby, it is claimed or assumed, improve health outcomes and care as well as 'empowering' citizens and providing the foundation for wealth creation. In previous chapters I have explored the various claims that attach to digital health. However, on the basis of the evidence and arguments presented in those chapters, and knowledge of the factors that shape health, one can question whether digital health will deliver much of what is promised, especially given that the term itself tends to be broadly defined, or left undefined, in policy statements and programs. However, related initiatives may have far-reaching deleterious consequences, as I will explain. My overall assessment is that digital health initiatives may benefit some people in certain respects but will likely not benefit the majority and have the potential to harm many. Let me explain, drawing on some themes covered in the preceding chapters.

The claim to make healthcare systems and practice more efficient and effective

It is often claimed that digital health will have its most immediate and profound impacts in transforming the effectiveness and efficiencies of healthcare systems by better 'connecting' data with those who are able to best analyse and use it, thereby improving the quality of their practices. As noted in Chapter 3, in recent years a number of countries, including Australia, the UK and the US, have given priority to establishing the basic infrastructure for the envisaged future networked healthcare system via investment in electronic health record (EHR) systems. Current processes of recording and sharing patient information in large, fragmented, information-intensive healthcare systems that have been, and continue to be, heavily reliant on paper-based records, are seen by policymakers and healthcare authorities to thwart the delivery of timely, effective treatment and care. While the history of medical records is characterized by conflict over methods of standardization, with past innovations often meeting opposition from clinicians who are wedded to long-established paper-based practices, pressures for change in recording systems began to build from the early twentieth century with the growing applications of scientific principles into medicine, which generated a mass of data on patients' symptoms, physical examination findings, laboratory and radiology test results, notes from various specialists, and more (Wachter, 2017: 35–41).

New systems of financial accountability and safety assessment during the twentieth century were also increasingly impacting healthcare practice. Bringing together in one place disparate items of information on a patient, including on current diseases/conditions, medical histories, allergies, medications, test results, risk factors and personal preferences (e.g. in relation to resuscitation)—often collected by many different providers scattered across a region—has been a major challenge for healthcare planners and a point of frustration for both health professionals and patients (ibid.: 43). It is here that digital technologies, especially EHR systems (Chapter 3), are seen to have considerable potential.

In practice, however, digitalization has not proved as straightforward as proponents generally envisage. The implementation of EHR systems provides an exemplary case for exploring the unanticipated consequences of digitalization. Robert Wachter (see Chapter 3), a medical clinician-researcher and close observer of digital developments in the US healthcare, observes that in the 1970s experts began to tout the computer as the 'savior for the [patient] note's many flaws and contradictions' (ibid.). However, while electronic systems might have been able to address each of the problems that he identifies, such as dealing with 'voluminous quantities of dynamic information' and 'the need to capture and promote accurate analyses of the patient's problems',

> the multifaceted demands made even these 'easy' problems devilishly difficult to solve electronically. This is because, in attempting to solve all of them, the electronic records that emerged weren't very good at solving *any* of them.
>
> (ibid.: 46; emphasis in original)

In his book *The Digital Doctor*, Wachter describes the diverse, multifarious impacts of digitalization and related changes on the healthcare system and healthcare practice in the US, with reference to areas such as EHR systems, doctor–patient interactions, diagnosis, and health information exchange between healthcare organizations. Wachter documents how reliance on digital technologies can lead to medical errors including misdiagnoses and inappropriate treatments, wastage of resources, distancing between clinicians and patients and between healthcare professionals, and fraudulent practices. He cites the example of radiology, which he describes as a 'crystal ball for the rest of the healthcare system' which, in the US, has been transformed by digital technologies, especially in imaging which has shifted from film-based to computerized systems (Picture Archiving and Communication System, PACS) allowing clinicians to see images and read radiologists' reports on their computers. As Wachter observes, while the advantages of PACS have been significant, the impact of this change on those who order X-rays and those who read them has been 'profound [...] and not all positive' (ibid.: 53–54). In his view, the nuanced, empathetic human interactions that previously characterized relations between clinicians and radiologists, and between both groups and patients in the clinical context, have been eroded. The trend to expand use of computerized systems in a cost-cutting environment offers a threat to the happiness and livelihoods of radiologists, who no longer have contact with patients and whose labours are vulnerable to outsourcing to less expensive providers. Moreover, the new systems potentially compromise patients' care since trainees no longer get the opportunity to talk to and learn from radiologists (ibid.: 54–63).

In Australia, an over-reliance on electronic medical records has been implicated in a number of deaths in recent years. In one case, a 41-year-old man died from a serious adverse drug reaction after being prescribed an immunosuppressant medication to treat his Crohn's colitis. The coroner's report on the case found that the blood tests ordered at the hospital had found that the man was unable to metabolize the drug 'due to two non-functioning copies of the TPMT gene'. The 'critical results' had been uploaded in the electronic health system with a 'red flag indicating an abnormal result [...] But by then the patient had been discharged and "due to systemic failures", clinicians were not alerted to the results' (Minion, 2017). The patient subsequently collapsed and died from 'septic shock and marrow aplasia', which was attributed to the toxicity of the drug. The coroner found that contributing factors to the death were poor communication between clinicians and rotating shifts combined with an over-reliance on 'electronic communications in an environment where clinicians routinely work on rotation and in team environments' (ibid.). In another Australian case, a 54-year-old man died after a routine knee surgery when an anaesthetist 'accidently misuse[d] a month-old electronic medical record at Macquarie University Hospital' and 'administered medication meant for another patient' (Minion, 2018c). Twenty-two alerts triggered by the electronic system (Inter-Systems TrakCare®) were 'manually overridden by the anaesthetist'.

While, it was reported, the doctor 'bears primary responsibility for the error', the electronic medical record 'made the medication mistake easier' since it enabled different patient records to be opened from a single terminal. The coroner noted that 'Prior to the introduction of electronic medical records, it was much more difficult to chart medication on the wrong patient file' (ibid.). And, in the UK in 2018, it was reported that 'a computer algorithm failure' going back to 2009 resulted in 450,000 women aged between 68 and 71 not being invited to their final breast cancer screening (Crouch, 2018b). While it is unclear whether the delayed diagnosis would have resulted in any avoidable harm or death—opponents of breast cancer screening question the claim (Bewley et al., 2018)—it was calculated that up to 270 women in England may have experienced shortened lives as a result (ibid.).

Cases such as these highlight the complex interactions that occur between humans and machines that can lead to medical errors, resulting in harm and sometimes death. Humans may rely too heavily on electronic communications, even where information is at variance from established clinical protocols; or electronic triggers that have been established to assist humans may be over-ridden because they become distracting or annoying. According to many designers, electronic communications and diagnostic tools are meant to *support rather than replace* clinical judgement—which, it has been argued, is the case with electronic medical record systems such as Isabel (Isabel Healthcare, n.d.). However, technologies tend to be introduced with little understanding of the contexts in which human decisions occur, involving time pressures, established traditions of clinical reasoning, emotional responses and system failures (Wachter, 2017: 93–114).

Despite the difficulties of implementing electronic health record systems, and problems associated with using them in clinical decision-making, policymakers' enthusiasm for the adoption of digital health technologies has remained steadfast. Comments by the New South Wales Health Minister in 2018 describing digital health as 'the golden way forward', and stating that health was 'the state government's top priority' to justify 'spending at an unprecedented level to deliver pioneering healthcare facilities' (Minion, 2018d), are not uncommon in recent policy announcements about investments in digital health. Described as the largest 'technology ecosystem' under way in Australia, New South Wales' spending on eplatforms 'outranks roads, schools and policing on the government's list of priorities'. Initiatives cited include Sydney's Sutherland Hospital introducing an Electronic Record for Intensive Care to replace paper documentation, which is 'now live throughout nine hospitals across the state'; clinicians' access to 'diagnostic-quality medical images' in a number of hospitals and services; and 'the modernising of existing infrastructure [and] the construction of new facilities' (ibid.). Typical of such announcements, it is claimed that this investment will both empower patients and put information at the 'fingertips' of clinicians (ibid.). Later I will consider the claim regarding 'patient empowerment'—a problematic concept, especially in the context of digitally mediated healthcare. However, the claim or assumption that clinicians will have better access to information that will improve health outcomes is one that is commonly made in relation to investment in EHR systems and other digital technology-related initiatives in healthcare, and should be closely scrutinized.

The claim to improve healthcare outcomes

The claim that digital health will transform the quality of healthcare is, on the face of it, the strongest argument for investment in related technologies, infrastructure and expertise. However, questions need to be asked: In what respects will such initiatives improve healthcare? What does improving health and care mean in practice? 'Health' is a highly contested concept, the meanings of which vary through time and across cultures, religions and geopolitical contexts. In the often-cited definition of the World Health Organization (WHO), 'Health is a state of complete physical, mental and social well-being and not merely the absence of disease or infirmity' (WHO, n.d.). This is one of a set of principles outlined in WHO's Constitution. Other WHO principles that are less often cited make reference to the politico-economic and socio-cultural conditions that facilitate the achievement of health. These include: 'The enjoyment of the highest attainable standard of health is one of the fundamental rights of every human being without distinction of race, religion, political belief, economic or social condition'; 'The extension to all peoples of the benefits of medical, psychological and related knowledge is essential to the fullest attainment of health'; and 'Governments have a responsibility for the health of their peoples which can be fulfilled only by the provision of adequate health and social measures' (ibid.).

While WHO's principles are widely accepted by governments and health authorities in the context of global health, as noted (Chapter 3), in practice the meanings and practices of healthcare have been colonized by high-tech biomedicine. Healthcare often equates with technological interventions (tests, treatments, devices) oriented to the biophysical body, which tends to be viewed in isolation from other aspects of being, including psychosocial and emotional experiences, which are profoundly shaped by socio-economic status, ethnicity, sexuality and other factors. The economic, political, socio-cultural and physical environmental factors that shape health, and that have long been known to have the greatest impact on health outcomes across populations (e.g. Bartley, 2004; Doyal, 1979; Townsend and Davidson, 1982; Wilkinson, 1996) are largely considered irrelevant in the practices of biomedically dominated healthcare. The molecular turn in medicine, which focuses attention on genetic susceptibility to disease and decisions based on data derived from gene testing and, increasingly, genomic sequencing and the identification of biomarkers, is reductionist and diverts attention from the broader factors that contribute to health in its widest sense. Further, with a growing tendency in many healthcare systems to rely on market-based mechanisms to deliver services, the responsibility of governments 'for the health of their peoples', envisaged in WHO's principles, above, is no longer taken for granted. As argued in Chapter 4, 'care', too, has a particular nuance in the context of biomedically dominated healthcare and has become increasingly commoditized, technologized and standardized, and less defined by the unique quality of intimate human-to-human contacts. The ways in which digital health is being, and is envisaged to be, enacted, with a growing reliance on technological mediation—artificial intelligence (AI) and algorithm-driven decisions, EHR systems, personal assistants, implants, monitors and telehealth devices—unsettles the established idealized conception of care that focuses on the whole person and the psychological, emotional and physical aspects of one's being.

The claim to empower patients

'Patient empowerment' or 'citizen empowerment' is very often invoked as justification for the introduction of new technologies in healthcare. This is not restricted to digital technologies, but has been used in relation to access to other technologies, such as genetics and, recently, whole-genome sequencing. However, a host of new digital health technologies, currently available or in development—including apps, wear-ables, self-diagnostic tools, voice recognition technologies, personalized medicines, and robots to deliver care—are widely promoted as means to empower citizens in general, or patients specifically. Governments and healthcare authorities argue that such technologies will allow people to gain more control over their health by being able to constantly monitor their body's functioning, gain feedback on or self-assess their risk factors, access timely information on health and treatments, and maintain autonomy when they get sick or as they age. The rhetoric of empow-erment seems compelling and resonates with the contemporary imperative that individuals should assume responsibility for their own health. Further, the rapidly growing amount of online information on health, including that curated by patient organizations, provides the illusion of virtually unlimited options in regards to lifestyles, treatment options and self-care. I have referred to some of these sources at various points in the preceding chapters, especially Chapter 2. However, as I explained in that chapter, those going online will be confronted with a glut of information, the veracity of which may be difficult if not possible to verify, espe-cially since much of it will be advertising that uses manipulative and deceptive devices oriented to *persuading* rather than informing users.

In Chapter 2, I referred to how search engines limit what can be known: the tendency for 'Google-knowing' (citing Lynch, 2016) to dominate other ways of knowing; and for the 'information cascades' that may develop with social media and blogs, whereby initial posts or expressions of opinion can establish the frame for later debates. The 'echo chamber' effect evident with social media, where self-reinforcing opinion becomes established as 'fact', is now well understood. Advertisers' use of algorithms to personalize information that citi-zens or patients are assumed to find useful, based on previous internet searches along with other information, brings into question the idealized notion of citizen or patient empowerment as portrayed by promoters of digital health—broadly, personal control over one's health and the knowledge required to advance it (Chapter 4). Growing corporate influence on the affairs of patient communities, and on the content of online resources available to those search-ing for information on health and on particular conditions and treatments (Chapters 2–4), undermines the claim that citizens or patients are empowered by digital media—if by this it is meant that their autonomy or freedom from external control will be enhanced. Insofar as citizens or patients could be said to be empowered, as I argued, this is via their enrolment in the broad project of datafication, whereby individuals actively contribute their personal informa-tion via the use of apps, wearables and monitors to big data projects that are avowedly for 'the public benefit'. In Chapters 3 and 4, I discussed the various ways in which citizens are being 'incentivized' to become 'digitally literate' and to integrate technologies into their daily lives. As I argued, the achievement of such self-subjection, self-objectification and self-mastery is integral to the emergent digital health economy that is expected to provide the foundation for future economic growth.

The claim to generate wealth creation

There is no doubt that 'digital health' already constitutes a substantial industry, and one that is expected to grow significantly in coming years. The questions of whether it is creating wealth, and for whom, are addressed later. First, however, it is worth examining the dimensions of the market, at least as portrayed by market researchers. According to one market research company, in 2016 the global digital health market was worth $US179.6 billion and was estimated to increase to $US536.6 billion by the end of 2025—a compound annual growth rate of 13.4 percent (HealthIsCool, 2017). This article cites Transparency Market Research (2017), which states that the market is 'assessed on the basis of the product, component, end user, and the geography'. As the report notes, the product market includes wearable devices and healthcare information systems—the latter identified as leading the global market 'due to the significant rise in the adoption of technological advanced products such as telehealth, EHR/EMR, and population health management' (ibid.). The health information segment is further bifurcated into 'clinical solutions' (including decision support systems, 'computerized physician order entry [a system that enables clinicians to enter instructions, for example for treatments or medicines, electronically rather than via paper charts], EHR/EMR, telehealth, mHealth [mobile health] and population health management'); and 'non-clinical solutions' (ibid.). The mHealth sector is identified as a significant growth area due to growing smartphone penetration across the world and growing awareness of health and fitness apps among people. In terms of the component, the market is categorized into software, hardware and services—with the latter seen as a higher growth area than the former two. Based on the end user, the market is categorized in terms of two segments—one comprising employers, payers and pharmaceutical companies ('the key contributor to this market over the last few years'), and the other patients and caregivers. Finally, the market is segmented in terms of geography, spanning six regions: Europe, Asia Pacific, Latin America, North America, the Middle East and Africa. While, the report notes, North America 'has been dominating the global market', other markets are expected to grow considerably in future years, especially Europe and Asia Pacific (which is described as offering 'lucrative opportunities for the growth of the global market for digital health in the near future') (ibid.).

Market reports such as this one are part of the promissory discourse attached to digital health, which shapes investment decisions. The information cited conveys the optimism for the field and its potential to attract venture capital and for businesses to profit from datafication. Market research companies themselves profit from the digital health industry, with the cited report, for example, starting at $US7,795 for a single user and rising to $US13,795 for a corporate licence (ibid.). Other parts of the market, not specifically mentioned in the report (although potentially part of the 'services' segment), include companies or organizations specializing in training, consultancy, standards and regulatory management, conference management, news production and academic research. The US company Corepoint Health, for example, offers various digital health-related services, including supporting organizations to integrate AI into healthcare systems (e.g. to aid administrative tasks) and to achieve interoperability (matching computer systems so they can be used together) (Corepoint Health, 2018). Australian publisher SAI Global claims, in its description of the *Digital Hospitals Handbook* (which sells for $AU172), that the publication 'develops a set of principles and recommendations that inform the design and implementation of digital hospitals, both new and refurbished, that enables innovative ways for providing healthcare services and supports positive outcomes for stakeholders now and into the future' (SAI Global, 2017).

Digital health provides the focus for a thriving conference market. The Digital Healthcare Show, hosted by Health Plus Care, a company specializing in hosting conferences in the healthcare arena, is trumpeted as a premiere event showcasing the latest digital technologies and case studies to illustrate their implementation. The conference, it is claimed, attracted 5,901 attendees in 2017, and its advertising suggests it provides not just an opportunity for networking but also for business to market their products and services. The webpage advertising the 2018 event, hosted in London, indicates that the event is oriented to offering solutions for implementing digital strategies. The site indicates that one can book a stand, or simply register for a fully-subsidised place, for a cost of £899 plus VAT. (Digital Healthcare Show, 2018) The annual HIMSS Global Conference and Exhibition is another major event in the digital health calendar. Its advertisement for its 2018 event claimed to attract over 40,000 health IT professionals, clinicians, executives, and vendors from around the world (HIMSS, 2018). Finally, a range of specialized journals and magazines focusing specifically on digital health have appeared in recent years. These include e-news magazines *digitalhealth, mobihealthnews, Healthcare IT News, British Journal of Healthcare Computing*, and *Becker's Health IT and CIO Report*, which are owned by large media or healthcare companies including eHealth Insider, HIMSS Media and Becker's Healthcare.

Academic research on digital health arguably has become an industry in its own right. While this research is mostly ostensibly undertaken within the public rather than the private sector, much involves close collaborations with industry partners and is often heavily reliant on private sector funding. In Australia, for example, recently initiated research centres include the Centre of Research Excellence in Digital Health, funded by the National Health and Medical Research Council for a period of five years, commencing in 2017; and the Digital Health Cooperative Research Centre (CRC), funded by the Department of Industry, Innovation and Science for seven years, commencing in 2018. The latter has attracted AU$111 million cash funding and AU$118 million in-kind funding over its duration, and includes numerous industry partners including genome sequencing companies, Telstra Health (an Australian telecommunications company with an interest in healthcare), other technology and software companies, pharmaceutical companies, insurance companies and health service providers, along with some not-for-profit organizations that operate healthcare businesses, government departments and agencies with a health and/or digital health remit, and health professional regulators and colleges. Arguably, these large research initiatives contribute to developing much-needed research capacity in digital health, while the research itself generates employment for individual researchers and products and services that may create profit and enhance the reputation and market position of the universities and other research institutions involved—although all this will likely be longer term and difficult to quantify.

For most governments, investment in digital health is integral to the advancement of the digital economy that is expected to underpin future growth. This economy, it is suggested, will be driven by technologies such as AI, quantum computing, cybersecurity and blockchain (see Chapter 3) (Australian Government, 2017c). Governments are already investing heavily in digital health technologies and are expected to invest considerably in years ahead. In the UK, for example, a Digital Health Intelligence market forecast report, published in May 2018, states that the NHS IT market is expected to rise year-on-year to reach £4 billion by 2022 in the effort to move the service away from 'paperless initiatives into areas such as cyber security and infrastructure' (digitalhealth, 2018). As noted in 2018 Australia announced a major multimillion-dollar research initiative in digital health, and is investing heavily in its EHR system, My Health Record. However, the questions arise: Who bears the cost of this investment? Will it pay dividends in terms of improved health outcomes and wealth creation?

In the view of Klaus Schwab, author of *The Fourth Industrial Revolution* (see Chapters 1 and 2), new technology has the potential to boost economic growth, which is seen to have slowed from its peak in 2007, before the global financial crisis, and to 'alleviate some of the major global challenges we collectively face' (2017: 35). He argues that 'digital connectivity' is 'fundamentally changing society' and the 'speed and scale of change for businesses' and that, while many jobs, especially routine and repetitive ones, will be automated and will disappear, new positions and professions will emerge and old power structures and ways of transacting business and social relations will be disrupted (ibid.: 50, 120). In Schwab's view, business leaders need to recognize that disruption affects both demand and supply sides of their businesses and consequently 'they must challenge the assumptions of their operating teams and find new ways of doing things. In short, they have to innovate continuously' (ibid.: 52). Further, he argues, while there may be 'downsides' to these changes, including rising inequality and potential new compulsions (e.g. by insurance companies) to wear devices that report health data, opportunities await those who are willing to embrace changes such as new ways of connecting and doing business, better decision making, more self-sufficiency and more civic participation (ibid.: 121–172).

In Chapter 1, I questioned Schwab's generally optimistic portrayal of 'digital disruption', which is technologically determinist and largely ignores the workings of politics and power and the role citizens may play in shaping futures. However, the World Economic Forum, of which he is Executive Chairman, has considerable influence among political, business and academic leaders, and so his views are likely to have considerable influence. At the Forum's Annual Meeting in Davos-Klosters, Switzerland in 2018, where there was much discussion about the prospects for the 'digital economy', the 'fourth industrial revolution' was often referred to as a given (World Economic Forum, 2018).

The health data economy

While digital health already constitutes a thriving market of products and services that generates profits and jobs for some companies and organizations, its potential contributions to the creation of *population* wealth is questionable. Indeed, the growing use of digital technologies in health, medicine and healthcare is likely to accentuate divisions arising from unequal access to the means of producing value from those technologies. One of the major promises of digital technologies in medicine and healthcare, and more generally, is to extract value from otherwise valueless data through combining information from different sources to offer individual consumers targeted (personalized) preventive advice and treatments (Mayer-Schönberger and Cukier, 2013). As Mayer-Schönberger and Cukier argue, 'the crux of data's worth is its seemingly unlimited potential for reuse: its option value' (ibid.: 122). Collecting information is one thing but, as they note, its value derives from its use rather than its possession. This sets data apart from resources such as coal, gas or iron ore, which are used once with their energy lost as heat or light, or converted, and which thus have no resale value, unless of course the residue can be somehow recycled.

Big data has been described in the media as the 'new oil' (or sometimes 'new gold') to highlight its value in contemporary economies: to 'power' the technologies (AI, predictive analytics) that will generate growth. The term is credited to Clive Humby, a British mathematician and businessman who argued that, while inherently valuable, data needs processing in the same way that oil needs refining before its value can be unlocked (Marr, 2018). However, as Marr correctly points out, the analogy is inaccurate—oil is a finite resource that requires other resources to transport it to where it is needed, whereas data can, in theory, be infinitely replicated, moved around the world at great speed and put to other uses (ibid.). The example Marr cites is medical data collected from patients, which is then used to diagnose and treat an individual, after which the data can be anonymized and fed into machine-learning systems to generate further insights that can used for other purposes. Increasingly, companies and organizations recognize the value of big data as a resource that can be bought, owned and rapidly exchanged by companies and organizations. Big technology companies, notably Google, Amazon and Microsoft, have recognized this, as reflected by their recent move into cloud computing, which provides the means to store big data and make it readily accessible to other companies, healthcare organizations and individual consumers (Chapters 3 and 4).

While much of the promise of big data is in improving individual patient care, as Wachter (2017) points out, there is another, more ambitious goal: creating a 'learning healthcare system' in which data is constantly mined for patterns and insights that may be used to improve the organization of clinical practice. Such data may eventually be used to help determine optimal staffing patterns, to assist efforts to prevent hospital-acquired infections, and to help estimate prognoses and risk factors, including for events such as heart attacks and readmissions (ibid.: 119).

Potential applications such as these are attracting the attention of large technology companies such as Google and IBM, which have moved into the healthcare field in recent years. Big health data is generally not considered to be a community resource, and its collection, storage and use is ultimately reliant on the investment of companies and other entities that hope and expect to profit from the health data economy. This means that any resulting treatments and other technologies will be sold, much like other products and services in the market—probably at relatively high prices due to patent protection, or at best subsidized through national health insurance or covered through private health insurance, for those who can afford it. However, the big data is generated and contributed by individual consumers themselves, either indirectly through the access that is provided to their health records, or directly via their wearables and monitors (Chapters 3 and 4).

New digital and data divides are emerging in healthcare, as they are in other fields. At the global level, 46 percent of the population do not use the internet—which may be largely because they do not have access to it. In 2018, the penetration rate of internet usage was 95 percent in North America and 85 percent in Europe, compared with nearly 35 percent in Africa and 48 percent in Asia (Miniwatts Marketing Group, 2018). Digitally mediated data is also unevenly distributed. Some writers make a distinction between the 'data rich', such as governments, institutions and commercial enterprises, and 'data poor', the individual citizens who both contribute the data and are the target of data collection efforts (e.g. Andrejevic, 2014; Van Dijck, 2014). However, this distinction is not as clear as has been presented since some groups and individuals are poorer or richer than others, depending on the context. Nevertheless, it is useful in highlighting the asymmetrical relations of knowledge and power that characterize the health data economy, which tend to be overlooked by digital optimists. Clearly, there will be winners and losers from the digital health economy. Indeed, divisions based on ownership versus non-ownership of data are already manifest in genomics medicine (described by the US National Institutes of Health as a 'subset of precision medicine') (National Institutes of Health, 2018) (Chapter 3), a field strongly reliant on commercial investment. As explained in a 2018 UK Government report *Genomics and Genome Editing in the NHS*, 'partnerships between the NHS and industry were needed in order for new medicines and diagnostics to be developed off the back of genomic data' (House of Commons Science and Technology Committee, 2017: 4.85) In fact, the NHS (like most other national healthcare systems) is *reliant* on industry support:

> Without the involvement of industry, the NHS and Genomics England would not be able to get the new medicines, treatments and diagnostics for patients that should come from this project. Medicines and diagnostics are always developed outside the NHS and government by the private sector.
>
> (ibid.)

Indeed, as this report conveys, the commercialization of genomic data is an end in itself (ibid.: 4.91). Those who contribute the data, namely the citizens whose genome has been sequenced, are unlikely to derive any immediate personal benefit and it is doubtful that many will receive any longer-term benefit from their contributions. However, the potential deleterious consequences of participation in genomics medicine and other digital health initiatives may be significant, as I will explain.

Digital technology use as a Faustian bargain

Citizens' relationship to digital technologies can be likened to a Faustian bargain, in that it involves the trading of 'something of supreme moral or spiritual importance, such as personal values or the soul, for some worldly or material benefit, such as knowledge, power, or riches' (Encylopaedia Brittanica, 2018) As this definition elaborates:

> A Faustian bargain is made with a power that the bargainer recognizes as evil or amoral. Faustian bargains are by their nature tragic or self-defeating for the person who makes them, because what is surrendered is ultimately far more valuable than what is obtained
>
> (ibid.).

What exactly is being traded? For digital health initiatives to gain traction, they rely on the consent of citizens to contribute their own data and to use technologies in prescribed ways. As noted, many citizens are already contributing data via wearable technologies, which is being encouraged by health authorities, insurers and technology companies. Further, governments are seeking to nurture 'digital literacy' among students, the elderly and more generally. While, as mentioned, internet usage remains uneven at the global level, many of those who do have access to the internet are evidently prepared to trade privacy and other risks of online use (potential loss of privacy, security) for convenience, the promise of empowerment, and the hope that they personally, or their families or communities, will derive health benefits from their digital connections. However, while citizens may recognize that there are risks associated with their growing use and reliance on digital technologies, they may not be fully aware that what they surrender may be far more valuable than what they obtain from the use of these technologies. As revealed by various academic literature and media reports, discussed below, the potential and actual harms is wide-ranging. Taken together, these sources suggest that citizens' engagements with digital health may not just present a risk to health and wealth, but may represent the quintessential Faustian pact: the trading of the most intimate aspects of one's self.

Harvesting of personal data

The Cambridge Analytica scandal, reported in 2018, highlights the ever-present danger that citizens' personal data may be harvested and used in ways unknown to them (Chapter 3). It also underlines the power of technology companies such as Facebook, whose income ultimately relies on tracking users' browsing history and the trading of the personal information acquired. Facebook users who are able to download the data kept by this company have been astounded by the amount of information collected, and also the difficulty of deleting information about oneself, such as birth dates and details of those whom one has 'unfriended'. One user discovered that Facebook had kept a permanent record of approximately 100 people that he had deleted from his friends list over the previous 14 years, including ex-partners (Chen, 2018). He also found that Facebook had an 'index' file that included 764 names and phone numbers of everyone in his iPhone's address book. Facebook also kept a history of each time he opened Facebook over the past two years, including the device and web browser used, and logged his locations. More troubling was the discovery that a large number of advertisers had his contact information, which he found could be harvested via various means, such as tracking technologies (e.g. cookies and invisible pixels that load in one's web browser), the purchase of data from data providers such as Acxiom, and credit card loyalty programs that may share information with third parties. Upon making this discovery, the user downloaded copies of his Google data and found that 'the datasets were exponentially larger than my Facebook data' and included details on the news articles that he had read and the apps he had opened on an Android phone over the previous three years, along with the date and time (ibid.).

As Taylor (2018) observes in regards to the growing trade in medical data and with reference to governments' deepening links with business (Chapter 4), despite the assurances, 'no large collection of information about individuals can be definitely anonymised'. The UK Government was reported to have sold hospital statistics pertaining to 47 million patients to insurance providers 'so that they could use the information to refine premiums' (ibid.). In the US, Taylor notes that for US$50 one can purchase a dataset that provides 'anonymised data on all hospitalisations in Washington State'. One researcher found that the data provided—including zip code, age, ethnicity and gender of patients—when matched with news stories in Washington State during a specified period (2011) containing the word 'hospitalisation', enabled 35 individuals whose data featured in the hospital data to be confidently identified as the person named in the report (ibid.). Taylor offers another interesting observation: the companies that have sold IT systems to hospitals are exploiting their privileged access to the data lodged in their systems, which may be used to generate products for the system to buy back. As he notes, the business model underpinning IT systems is predicated on the introduction of new practices, apps and monitoring devices that drive down costs in the system as a whole, which these companies are well positioned to profit from (ibid.).

As the Cambridge Analytica scandal makes clear, individuals cannot take issues of privacy and security for granted when commercial or (in this case) political interests are involved in decisions about data usage. Facebook and Google, and other big technology companies, have a business model that is fundamentally in conflict with users' interests in regards to ownership of their data, since their profits are generated through the use of such data to develop algorithm-driven personalized advertising. Moreover, they have designed their technologies in a way that some have argued leads users to become 'addicted'. While one may question use of the term addiction—taken from the field of drug studies—to describe people's obsessions with digital technologies, it does serve to highlight the potential harms associated with citizens' growing dependence on digital technologies in health and medicine, and other spheres.

Tristan Harris, who claims to have left Google in 2016 with the intention of 'work [ing] full-time on reforming the attention economy' and subsequently founded the Center for Humane Technology, is one of a number of activists/writers who have drawn attention to technology's 'addictions'—although in his case, this itself has become the basis for a business, with patents from his work held by Apple, Wikia, Apture and Google (Harris, n.d.) The website of his Center proclaims: 'Our society is being hijacked by technology' and that 'What we feel is addiction is something much bigger'. It is noted that while Facebook, Twitter, Instagram and Google have produced valuable products, they are 'caught in a zero-sum race for our finite attention, which they need to make money'. This race means that 'they must use increasingly persuasive techniques to keep us glued' and that 'They point AI-driven news feeds, content, and notifications at our minds, continually learning how to hook us more deeply— from our own behaviour' (Center for Humane Technology, 2018).

Sherry Turkle (2015), a US psychologist who writes on technology, argues that citizens, especially children, have become so reliant on their digital tools that they have lost the art of conversation. In Turkle's view, children's attention spans have been reduced by their addictions to mobile devices and their tendency to multi-task, and they have come to value their digital conversations more than their face-to-face ones. Drawing on research from cognitive psychology, she observes that when children use social media such as Facebook, the range of emotional experiences is limited since 'everyone learns to share the positive' (ibid.: 41). However, Turkle contends that one should not despair since parts of the brain that process emotion—likened to a muscle that may 'atrophy if not exercised'—'can be strengthened through face-to-face interaction' (ibid.). Also writing in the US context, Adam Alter argues that we live in an age of 'behavioural addiction', the product of digital devices and other consumer products that are designed to keep us hooked. In his book, Alter cites technology designers, including one of Instagram's founding engineers, who realized that they were 'building an engine for addiction', and Steve Jobs, founder of Apple, who refused to allow his own children to use an iPad purportedly because of the attention-sapping design of the technology (Alter, 2017: 1–3). Alter also refers to statistics suggesting that 'Most people spend between one and four hours on their [mobile] phones each day—and many far longer' (ibid.: 15).

As noted in Chapter 2, McLuhan and Fromm expressed sentiments similar to these in the 1960s, at the beginnings of the electronic age. These writers anticipated that human thought would be profoundly impacted by cybernetics and automation, which would lead to a radically new kind of economic and social organization dominated by large enterprises, and so they would likely not be surprised by the socio-technical changes and psychological impacts associated with the new digital technologies. Fromm observed the compulsions attached to the use of technologies—'that something *ought* to be done because it was technically *possible* to do it'—and the striving for '*maximal efficiency and output*' involving the reduction of individuals to 'quantifiable units whose personalities can be expressed on punch cards' (Fromm, 2010 [1968] 43). In the workplace, Fromm saw the danger of dehumanization and the ultimate loss of individuality and individual freedom associated with new methods of 'recording operators' contacts with customers and asking customers to evaluate workers' performance and attitudes, and so forth—all aimed at instilling "proper" employee attitude, standardizing service, and increasing efficiency' (ibid.: 44). This standardization, loss of individuality and surveillance is evident with digital technologies in general, and digital health specifically. However, I would suggest that it is manifesting in ways that are more subtle, diffuse and variegated than portrayed by either Fromm or McLuhan.

New forms of surveillance and control

As a number of scholars have rightly argued, the term 'surveillance' is too 'optically freighted' since it suggests a coercive and a centrally organized phenomenon that does not adequately capture the character of contemporary networked society, involving the continuous tracking and algorithmic analysis of personal data and propose, instead, the use of 'dataveillance' (Ruckenstein and Schüll, 2017; see also Van Dijck, 2014). As Ruckenstein and Schüll observe, rather than originating from a single source, dataveillance is distributed across different parties, such as clinicians, insurers, caregivers, pharmacies, and data aggregator and analytics companies and the individuals who provide the information (Ruckenstein and Schüll, 2017: 264). Another distinguishing feature of dataveillance, the authors note, is the use of predictive analytics to track emergent patterns and sort, categorize and differentially charge users for services, to assess patients on the basis of their risk, expense and/or non-compliance with medications, and to incentivize citizens on the basis of information fed back to them (ibid.: 264).

The growing use of personal voice assistants provides one context where dataveillance has the potential to upturn established conceptions of privacy, especially given their omnipresent character and the growing role in this field of big technology companies such as Amazon, Apple, Google, Samsung and Microsoft. As noted in Chapter 4, it has already been suggested that some companies may use these technologies to collect information that could be used for intrusive digital advertising. If, as predicted, devices become increasingly connected and interact with other devices via the Internet of Things, it may become increasingly difficult to control the flow of data between healthcare and other domains, such as business and crime detection. Inadvertent or malicious data leakage from healthcare to other contexts, such as business or criminal investigation, is an ever-present possibility. The recent case of NHS Digital sharing patients' demographic and administrative data with the UK's Home Office to help identify immigration offenders highlights the potential for such leakage to occur (Postelnicu, 2018). As Lucas argues, 'The "internet of things" is already churning out problems before it has even begun to reach its full potential' (Lucas, 2015: 166). It has already been demonstrated that it is possible to convert a domestic thermostat into a spying device within fifteen seconds of access to it (ibid.: 166). An attacker could, for example, gain access to a device at some point between manufacture and installation. According to the researchers who discovered the vulnerability in the thermostat, 'more than 750,000 spam and "phishing" emails (those containing malware or links to toxic sites) have been sent out from seemingly innocent devices such as fridges and televisions' (ibid.).

Data breaches

In this context, personal data collected for avowedly health reasons may be difficult if not impossible to regulate so as to both ensure privacy and guard against the exchange or selling of data to unauthorized third parties. Data breaches in the healthcare system, reported in recent years, highlight that data security is an ongoing issue, and may or may not be due to hacking. Healthcare datasets are especially vulnerable to hacking, given the personal nature of the information collected. One estimate by the Office of the Australian Information Commissioner indicates that one-third of all reported hacking occurred in this field in the six weeks following the introduction of a new notifiable data breach scheme (Office of the Australian Information Commissioner, 2018: 3). Further, according to a US analysis of the statistics available between 2009 and 2017, there has been an upward trend in healthcare data breaches (HIPAA Journal, 2018). Authorities intent on establishing EHR systems may not be keen to highlight the risks of hacking, or other risks. In 2018 in Australia, it was reported that shortly before the announcement of the My Health Record opt-out period (Chapter 4), a member of the steering group leaked information that the Australian Digital Health Agency had decided that associated risks for consumers, including the potential for cyber attacks and the secondary use of My Health data, 'will not be explicitly discussed on the website' (Minion, 2018e). It was reported that 'the agency moved swiftly to have [the member] delete the paragraph relating to secondary use' (ibid.).

Unintentional breaches may present a significant risk. In early 2018, it was announced that Australia's federal Department of Health had '"unintentionally" breached privacy laws when it published de-identified health records of 2.5 million people, online' (Han, 2018). The report noted that de-identified data of 10 percent of the population from the Medicare Benefits Scheme and the Pharmaceutical Benefits Scheme had been made available on the Government's open data website for 'research purposes'. However, a month later, researchers at the University of Melbourne revealed that 'the data could be re-identified' by 'cross-referencing the dataset with other sources such as Wikipedia, Facebook and news websites', and that 'they had pinpointed unique patient records matching seven well-known Australians, including three former or current MPs and an AFL footballer (ibid.). This followed an earlier report that the Australian Red Cross Blood Service had suffered a similar data breach (Office of the Australian Information Commissioner, 2017). In that case, a file containing information relating to approximately 550,000 people 'was saved to a publicly accessible portion of a webserver managed by a third party provider'; namely Precedent. This information included contact details such as physical address, email address and phone number, answers to questions about the individual's eligibility to donate blood, and sensitive and health information such as whether they were taking antibiotics, had engaged in risky sexual behaviour or had been pregnant in the past nine months. According to the Information Commissioner's report, the above incident was 'an important reminder that you cannot outsource privacy obligations' (ibid.).

As recent events indicate, hacking and the implanting of malware are ever-present risks. In 2018, for example, it was reported that security researchers had identified a hacking group, dubbed Orangeworm, that had been targeting hospitals with malware used to remotely access medical equipment such as MRI and X-ray machines as well as devices that are used to assist patients to complete consent forms for medical procedures (Hughes, 2018b). However, the growing links between businesses seeking to extract value from patient data and hospitals and other healthcare institutions may also present a risk of data being collected, shared and mined for unauthorized purposes. In 2017, a Cambridge University academic, Julia Powles, and a science journalist, Hal Hodson, drew attention to some 'inexcusable' mistakes made by DeepMind Health, a wholly owned subsidary of the Google-owned Alphabet Inc. and the Royal Free London NHS Foundation Trust, in a collaborative research project focusing on the management of acute kidney injury (Powles and Hodson, 2017). The authors argued that while the project was 'initially received with great enthu-siasm, the collaboration has suffered from a lack of clarity and openness, with issues of privacy and power emerging as potent challenges as the project has unfolded' (ibid.: 351). They contend that in the first year of the project identifiable patient records were transferred 'across the entire Trust, without explicit consent, for the purpose of developing a clinical alert app for kidney injury'. Further, in their view, the institu-tional and regulatory responses were 'insufficiently robust and agile to properly respond to the challenges presented by data politics and the rise of algorithmic tools in healthcare' (ibid.). The authors stated that they were interested in exploring the lessons that could be drawn when transferring 'population-derived datasets to large private prospectors [...] as healthcare moves into an algorithmic age'.

This was DeepMind's first major health project and the criticism was evidently not welcome, with both the company and the Royal Free quickly providing a joint statement challenging the claims (Stevens, 2018). Regardless of the veracity of these contending claims, the authors' intent in undertaking the study is well founded, given the growing interest of big technology companies in personal health data and the danger this presents for its unauthorized use. In 2018, for example, Facebook was reported to have approached US medical academies about 'a project that would see patient records linked to users' profiles' (Hughes, 2018c). According to the article reporting the request, Facebook planned to 'correlate this data against Facebook users to find out whether it could be used within targeted care scenarios'; however, the project was halted after the Cambridge Analytica scandal placed its privacy policy under scrutiny (ibid.).

The dangers associated with digital health mentioned above, such as the mon-etizing and harvesting of personal data, growing surveillance and data breaches, are already in evidence. This is a rapidly growing field, and developments are occur-ring ahead of wide public deliberation on the implications of technologies and regulatory efforts to ensure the safety and security of information and the avoidance of unwarranted intrusions into people's lives. While it is difficult to envisage where technological developments are leading, some technologies in their early stage application would seem to present unique risks.

Dangers on the horizon

As noted in Chapter 4, personal voice assistants are starting to find growing application in healthcare and they give rise to a specific set of concerns. One issue to arise from the use of these technologies is the potential for companies to capture new kinds of data on users and build more personal 'behavioural profiles'—summaries of consumers' interests and preferences based on interactions—with which to target consumers for advertising, and potentially other purposes (Kelly and Letheren, 2018). As with all digital technologies, privacy is a major concern, especially where personal health information is involved. Commercially available voice assistants are designed for group settings such as homes and hospitals, where the control over information is likely to be difficult to regulate (Siwicki, 2018b). This is a particular concern given the current development of the technology, which cannot always easily distinguish between individuals who are speaking, or between different accents (ibid.). In 2017, a study of patent applications filed by Amazon and Google, undertaken by the US-based non-profit organization Consumer Watchdog, highlighted the potential for the devices to be used for 'massive information collection and intrusive digital advertising' (Simpson, 2017). As the article points out, while the filings of patents do not necessarily mean that a company will implement the concept, they do 'reflect a company's ambitions' and 'nothing prevents them from implementing those changes once the devices are in your home' (ibid.).

Consumer Watchdog (2018) has raised a number of concerns about voice assistants. One is that the devices can still be 'awake' despite users believing they aren't listening. Amazon envisages that Alexa will use information on anyone in a room to sell them goods, and has filed a patent for an algorithm that will allow it to identify 'statements of interest' that will enable the speaker to be surveilled and targeted for related advertising. The study's Executive Summary notes that the technologies detailed in the patent application include: 'Multiple systems for identifying speakers in a conversation and building interest profiles for each one'; 'A method for inferring users' showering habits and targeting advertising based on that and other data'; and 'A methodology for "inferring child mischief" using audio and movement sensors' (ibid.). Another reported concern is that the devices can connect to other internet-enabled home systems that will allow monitoring of family members, with one Google patent application describing a 'smart home system to monitor and control screen time, hygiene habits, meal and travel schedules, and other activity' (Simpson, 2017). Researchers have shown that such assistants can be controlled by commands of third parties that are undetectable to the human ear and may be used to dial phone numbers and open websites 'simply with music playing over the radio' (Smith, 2018). It was reported that researchers at the University of California at Berkeley and Georgetown University 'could hide commands in white noise played over loudspeakers and through YouTube videos to get smart devices to turn on airplane mode or open a website'. And, while the researchers had no evidence that these techniques were being used as yet, 'it may be only a matter of time before someone starts exploiting them' (ibid.).

Apart from these intrusive uses of personal voice assistants, there is the danger that users may become overly dependent on and trusting of the technologies, and even begin treating them like humans. The futuristic film *Her*, released in 2013, produced by Spike Jonze, has characterized this human–technology interaction, with the main character, Theodore Twombly, a lonely writer, developing an intimate relationship with an intelligent computer operating system, Samantha, which meets his every need (see Chapter 2). It has been suggested that 'voice is the new touch' and that the appeal of personal voice assistants is that they allow 'frictionless connectivity' that feels 'human' and there is no technology to learn (Leong, 2017). Leong observes that voice assistants have particular appeal among those who are 55 or older.

The growing use of facial recognition technology is another looming danger confronting digital technology users and for society at large, although some argue that the benefits are significant. In healthcare there is growing interest in this technology, with early stage research in areas such as using family photos to help diagnose rare genetic conditions, and analysing a person's future health prospects based on the ageing of their face, with more medical and health applications expected in the future (Mohapatra, 2016: 1022–1023). Some research has been undertaken on using facial shape analysis to detect markers of physiological health among 270 individuals of different ethnicities. The researchers concluded that 'facial shape provides a valid cue to aspects of physiological health' (Stephen et al., 2017). Perhaps the strongest argument for the use of this technology, however, is securing the privacy of health consumers. Some argue that facial recognition will become the standard for authenticating users on mobile devices and is a 'virtually spoof proof' solution to gaining secure access to medical records, lab results, patient data portals and patient ID confirmation (Brostoff, 2017). However, while facial recognition technology has been so lauded, like all technologies it reflects cultural assumptions and biases, which may serve to discriminate against certain groups. Some research has found that facial recognition is mostly accurate if the photo is a white man, but the darker the skin of the person, the more errors arise. The researchers estimated that the error rate was up to 35 percent for images of darker-skinned women (Lohr, 2018).

Facial recognition is already finding application in a number of areas, especially law enforcement, and has become a feature of Apple's iPhone X, released in December 2017. In Apple's advertising the facial recognition technology is being marketed as a convenience, a means of biometric authentication that obviates the need for passwords, security dongles or authentication apps (Macworld, 2017). This purported convenience for authentication is a major selling point for this technology and arguably facilitates its introduction into healthcare and other areas. However, once the 'path dependency' for the technology becomes established, facial recognition may be used more generally, despite its flaws. The technology is already being widely used in the US and China for crime detection, and has been taken to a new level by Chinese authorities using it as part of state surveillance apparatus to identify criminals and to publicly shame those accused of jaywalking and other misdemeanors. In 2018, it was reported that the southern Chinese city of Shenzhen had instantly displayed photographs of pedestrians caught in the act of jaywalking on LED screens installed at road junctions (Xiuzhong and Xiao, 2018). In another case, facial recognition technology had been used to identify a 31-year-old man wanted by the police for 'economic crimes'. The man had been identified among a crowd of 60,000 people attending a sports centre for a music concert (Wang, 2018). Also in 2018, it was reported that 'A Chinese school has installed facial recognition technology to monitor how attentive students are in class' and that 'cameras positioned above the blackboard' were able to detect students' facial expressions, with the information being fed into a computer 'which assesses if they are enjoying lessons or if their minds are wandering' (Connor, 2018).

In the US, an estimated 117 million adults are in facial recognition networks used by law enforcement agencies, which are 'exploring real-time face recognition on live surveillance camera video' (Garvie et al., 2016). As this report concluded, law enforcement agencies do little to ensure their facial recognition systems are accurate, and their use is likely to disproportionately affect African Americans (ibid.). There are two major risks associated with the use of this technology in healthcare: over-reliance on the data for healthcare decisions (diagnosis, treatment, care), especially given the potential for errors and biases of the kind referred to earlier; and the potential for data to be used eventually for other purposes, such as crime control, identity theft and insidious surveillance, which is an ever-present possibility as technologies become increasingly interconnected and locked in.

The future

In this chapter, I have identified a number of trends in digital health, questioned a number of its claimed potential benefits, and pointed to a number of dangers. I have likened citizens' relationship with digital technologies to a Faustian bargain, in that it involves them surrendering more than they are likely to receive in return. Notwithstanding the promises that attach to digital health, the evidence suggests that any benefits of the use of technologies will mostly accrue to those who have ready access to the internet, namely the inhabitants of the richer, urban parts of the developed and developing worlds, while the potential harms to many individuals and groups across the world are significant. However, as I have argued, there is nothing inevitable in the development and application of technologies since, as noted in Chapter 1, they are socially produced and mediated. Community responses will shape how technologies are applied and used. Thus, while the pro-missory discourse surrounding digital health has considerable performative power in mobilizing actions, including investment decisions, for various reasons—politico-economic and socio-cultural—developments may, and in all likelihood will, play out in ways currently unimagined. Performativity may fail to produce what is promised, and futures will unfold differently from that imagined by technology designers and advocates (Chapter 1). Indeed, the conditions for performative failure are increasingly apparent: a decline of trust in digital technology companies, espe-cially in the wake of the Cambridge Analytica scandal; growing concerns about privacy and exploitation online and in relation to various widely publicized data breaches; and growing questioning of notions of truth and the claims of credentialled experts and related expertise. Citizens are encouraged to become 'informed consumers' and to become digitally literate and, in some cases, this is manifest in cautious, subversive and resistive practices. In the Web 2.0 era, citizens may use the internet and social media and draw on diverse knowledge, as 'evidence-based activists' (Chapter 2), both to press their claims to access information and treatments (e.g. on the grounds of 'compassionate access') (Chapter 3), and to challenge established knowledge and expertise.

Acts of resistance and calls for accountability

Various acts of resistance to the internet, social media or particular digital devices, and calls for digital companies or to be more accountable for their operations, are increasingly evident, although these are often disparate and uncoordinated at national and global levels. One of the characteristics of the internet is its tendency to divide populations into unconnected communities of interest and affiliation, making it difficult to mobilize at national and international levels. There exist, in a sense, parallel internets, which sometimes intersect yet often exist in relative isolation. The terms splinternet and cyber- or internet-balkanization have been used to convey this fragmentation of communications and communities. The rise of social media and their associated 'echo chambers' with self-reinforcing effects have arguably exacerbated this fragmentation. The idea of collective, coordinated action, associated with the social movements of the pre-internet era, is less evident online, although the internet is often used to complement offline advocacy work. Examples of these acts of resistance or calls for accountability are numerous, with some focusing on problematic technologies, others on companies or governments and their operations.

Algorithmic accountability

Many concerns focus on the potential for algorithms to have an undue influence over our lives. I mentioned the work of Cathy O'Neil (2016) who has highlighted the tendency for algorithms to discriminate against certain groups because of the human biases that are introduced in their development. O'Neill's warnings are part of a broader call for 'algorithmic accountability'. One group that has been active in this regard is the World Wide Web Foundation, established in 2009 by Tim Berners-Lee, the founder of the Web, who, as mentioned (Chapter 1), has become increasingly disillusioned with the direction of the internet in terms of its domination by big technology companies, the monetization of people's data and the restrictions on free speech. The group claims to be committed to advancing digital equality, undertaking research and supporting initiatives such as women's rights online, open data labs, and reducing the cost of internet access. One of its stated concerns is the influence of algorithms on public discourse (World Wide Web Foundation, n.d.); for example, it has undertaken recent research on how Facebook's news feed shapes 'our information diets' (World Wide Web Foundation, 2018).

In its report *Algorithmic Accountability*, published in July 2017, the Foundation offers examples of 'algorithms by function' in low- and middle-income countries, and how these 'may be applied to populations that are geographically and culturally distant to the places where the algorithms were designed', which increases the chances of them causing harm. In its report, the Foundation defines accountability as 'the duties that governments and other authorities have to present themselves before those whose interests they represent or are otherwise bound to, and justify how power was exercised, and resources were used' (World Wide Web Foundation, 2017: 10). The report outlines various 'principles of accountable algorithms' (accuracy, explainability, auditability, responsibility) and some areas for action. However, the emphasis so far has been on measures such as transparency, education and citizen engagement, and the risks associated with algorithmic decision-making, rather than challenging the data economy itself upon which algorithmic decision-making relies. It is here that data activists may play a role in challenging how and what data gets collected and the purposes to which it is put.

Data activism

Some data activists are developing their own databases using publicly available information to offer alternative sources to those of technology companies, thus challenging the operations and assumptions of their algorithm-driven decision-making. One example is Inside Airbnb, which 'provides filters and key metrics so you can see how Airbnb is being used to compete with the residential housing market' and relies on the contributions of volunteers and donations (Inside Airbnb, 2018). Efforts have also been made to hold companies to account for their practices. In the US, the National Fair Housing Alliance and other fair housing advocates were reported to be suing Facebook for allowing landlords and real estate brokers to target advertising that served to discriminate against families with children, women and people with disabilities (Neumeister, 2018). Also in the US, child advocacy groups fielded a complaint with the Federal Trade Commission against the Google-owned platform YouTube, on the grounds that it collects many types of personal information on children under the age of 13, including 'geo-location, unique device signifiers, mobile phone numbers' (della Carva, 2018). A more direct form of citizen response is to deregister from services offered by technology companies. In the wake of the Cambridge Analytica scandal there were calls to boycott Facebook, with some well known business people, such as Apple co-founder Steve Wozniak, announcing they were leaving the platform reportedly 'out of concern for the carelessness with which Facebook and other internet companies treat the private information of users' (Guynn and McCoy, 2018). However, deregistering has often proved difficult since Facebook is technologically embedded with third-party apps and social media platforms and, for many people, using Facebook is a required part of their job or education (Romano, 2018).

Citizens have also resisted specific technologies that have been promoted as 'tools of empowerment' where these are seen to have a deleterious impact on services. In early 2018 in the UK, patients joined GPs and NHS staff to protest against 'GP at Hand', a video consultation service for those suffering a range of stipulated medical conditions, which had been promoted on the basis that it cut GP waiting times and allowed patients to book appointments and talk to their doctor via their smartphone at short notice. Media coverage reported that angry patients had contacted their surgeries after discovering they had been deregistered from their usual surgery once they began using GP at Hand, while one GP argued that the service was 'cherry-picking younger, healthier patients' and taking resources from local NHS general practices. Concerns were also raised about the safety of online consultation providers, with a cited report from the UK's Care Quality Commission showing that '43% of online consultation providers are not deemed to be safe' (Crouch, 2018c).

Regulation

In addition to various acts of resistance and calls for accountability, there have been growing demands for an improved regulatory framework for internet platforms that have been able to proliferate in a relatively unregulated environment. In the view of Roger McNamee, who says he 'used to be a technology optimist' and 'mentor to Facebook founder Mark Zuckerberg from 2006 to 2010', 'With little or no regulatory supervision in most of the world, companies like Facebook, Google, Amazon, Alibaba, and Tencent used techniques common in propaganda and casino gambling, such as constant notifications and variable rewards, to foster psychological addiction' (McNamee, 2018). In McNamee's view, social media could be treated in a manner similar to tobacco and alcohol, involving a combination of education and regulation. We are witnessing the beginnings of such regulation in some countries or regions, particularly Europe, with new EU data protection rules (operating from 25 May 2018) that will limit how internet companies collect, secure and use information, and allow people to withdraw their permission for a company or organization to use their personal data (Europa.eu, 2018). However, clearly, much more needs to be done at the global level to protect citizens from the exploitations associated with unauthorized or inappropriate use and monetization of personal data.

A final word

Technological development and the emergent health data economy promise to enable humans to achieve what was unimaginable until relatively recently—ultimate control over nature, time, space, and economic and social uncertainty. Yet the digital health imaginary of a fully networked, empowering, personalized healthcare is underpinned by a deeply troubling vision of technologically and commercially dominated societies of a character not dissimilar to that portrayed by McLuhan and Fromm five decades ago. In these societies, citizens are essentially automatons whose thinking is handed over to machines. As noted in Chapter 2, in the depictions of these early writers, citizens have limited agency and are manipulable and passive. While recent developments of the kind outlined earlier indicate that citizens are certainly exploitable, the examples I cite of resistance, and of efforts to hold authorities to account, demonstrate that they are far from passive and have the capacity to shape events. Indeed, such examples underline the potential for citizens to mobilize to create alternative futures—potentially societies oriented to fulfilling human needs rather than techno-utopian visions that will do little to address the fundamental conditions affecting health in its widest sense.

REFERENCES

Abbott, A. (2013) 'Stem-cell ruling riles researchers', *Nature*, 495: 418–419. doi:10.1038/495418a.

Abraham, J. (2010) 'Pharmaceuticalization of society in context: theoretical, empirical and health dimensions', *Sociology*, 44, 4: 603–622.

Abrahams, E. (2011) 'The history of personalized medicine', in E. Gordon and S. Koslow (eds) *Integrative Neuroscience and Personalized Medicine*. Oxford University Press: New York.

AC Wellness (2018a) 'About'. https://www.acwellness.com/about (Accessed 20 March, 2018).

AC Wellness (2018b) 'Careers'. https://www.acwellness.com/careers (Accessed 20 March, 2018).

Accenture (2015) 'Insurers set to embrace wearable technologies, which they believe will have a significant impact on their industry', News release, 5 May. https://newsroom.accenture.com/news/insurers-set-to-embrace-wearable-technologies-which-they-believe-will-have-a-significant-impact-on-their-industry-according-to-accenture-insurance-technology-vision-2015.htm (Accessed 3 March, 2018).

ActiveHealth Management (2015) 'Engaging employees with wearable fitness devices'. http://go.activehealth.com/rs/661-IGJ-073/images/AHM_Wearable%20Device%20Flyer_FINAL.pdf (Accessed 4 March, 2018).

Akerlof, G. A. and Shiller, R. J. (2015) *Phishing for Phools: The Economics of Manipulation and Deception*. Princeton University Press: Princeton, NJ.

Alter, A. (2017) *Irresistible: The Rise of Addictive Technology and the Business of Keeping Us Hooked*. Penguin: New York.

Anderson, A., Petersen, A., Wilkinson, C. and Allan, S. (2009) *Nanotechnology, Risk and Communication*. Palgrave Macmillan: Basingstoke, UK.

Andrejevic, M. (2014) 'The big data divide', *International Journal of Communication*, 8: 1673–1689.

AnxietyBC® (2018) 'MindShift™ App'. https://www.anxietybc.com/resources/mindshift-app (Accessed 8 March, 2018).

Aouad, A. and Beaver, L. (2018) 'Digital health briefing', *Business Insider Australia*, 1 March. https://www.businessinsider.com.au/digital-health-briefing-apple-unveils-health-clinic-fitbit-misses-earnings-amid-pivot-samsungs-new-phone-will-have-in-built-health-trackers-2018-2 (Accessed 20 March, 2018).

Apple Inc. (2018) 'A bold way to look at your health'. https://www.apple.com/au/ios/hea lth/ (Accessed 1 March, 2018).

Arlington, K. (2017) '"It's not just me": how a lonely and ill Luke found support on the internet', *The Age*, 13 March, p.8.

Aronowitz, R. (2015) *Risky Medicine: Our Quest to Cure Fear and Uncertainty*. University of Chicago Press: Chicago and London.

ACOLA (2017) *The Future of Precision Medicine in Australia*. Australian Council of Learned Academies: Melbourne.

Aetna (2016) 'Atena to transform members' consumer health experience using iPhone, iPad and Apple Watch'. https://news.aetna.com/news-releases/aetna-to-transform -members-consumer-health-experience-using-iphone-ipad-and-apple-watch/ (Accessed 3 March, 2018).

Australian Digital Health Agency (n.d.a) 'About the Agency'. http://www.digitalhealth.gov. au/about-the-agency (Accessed 24 August 2018).

Australian Digital Health Agency (n.d.b) *Safe, Seamless and Secure: Evolving Health and Care to Meet the Needs of Modern Australia. Australia's National Digital Health Strategy*. Australian Digital Health Agency: Canberra. https://conversation.digitalhealth.gov.au/sites/default/ files/adha-strategy-doc-2ndaug_0_1.pdf (Accessed 10 August, 2018).

Australian Digital Health Agency (n.d.c.) *Corporate Plan 2016–2017*. February 2017. Australian Digital Health Agency: Sydney.

Australian Digital Health Agency (2018) 'New global digital health partnership', Media release, February. https://www.digitalhealth.gov.au/news-and-events/news/media-relea se-new-global-digital-health-partnership (Accessed 10 April, 2018).

Australian Genomics Health Alliance (2018) 'A "world of knowledge" to help Australian doctors better diagnose inherited diseases', Media release, 18 October. https://www.austra liangenomics.org.au/news-events/media-releases/2017/a-world-of-knowledge-to-help -australian-doctors-better-diagnose-inherited-diseases/ (Accessed 31 January 2018).

Australian Government (2017a) *Australia 2030: Prosperity Through Innovation*. Commonwealth of Australia: Canberra.

Australian Government (2017b) *National Health Genomics Policy Framework* (Consultation Draft). Commonwealth of Australia: Canberra.

Australian Government (2017c) *The Digital Economy: Opening Up the Conversation*. Consulation Paper. https://industry.gov.au/innovation/Digital-Economy/Documents/Digital-Econom y-Strategy-Consultation-Paper.pdf (Accessed 23 April, 2018; no longer available online).

Baers, L. (2018) *Digital Health 2018: Trends, Opportunities and Outlook*. IDTechEx: Boston, MA. https://www.idtechex.com/research/reports/digital-health-2018-trends-opportuni ties-and-outlook-000590.asp (Accessed 3 August 2018).

Baird, J. (2016) 'Facts are dead, long live facts: there's no simple solution for how to dissolve the fog of lies', *The Age*, 3 December. http://www.theage.com.au/comment/facts-a re-dead-long-live-facts-theres-no-simple-solution-for-how-to-dissolve-the-fog-o f-lies-20161201-gt1wpp.html (Accessed 15 December 2016).

Bajkowski, J. (2014) 'NeHTA set to be scrapped in radical eHealth overhall', *Government News*, 20 May. http://www.governmentnews.com.au/2014/05/nehta-set-scrapped-radica l-ehealth-overhaul/ (Accessed 24 April 2017).

Bartley, M. (2004) *Health Inequality: An Introduction to Theories, Concepts and Methods*. Polity: Cambridge.

Baudrillard, J. (1998 [1970]) *The Consumer Society: Myths and Structures*. Sage: London.

BBC News (2017) 'Charlie Gard: parents to appeal withdrawal of life support', *BBC News*, 2 May. http://www.bbc.com/news/uk-england-london-39777073 (Accessed 8 August, 2017).

Bewley, S., Ross, N. and McCartney, M. (2018) 'Impact of mass breast cancer screening has been overrated', *The Guardian* Letters, 8 May.https://www.theguardian.com/society/2018/may/07/impact-of-mass-breast-cancer-screening-has-been-overrated (Accessed 11 May, 2018).

Bianchi, A. (2012) 'Pharma 3.0 pulls companies into the digital future', *Cutting Edge Information*, 17 December. https://www.cuttingedgeinfo.com/2012/pharma-3-0/ (Accessed 19 March, 2018).

BlueCross (2018) 'Ageing in place'. https://www.bluecross.com.au/residential-care/care-ser vices/ageing-in-place (Accessed 27 February, 2018).

Bookman, M. Z. and Bookman, K. R. (2007) *Medical Tourism in Developing Countries*. Palgrave: New York and Houndmills.

Brostoff, G. (2017) '3D facial recognition gives healthcare data a new look', *Clinical Informatics News*, 6 October. http://www.clinicalinformaticsnews.com/2017/10/06/3d-facial-recognition-gives-healthcare-data-a-new-look.aspx (Accessed 5 May, 2018).

Brown, N. (2003) 'Hope against hype: accountability in biopasts, presents and futures', *Science Studies*, 16, 2: 3–21.

Browne, R. (2017) '"The ultimate in preventative treatment": push for government to fund genetic testing', *The Sydney Morning Herald*, 4 August. http://www.smh.com.au/national/health/the-ultimate-in-preventative-treatment-push-for-government-to-fund-genetic-tes ting-20170804-gxpazi.html (Accessed 8 August, 2017).

Butler, J. (2010) 'Performative agency', *Journal of Cultural Economy*, 3, 2: 147–161.

Cancer Research UK (2018) 'Screening for cancer'. http://www.cancerresearchuk.org/a bout-cancer/screening (Accessed 2 March, 2018).

Canguilhem, G. (2012) *Writings on Medicine*. Translated and with an introduction by S. Geroulanos and T. Meyers. Fordham University Press: New York.

Capra, F. (1983) *The Turning Point: Science, Society and the Rising Culture*. Bantam Books: London.

Cardon, L. (2009) 'Translating complex disease genes into new medicines', paper delivered at the Colston Symposium, The New Genomics: Public Health, Social and Clinical Implications, 4–5 June, Bristol University, UK.

Castells, M. (2010 [1996]) *The Rise of the Network Society*. Volume One, second edition. John Wiley & Sons: Chichester.

CCS Insight (2014) 'Smartwatches and smart bands dominate fast-growing wearables market'. https://www.ccsinsight.com/press/company-news/1944-smartwatches- (Accessed 4 March, 2018).

Center for Humane Technology (2018) 'Our society is being hijacked by technology'. http://humanetech.com/problem/ (Accessed 1 May, 2018).

Centers for Disease Control and Prevention (2018) 'Healthy places terminology'. https://www.cdc.gov/healthyplaces/terminology.htm (27 February, 2018).

Centre for Public Impact (2017) 'The Electronic Health Records System in the UK', 3 April. https://www.centreforpublicimpact.org/case-study/electronic-health-records-sys tem-uk/ (Accessed 27 February, 2018).

Chen, B. X. (2018) 'I downloaded the information that Facebook has on me. Yikes', *The New York Times*, 11 April. https://www.nytimes.com/2018/04/11/technology/personaltech/i-downloa ded-the-information-that-facebook-has-on-me-yikes.html (Accessed 25 April, 2018).

Chokshi, N. (2016) 'Hack of quest diagnostics app exposes data of 34,000 patients', *The New York Times*, 13 December. https://www.nytimes.com/2016/12/12/us/hack-of-quest-dia gnostics-app-exposes-data-of-34000-patients.html (Accessed 16 December 2016).

Choosing Wisely (n.d) 'History'. http://www.choosingwisely.org/about-us/history/ (Accessed 26 September, 2017).

Clover, J. (2018) 'Apple launching "AC Wellness" medical clinics for its employees', *MacRumors*, 26 February. https://www.macrumors.com/2018/02/27/apple-ac-well ness-medical-clinics/ (Accessed 20 March, 2018).

Cohen, J. D., Wang, L.L. Y., Thoburn, C., Afsari, B., et al. (2018) 'Detection and locali-
zation of surgically resectable cancers with a multi-analyte blood test', *Science*, 18 January.
doi:10.1126/science.aar3247.

Connor, N. (2018) 'Chinese school uses facial recognition to monitor student attention in
class', *The Telegraph*, 17 May. https://www.telegraph.co.uk/news/2018/05/17/chine
se-school-uses-facial-recognition-monitor-student-attention/ (Accessed 28 August 2018).

Consumer Watchdog (2018) 'Google, Amazon patent filings reveal digital home assistant
privacy concerns'. http://www.consumerwatchdog.org/sites/default/files/2017-12/Digita
l%20Assistants%20and%20Privacy.pdf (Accessed 22 March, 2018).

Corepoint Health (2018) 'How health IT can handle AI and telemedicine workflows'. https://
corepointhealth.com/ai-telemedicine-healthcare-integration (Accessed 23 April, 2018).

Crawford, R. (1980) 'Healthism and the medicalization of everyday life', *International Journal
of Health Services*, 10(3): 365–388.

Crouch, H. (2018a) 'Public Health England launches Alexa service for breastfeeding mums',
digitalhealth, 8 March.https://www.digitalhealth.net/2018/03/public-health-england-alexa
-breastfeeding-mums/ (Accessed 24 March, 2018).

Crouch, H. (2018b) 'Hunt: IT error "could have cut short the lives of up to 270 women"',
digitalhealth, 2 May. https://www.digitalhealth.net/2018/05/hunt-it-error-breast-cancer/
(Accessed 10 May, 2018).

Crouch, H. (2018c) 'Patients and GPs gather for protest against GP at Hand', *digitalhealth*, 30
March.https://www.digitalhealth.net/2018/03/gp-at-hand-protests-east-london/ (Accessed 7 May, 2018).

Cyranoski, D. (2010) 'Korean deaths spark inquiry', *Nature*, 468, 7323: 485.

Daley, G. (2012) 'The promise and perils of stem cell therapeutics', *Cell Stem Cell*, 10, 6:
740–749.

Davidson, J. (2017) 'Mega phone, mega price', *The Australian Financial Review*, 14 September, 44–45.

Davies, A. (2018) 'Australian regulator investigates Google data harvesting from Android
phones', *The Guardian*, 14 May.https://www.theguardian.com/technology/2018/may/
14/australian-regulator-investigates-google-data-harvesting-from-android-phones (Accessed 15 May, 2018).

DeepMind Health (n.d.a) 'About DeepMind Health', https://deepmind.com/applied/
deepmind-health/about-deepmind-health/ (Accessed 12 September, 2017; no longer
available online).

DeepMind Health (n.d.b) 'Working with the NHS', https://deepmind.com/applied/deepm
ind-health/ (Accessed 12 September, 2017; no longer available online).

DeepMind Health (n.d.c) 'DeepMind Health and research collaborations', https://deepmind.
com/applied/deepmind-health/working-partners/health-research-tomorrow/ (Accessed 12
September, 2017; no longer available online).

DeepMind Health (n.d.d) 'DeepMind Health and de-personalised research data', https://
deepmind.com/applied/deepmind-health/data-security/depersonalised-data/ (Accessed
12 September, 2017).

della Carva, M. (2018) 'YouTube illegally collects personal info from kids and should be
fined, advocacy groups charge', *USA Today*, 9 April. https://www.usatoday.com/story/
tech/2018/04/09/youtube-hit-complaint-child-advocacy-groups-which-say-illegally-ta
rgets-kids/482024002/ (Accessed 7 May, 2018).

Dellot, B. and Wallace-Stephens, F. (2017) *The Age of Automation: Artificial Intelligence,
Robotics and the Future of Low-Skilled Work*. Royal Society of Arts: London.

Deloitte (2015) *Mobilizing MedTech for mHealth: Market Trends and Potential Opportunities*.
Deloitte Development LLC: New York. https://www2.deloitte.com/content/dam/

Deloitte/us/Documents/life-sciences-health-care/us-lshc-mobilizing-mhealth-genera
l-paper.pdf (Accessed 28 August 2018).

Deloitte (2016) *Mobile Consumer Survey 2016. The Australian Cut. Hyper Connectivity: Clever
Consumption.* Deloitte Touche Tohmatsu: Sydney. http://landing.deloitte.com.au/rs/
761-IBL-328/images/tmt-mobile-consumer-2016-final-report-101116.pdf (Accessed 3
March, 2018).

Deloitte (2018) *2018 Global Life Sciences Outlook.* Deloitte Touche Tohmatsu: New York.
https://www2.deloitte.com/global/en/pages/life-sciences-and-healthcare/articles/globa
l-life-sciences-sector-outlook.html (Accessed 20 March, 2018).

Department of Health (2018a) *National Health Genomics Policy Framework 2018–2012—Fact
Sheet.* Department of Health: Canberra. http://www.health.gov.au/internet/main/publ
ishing.nsf/Content/National%20Health%20Genomics%20Policy%20Framework%
202018-2021-fact-sheet (Accessed 8 February, 2018).

Department of Health (2018b) *Framework to Guide the Secondary Use of My Health Record
System Data.* Department of Health: Canberra. http://www.health.gov.au/internet/ma
in/publishing.nsf/Content/F98C37D22E65A79BCA2582820006F1CF/$File/MHR_
2nd_Use_Framework_2018_ACC_AW3.pdf (Accessed 18 May, 2018).

Digital Health Enterprise Zone (n.d.) 'Vision: A vision for improved health'. http://www.
dhez.org/about/vision/ (Accessed 24 April, 2017; no longer available online).

digitalhealth (2018) 'Digital Health Intelligence forecast NHS IT market to hit £4bn by
2022', *News*, 3 May. https://www.digitalhealth.net/2018/05/digital-health-intelligence-
forecast-nhs-it-4bn-2022/ (Accessed 24 August 2018).

Digital Healthcare Show (2018) 'Registration' link. https://www.digitalhealthcareshow.
com/welcome (Accessed 23 April, 2018).

Douglas, M. (2016) 'Google expands the "right to be forgotten", but Australia doesn't
need it', *The Conversation*, 7 March. https://theconversation.com/google-expa
nds-the-right-to-be-forgotten-but-australia-doesnt-need-it-54887 (Accessed 14 June,
2017).

Doyal, L. with Pennell, I. (1979) *The Political Economy of Health.* Pluto Press: London.

Dudley-Nicholson, J. (2016) 'Red Cross Blood Service exposes more than 550,000 medical
records in record data breach', *News.com.au*, 28 October. http://www.news.com.au/technol
ogy/red-cross-blood-service-exposes-more-than-550000-medical-records-in-record-data
-breach/news-story/bafc5218c7cba1238f87dab6db8b7238 (Accessed 1 May 2017).

Economist (2017) 'Japan is embracing nursing-care robots', *The Economist*, 23 November.
https://www.economist.com/news/business/21731677-around-5000-nursing-care-hom
es-across-country-are-testing-robots-japan-embracing (Accessed 2 March, 2018).

Eensaar, R. (2008) 'Estonia: ups and downs of a biobank project', in H. Gottweis and A.
Petersen (eds) *Biobanks: Governance in Comparative Perspective.* Routledge: Abingdon and
New York, 56–70.

Eggers, D. (2013) *The Circle.* Vintage Books: New York.

Eggleton, M. (2017) 'Putting more choice and control with users paramount', Special
report—digitalising government services, *The Australian Financial Review*, 11 April, 26.

Encylopaedia Brittanica (2018) 'Faustian bargain'. https://www.britannica.com/topic/Faustia
n-bargain (Accessed 25 April, 2018).

Equifax (2017) 'Equifax announces cybersecurity incident involving consumer information'.
https://investor.equifax.com/news-and-events/news/2017/09-07-2017-213000628
(Accessed 10 April, 2018).

Ernst & Young (2018) 'Progressions: building Pharma 3.0'. http://www.ey.com/gl/en/
industries/life-sciences/progressions–building-pharma-3-0 (Accessed 19 March, 2018).

Europa.eu (2018) 'Data protection and online privacy'. https://europa.eu/youreurope/citi zens/consumers/internet-telecoms/data-protection-online-privacy/index_en.htm (Accessed 22 May, 2018).

Evanstad, L. (2016) 'NHS England scraps controversial Care.data programme', *Computer Weekly. com*, 6 July. http://www.computerweekly.com/news/450299728/Caldicott-review-recomm ends-eight-point-consent-model-for-patient-data-sharing (Accessed 27 February, 2018).

Evenstad, L. (2018) 'NHS England on the cusp of launching first citizen identity pilot', *ComputerWeekly.com*, 16 May. https://www.computerweekly.com/news/252441212/NHS-En gland-on-the-cusp-of-launching-first-citizen-identity-pilot (Accessed 20 August, 2018).

Farr, C. (2014) 'Startup launches "first wearable health record" for Google Glass', *Reuters*, Technology News, 13 June. https://www.reuters.com/article/us-google-health/startup-la unches-first-wearable-health-record-for-google-glass-idUSKBN0EN2MG20140612 (Accessed 18 September, 2017).

Farr, C. (2017) 'Apple is working with Stanford and American Well to test whether its watch can detect heart problems', *CNBC*, 11 September.https://www.cnbc.com/2017/09/11/apple-wa tch-caridac-arrhythmia-tests-stanford-american-well.html (Accessed 18 September, 2017).

Farr, C. (2018a) 'Google rolls out a new tool to help health providers solve the medical record mess', *CNBC*, 5 March. https://www.cnbc.com/2018/03/05/google-cloud-hea lthcare-api-to-address-medical-reord-interoperability.html (Accessed 22 March, 2018).

Farr, C. (2018b) 'Apple will let you keep your medical records on your iPhone', *CNBC*, 24 January. https://www.cnbc.com/2018/01/24/apple-coo-williams-says-new-health-re cord-beta-is-right-thing-to-do.html (Accessed 22 March, 2018).

Ford, M. (2016) *The Rise of the Robots: Technology and the Threat of Mass Unemployment*. OneWorld Publications: London.

Foucault, M. (1975) *The Birth of the Clinic: An Archaeology of Medical Perception*. Vintage Books: New York.

Fox, R. (2003) 'Medical uncertainty revisited', in G. L. Albrecht, R. Fitzpatrick and S. Scrimshaw (eds) *The Handbook of Social Studies of Health and Medicine*. Sage: London and Thousand Oaks, CA.

Fox, R. and Swazey, J. P. (2008) *Observing Bioethics*. Oxford University Press: Oxford.

Fox, S. (2014) 'The social life of health information', *Pew Research Center, Fact Tank*, 15 January. http://www.pewresearch.org/fact-tank/2014/01/15/the-social-life-of-health-in formation/ (Accessed 30 March, 2018).

Frenkel, S. (2018) 'Scholars have data on millions of Facebook users. Who's guarding it?', *The New York Times*, 6 May. https://www.nytimes.com/2018/05/06/technology/fa cebook-information-data-sets-academics.html?emc=edit_th_180507&nl=todayshea dlines&nlid=705100570507 (Accessed 10 May, 2018).

Friedl, R. (2007) *A Culture of Improvement: Technology and the Western Millennium*. MIT Press: Cambridge, MA.

Fromm, E. (1968 [2010]) *The Revolution of Hope: Toward a Humanized Technology*. American Mental Health Foundation Books: New York.

Gartner (2017) 'Gartner survey shows wearable devices need to be more useful', Press Release, 7 December. http://www.gartner.com/newsroom/id/3537117 (Accessed 16 September, 2017).

Gartner Consulting (2016) *Why Gartner?*https://www.gartner.com/en/research/methodolo gies/gartner-hype-cycle (Accessed 24 August 2018).

Garvan Institute of Medical Research (2017) 'Genomic Cancer Medicine Program'. https:// www.garvan.org.au/foundation/our-work/genomic-cancer-medicine-program/ (Accessed 2 September, 2017).

Garvie, C., Bedoya, A. and Frankel, J. (2016) *The Perpetual Line Up: Unregulated Police Face Recognition in America*. Centre on Privacy and Technology at Georgetown Law, 18 October. https://www.perpetuallineup.org/ (Accessed 5 May, 2018).

GeneWatch (2010) *Bioscience for Life?: Who Decides What Research is Done in Health and Agriculture*. GeneWatch UK: Buxton.

Genome.One (2018a) 'Clinical service'. https://www.genome.one/clinical-service (Accessed 31 January, 2018; no longer available online).

Genome.One (2018b) 'Introducing Genome.One'. https://www.genome.one/about-us (Accessed 31 January, 2018; no longer available online).

Genomics England (2018) 'The 100,000 Genomes Project by numbers'. https://www.genomicsengland.co.uk/the-100000-genomes-project-by-numbers/ (Accessed 31 January, 2018).

Gibbs, P. (2018) 'A new blood test can detect eight different cancers in their early stages', *The Conversation*, 19 January. https://theconversation.com/a-new-blood-test-can-detect-eight-different-cancers-in-their-early-stages-90221 (Accessed 30 January, 2018).

Gibson, I. (2002) 'Petition on 'Biobank', *House of Commons Hansard Debates*, 3 July. https://publications.parliament.uk/pa/cm200102/cmhansrd/vo020703/debtext/20703-43.htm (Accessed 24 August 2018).

Global Alliance for Genomics and Health (2018) 'About us'. https://www.ga4gh.org/aboutus/ (Access 31 January, 2018).

Goldacre, B. (2012) *Bad Pharma: How Medicine is Broken, and How We Can Fix It*. Fourth Estate: London.

Google (2007) 'Systems and methods for patient identification using mobile face recognition'. https://www.google.com/patents/US20090136094 (Accessed 15 September, 2017).

Google Genomics (n.d.a) 'Power your science'. https://cloud.google.com/genomics/ (Accessed 10 April, 2018).

Google Genomics (n.d.b) *Genomic Data is Going Google: Ask Bigger Biological Questions*. Google Cloud Platform: Mountain View, CA. https://cloud.google.com/genomics/resources/google-genomics-whitepaper.pdf (Accessed 10 April, 2018).

Gottweis, H. and Petersen, A. (eds) (2008) *Biobanks: Governance in Comparative Perspective*. Routledge: London and New York.

Gray, C. H. (2002) *Cyborg Citizen: Politics in the Posthuman Age*. Routledge: New York and London.

Greenfield, A. (2017) *Radical Technologies: The Design of Everyday Life*. Verso: London and New York.

Greenwood, S., Perrin, A. and Duggan, M. (2016) 'Social media update 2016', *Pew Research Center, Internet and Technology*, 11 November. http://www.pewinternet.org/2016/11/11/social-media-update-2016/ (Accessed 29 May, 2017).

Guynn, J. and McCoy, K. (2018) 'Apple co-founder Steve Wozniak says he's left Facebook over data collection', *CNBC*, 9 April.https://www.cnbc.com/2018/04/09/apple-co-founder-steve-wozniak-says-hes-left-facebook-over-data-collection.html (Accessed 7 May, 2018).

Han, E. (2018) 'Guilty: Health Department breached privacy laws publishing data of 2.5m people', *The Sydney Morning Herald*, 29 March.https://www.smh.com.au/national/guilty-health-department-breached-privacy-laws-publishing-data-of-2-5m-people-20180329-p4z6wf.html (Accessed 1 May, 2018).Haraway, D. J. (1991) *Simians, Cyborgs, and Women: The Reinvention of Nature*. Routledge: New York and Oxford.

Haraway, D. (1999) 'Modest_Witness@Second_Millenium', in D. MacKenzie and J. Wajcman (eds) *The Social Shaping of Technology*, second edition. Open University Press: Buckingham and Philadelphia, PA.

Harris, I. (2016) *Surgery, the Ultimate Placebo*. University of New South Wales Press: Sydney.

Harris, T. (n.d.) 'About Tristan Harris'. http://www.tristanharris.com (Accessed 1 May, 2018).

Harvey, D. (1989) *The Condition of Postmodernity: An Enquiry into the Origins of Cultural Change*. Blackwell: Cambridge, MA and Oxford.

Health Informatics Society of Australia (n.d.) 'Digital health links'. https://www.hisa.org.au/links/ (Accessed 10 April, 2018).

HealthIsCool (2017) 'Digital health: Current state & future growth 2017–2025', *Health Standards*, 25 October. http://healthstandards.com/blog/2017/10/25/digital-health-trends-2025/ (Accessed 23 April, 2018).

Health Sociology Review (2017) Special issue: 'Self-tracking, health and medicine', 26, 1.

Health Wizz (2017) 'Health Wizz launches decentralized mobile platform to enable patients to take control over their health data', *Cision PR Newswire*, 30 November. https://www.prnewswire.com/news-releases/health-wizz-launches-decentralized-mobile-platform-to-enable-patients-to-take-control-over-their-health-data-300563347.html (Accessed 16 March, 2018).

Health Wizz (2018) 'About Us'. https://www.healthwizz.net/#about-us (Accessed 16 March, 2018; quoted text no longer available online).

HealthIT.gov (2018) 'Health IT Legislation'. https://www.healthit.gov/policy-researchers-implementers/health-it-legislation (Accessed 22 March, 2018).

Hedgecoe, A. M. (2004) *The Politics of Personalised Medicine: Pharmacogenetics in the Clinic*. Cambridge University Press: Cambridge.

HIMSS (2018) 'HIMSS18: About'. http://www.himssconference.org/about/general-info (Accessed 24 April, 2018).

HIMSS Insights (2018) 'Estonia offers 100,000 citizens free genetic testing as it builds its personalised medicine program', *Healthcare IT News*, 27 March.https://www.healthcareit.com.au/article/estonia-offers-100000-citizens-free-genetic-testing-it-builds-its-personalised-medicine (Accessed 10 April, 2018).

HIPAA Journal (2018) 'Healthcare Data Breach Statistics'. https://www.hipaajournal.com/healthcare-data-breach-statistics/ (Accessed 18 May, 2018).

Hochschild, A. R. (1983) *The Managed Heart: The Commercialization of Human Feeling*. University of California Press: Berkeley, CA.

Hof, R. D. (2013) 'Deep learning: with massive amounts of computational power machines can now recognize objects and translate speech in real time. Artificial intelligence is finally getting smart', *MIT Technology Review*. https://www.technologyreview.com/s/513696/deep-learning/ (Accessed 14 September, 2017).

Hoffman, B., Tomes, N., Grob, R. and Schlesinger, M. (eds) (2011) *Patients as Policy Actors*. Rutgers University Press: New Brunswick, NJ and London.

Holtzman, N. A. and Marteau, T. (2000) 'Will genetics revolutionize medicine?', *New England Journal of Medicine*, 343, 2: 141–144.

Hosanagar, K. (2016) 'Blame the echo chamber of Facebook. But blame yourself, too', *Wired Business*, 25 November. https://www.wired.com/2016/11/facebook-echo-chamber/ (Accessed 29 May, 2017).

House of Commons (2016) *A Paperless NHS: Electronic Health Records*. Briefing Paper 07572, 25 April. http://researchbriefings.parliament.uk/ResearchBriefing/Summary/CBP-7572 (Accessed 3 August, 2018).

House of Commons Science and Technology Committee (2017) *Genomics and Genome Editing in the NHS*. Parliamentary Report. https://publications.parliament.uk/pa/cm201719/cmselect/cmsctech/349/34902.htm (24 April, 2018).

Howard, P. and Gorwa, R. (2017) 'Facebook should share data on election interference', *The Age*, 22 May.

Hughes, O. (2018a) 'Only 17% of NHS trusts expect financial return from public cloud adoption', *digitalhealth*, 28 February.https://www.digitalhealth.net/2018/02/foi-17-nhs-trusts-expect-financial-return-public-cloud-adoption/ (Accessed 11 May, 2018).

Hughes, O. (2018b) 'Orangeworm: Hospitals worldwide warned of "aggressive" malware', *digitalhealth*, 30 April.https://www.digitalhealth.net/2018/04/orangeworm-malware-targe ting-hospitals-worldwide/ (Accessed 8 May, 2018).

Hughes, O. (2018c) 'Facebook approached US medical academies about sharing patient data', *digitalhealth*, 11 April.https://www.digitalhealth.net/2018/04/facebook-approache d-us-medical-academies-about-sharing-patient-data/ (Accessed 5 May, 2018).

Hunter, D. J. (2016) 'Uncertainty in the era of precision medicine', *New England Journal of Medicine*, 375, 8: 711–713.

Huxley, A. (1955 [1932]) *Brave New World*. Penguin Books: Harmondsworth, UK.

IBM (2018) 'The prescription for better healthcare is in the cloud'. https://www.ibm.com/ cloud/healthcare (Accessed 28 August 2018).

IBM Watson Health (2017a) 'Empowering heroes, transforming health'. https://www.ibm. com/watson/health/ (Accessed 21 September, 2017).

IBM Watson Health (2017b) 'IBM Watson for Genomics helps doctors give patients new hope', https://www.ibm.com/watson/health/oncology-and-genomics/genomics/ (Acces sed 21 September, 2017; no longer available online).

Illich, I. (1974) *Limits to Medicine. Medical Nemesis: The Expropriation of Health*. Calder and Boyars: London.

Information Age (2015) 'Why insurers are in love with wearables'. *Information Age*, 14 May. https://ia.acs.org.au/article/2015/why-insurers-are-in-love-with-wearables.html (Acces sed 3 March, 2018).

Inside Airbnb (2018) 'About Inside Airbnb'. http://insideairbnb.com/about.html (Accessed 7 May, 2018).

Irwin, A. and Michael, M. (2003) *Science, Social Theory and Public Knowledge*. Open University Press: Maidenhead, UK.

Isabel Healthcare (n.d.) 'Isabel EMR Integrations'. https://www.isabelhealthcare.com/p roducts/emr-integration (Accessed 1 May, 2018).

Jacobs, W., Amuta, A. O., Jeon, K. C. and Alvares, C. (2017) 'Health information seeking in the digital age: an analysis of health information seeking behavior among US adults', *Cogent Social Sciences*, 3, 1: 1302785. doi:10.1080/23311886.2017.1302785.

Janssen (2017) 'Health Consumer Organisation (HCO) Support'. http://www.janssen.com/a ustralia/partnerships/healthcare-organisation-support (Accessed 14 June, 2017).

JASON (2017) *Artificial Intelligence for Health and Health Care*. MITRE Corporation: McLean, VA. https://www.healthit.gov/sites/default/files/jsr-17-task-002_aiforhealthandhealthca re12122017.pdf (Accessed 5 April, 2018).

Kaufman, D. J., Baker, R., Milner, L. C., Devaney, S. and Hudson, K. L. (2016) 'A survey of U.S. adults' opinions about conduct of a nationwide Precision Medicine Initiative® cohort study of genes and environment', *PLOS One*, 11, 8: e0160461. doi:10.1371/ journal.pone.0160461.

Keen, A. (2015) *The Internet is Not the Answer*. Atlantic Books: London.

Kelly, L. and Letheren, K. (2018) 'Voice assistants must earn consumers' trust to track them', *ABC News*, 19 March.http://mobile.abc.net.au/news/2018-03-13/voice-assistants-must- build-trust-consumers/9542446?pfmredir=sm (Accessed 19 March, 2018).

Knowles, K. (2018) 'NHS offshore data deal is bad for British business – and dangerous for you', *The Memo*, 28 January.https://www.thememo.com/2018/01/24/nhs-offshore-data -sharing-cloud-storage-patient-privacy-google-amazon-health/ (Accessed 11 May, 2018).

Koene, A. (2017) 'Machine gaydar: AI is reinforcing stereotypes that liberal societies are trying to get rid of', *The Conversation*, 12 September.https://theconversation.com/machi ne-gaydar-ai-is-reinforcing-stereotypes-that-liberal-societies-are-trying-to-ge t-rid-of-83837 (Accessed 15 September).

Kosinski, M. and Wang, Y. (2017) 'Deep neural networks are more accurate than humans at detecting sexual orientation from facial images', *Journal of Personality and Social Psychology*, 114, 2: 246–257.

Kurzweil, R. (2012) *How To Create a Mind: The Secret of Human Thought Revealed*. Penguin Books: New York.

Lanchester, J. (2017) 'You are the product', *London Review of Books*, 39, 16: 3–10.

Laqueur, T. (1990) *Making Sex: Body and Gender from the Greeks to Freud*. Harvard University Press: Cambridge, MA.

Law Council of Australia (2017) 'Development of a Framework for Secondary Use of My Health Record Data Public Consulation Paper', Submission to HealthConsult, 17 November.https://www.lawcouncil.asn.au/resources/submissions/development-of-a -framework-for-secondary-use-of-my-health-record-data-public-consultation-paper (Accessed 10 May, 2018).

Leong, L. (2017) 'Why personal voice assistants are the next big marketing platform', *AppLovin*, 9 November. https://blog.applovin.com/personal-voice-assistants-marketing-p latform/ (Accessed 19 March, 2018).

Lister, C., West, J. H., Cannon, B., Sax, T. and Brodegard, D. (2014) 'Just a fad?: gamification in health and fitness apps', *JMIR Serious Games*, 2, 2: e9. doi:10.2196/games.3413.

Lock, M. and Nguyen, V.-K. (2010) *An Anthropology of Biomedicine*. Wiley-Blackwell: Chichester, UK.

Lohr, S. (2018) 'Facial recognition is accurate, if you're a white guy', *The New York Times*, 9 February. https://www.nytimes.com/2018/02/09/technology/facial-recognition-race-a rtificial-intelligence.html?emc=edit_th_180210&nl=todaysheadlines&nlid=70510057 (Accessed 5 May, 2018).

Lovett, L. (2018) 'In-depth: cryptocurrency's digital health potential for data sharing, behavioural incentives', *mobihealthnews*, 23 February. http://www.mobihealthnews.com/con tent/depth-cryptocurrencys-digital-health-potential-data-sharing-behavior-incentives (Accessed 16 March, 2018).

Lucas, E. (2015) *Cyberphobia: Identity, Trust, Security and the Internet*. Bloomsbury: London and New York.

Lupton, D. (2016) *The Quantified Self: The Sociology of Self-Tracking*. Polity: Cambridge.

Lynch, M. P. (2016) *The Internet of Us: Knowing More and Understanding Less in the Age of Big Data*. Liveright Publishing Corporation: New York.

MacGregor, C., Petersen, A. and Parker, C. (2017) 'Hyping the market for "anti-ageing" in the news: from medical failure to success in self-transformation', *BioSocieties*, 13, 1, 64–80. doi:10.1057/s41292-017-0052-5.

MacKenzie, D., Muniesa, F. and Siu, L. (2007) *Do Economists Make Markets?: On the Performativity of Economics*. Princeton University Press: Princeton and Oxford.

Macworld (2017) 'Face ID on the iPhone X: everything you need to know about Apple's facial recognition', *Macworld*, 25 December. https://www.macworld.com/article/ 3225406/iphone-ipad/face-id-iphone-x-faq.html (Accessed 5 May, 2018).

Maguire, L. (2017) 'Analytics crucial for dispensing change', Special report—digitising government services', *The Australian Financial Review*, 11 April, 41.

Mann, S. (1998) 'Humanistic computing: "WearComp" as a new framework and application for intelligent signal processing', *Proceedings of the IEEE*, 86, 11: 2123–2151.

Mann, S., Manders, C. and Fung, J. (2002) 'Painting with looks: photographic images from video using quantimetric processing', in *ACM Multimedia '02: Proceedings of the Tenth ACM International Conference on MultiMedia*, 117–126.

Margo, J. (2017) 'This brilliant Australian could save big pharma billions', *The Australian Financial Review*, 9 August, 45.

Margo, J. (2018) 'Maps to forecast the arrival of flu', *The Australian Financial Review*, 7 March, 36.

Marr, B. (2018) 'Here's why data is not the new oil', *Forbes*, 5 March. https://www.forbes.com/sites/bernardmarr/2018/03/05/heres-why-data-is-not-the-new-oil/#64aab4913aa9 (Accessed 4 May, 2018).

Mattick, J. S. (2018) 'Four ways precision medicine is making a difference', *The Conversation*, 2 February. https://theconversation.com/four-ways-precision-medicine-is-making-a-dif ference-90459 (Accessed 5 February, 2018).

Mayer-Schönberger, V. and Cukier, K. (2013) *Big Data: A Revolution That Will Transform How We Live and Think*. John Murray: London.

McCoy, M. S., Carniol, M., Chockley, K., Urwin, J. W., Ezekiel, J., Emanuel, M. D. and Schmidt, H. (2017) 'Conflicts of interest for patient-advocacy organizations', *The New England Journal of Medicine*, 376, 9: 880–885.

McDuling, J. and Mason, M. (2017) 'How Google and Facebook's trillion-dollar duopoly strangles the internet', *Financial Review*, April 7. https://www.afr.com/business/media -and-marketing/advertising/how-google-and-facebooks-trillion-dollar-duopoly-strangles-the-internet-20170328-gv7zxi (Accessed 28 August 2018).

McLuhan, M. and Fiore, Q. (1967) *The Medium is the Massage: An Inventory of Effects*. Gingko Press: Corte Madera, CA.

McNamee, R. (2018) 'Warning labels for social media, just like tobacco and alcohol', *The Australian*, 30 January, 9. https://www.theaustralian.com.au/news/world/warning-labels-for-social-media-just-like-tobacco-and-alcohol/news-story/3b22753a 410972060b262ed62ba742a4 (Accessed 10 August, 2018).

Meeker, M. (2017) *Internet Trends 2017—Code Conference*. Presentation 31 May. Kleiner Perkins: Menlo Park, CA. http://dq756f9pzlyr3.cloudfront.net/file/Internet+Trends +2017+Report.pdf (Accessed 6 June, 2017).

Minion, L. (2017) 'Electronic medical record blamed in death of 41-year-old WA man', *Healthcare IT News*, 9 October.http://www.healthcareit.com.au/article/electronic-medica l-record-blamed-death-41-year-old-wa-man (Accessed 25 April, 2018).

Minion, L. (2018a) 'Genome.One seeks investors as it scales up for a 2018 trial of genomics in GP software', *Healthcare IT News*, 18 April. https://www.healthcareit.com.au/article/genom eone-seeks-investors-it-scales-2018-trial-genomics-gp-software (Accessed 19 April, 2018).

Minion, L. (2018b) 'Outgoing head of the Garvan talks about the rapid, inevitable trans-formation of the "last of the great cottage industries"', *Healthcare IT News*, 2 May. http://www.healthcareit.com.au/article/outgoing-head-garvan-talks-about-rapid-inevitable-tra nsformation-%E2%80%9Clast-great-cottage (Accessed 8 May, 2018).

Minion, L. (2018c) 'Electronic prescribing error in month-old HER responsible for death of NSW man, State Coroner finds', *Healthcare IT News*, 6 April. https://www.healthcareit.com.au/article/electronic-prescribing-error-month-old-ehr-responsible-death-nsw-ma n-state-coroner-finds (Accessed 25 April, 2018).

Minion, L. (2018d) '"The golden way forward": NSW health minister on the state's digital health transformation', *Healthcare IT News*, 28 March. https://www.healthcareit.com.au/a rticle/"-golden-way-forward"-nsw-health-minister-state's-digital-health-transformation (Accessed 19 April, 2018).

Minion, L. (2018e) 'New My Health Record opt out and secondary use details leak, as announcements loom', *Healthcare IT News*, 4 May.https://www.healthcareit.com.au/a rticle/new-my-health-record-opt-out-and-secondary-use-details-leak-announcem ents-loom (Accessed 18 May, 2018).

Miniwatts Marketing Group (2018) 'Internet world statistics: usage and population statistics'. https://www.internetworldstats.com/stats.htm (Accessed 25 April, 2018).

Mirowski, P. (2011) *Science-Mart: Privatizing American Science*. Harvard University Press: Cambridge, MA.

Mittlestadt, B. D., Allo, P., Taddeo, M., Wachter, S. and Floridi, L. (2016) 'The ethics of algorithms: mapping the debate', *Big Data and Society*, July–December: 1–21.

Miyazaki, H. (2004) *The Method of Hope: Anthropology, Philosophy, and Fijian Knowledge*. Stanford University Press, Stanford, CA.

Mohapatra, S. (2016) 'Use of facial recognition technology for medical purposes: balancing privacy with innovation', *Pepperdine Law Review*, 43: 1016–1061.

Mol, A. (2007) *The Body Multiple: Ontology in Medical Practice*. Duke University Press: Durham, NC.

Mol, A., Moser, I. and Pols, J. (2010) 'Care: putting practice into theory', in A. Mol, I. Moser and J. Pols (eds) *Care in Practice: On Tinkering in Clinics, Homes and Farms*. Transcript Verlag: Bielefeld, Germany.

Monegain, B. (2018) '"Digital doctor" Robert Wachter changes his tune, sees real progress in digital health', *HealthITNews*, 5 March. https://www.healthcareitnews.com/news/digital-doctor-robert-wachter-changes-his-tune-sees-real-progress-digital-health (Accessed 22 March, 2018).

Moore, G. J. (2018) 'Google Cloud for Healthcare: new APIs, customers, partners and security updates', 5 March. https://www.blog.google/products/google-cloud/google-cloud-healthcare-new-apis-customers-partners-and-security-updates/ (Accessed 2 October, 2018).

Moynihan, R. and Bero, L. (2017) 'Toward a healthier patient voice: more independence, less industry funding', *JAMA Internal Medicine*, 177, 3: 350–351.

Müller, M. U. (2017) 'Doctor in your pocket', *The Australian Financial Review*, 29–30 July, 36–38.

Muoio, D. (2018) 'Google and Fitbit partner to integrate wearables with electronic health records for "bi-directional" data exchange', *Healthcare IT News*, 1 May. https://www.healthcareit.com.au/article/google-and-fitbit-partner-integrate-wearables-electronic-health-records-bidirectional-data (Accessed 8 May, 2018).

MyQuest Diagnostics (2017) MyQuest™. https://myquest.questdiagnostics.com/web/home (Accessed 21 September, 2017).

National Health Service (2016) 'Inclusion health and digital health', presented at Health and Care Innovation Expo 2016, Manchester, 7–8 September. https://www.england.nhs.uk/wp-content/uploads/2017/02/inclusion-hlth-expo.pdf (Accessed 24 April 2017).

National Health Service (2017) *Next Steps on the NHS Five Year Forward View*. NHS England: Leeds. https://www.england.nhs.uk/wp-content/uploads/2017/03/NEXT-STEPS-ON-THE-NHS-FIVE-YEAR-FORWARD-VIEW.pdf (Accessed 22 April, 2017).

National Health Service (2018) 'Empower the person: roadmap for digital health and care services'. NHS England: Leeds. https://indd.adobe.com/view/ab41d569-956d-4d45-a70a-940861e48f1b (Accessed 10 April, 2018).

National Human Genome Research Institute (2018) 'What is genomic medicine?'. National Institutes of Health: Bethesda, MD. https://www.genome.gov/27552451/what-is-genomic-medicine/ (Accessed 25 April, 2018).

National Institutes of Health (2017) 'Scientific opportunities'. https://allofus.nih.gov/about/scientific-opportunities (Accessed 4 September, 2017).

National Institutes of Health (2018) 'What is genomic medicine?'. https://www.genome.gov/27552451/what-is-genomic-medicine/ (Accessed 28 August 2018).

Neotiv (2017) 'Learning new things, remembering experiences'. https://www.neotiv.com/en/ (Accessed 15 September, 2015).

Neumeister, L. (2018) 'Facebook sued by housing advocates alleging discrimination', *PhysOrg*, 27 March. https://phys.org/news/2018-03-fair-housing-advocates-sue-facebook. html (Accessed 7 May, 2018).

Nicol, D., Bubela, T., Chalmers, D., Charbonneau, J., et al. (2016) 'Precision medicine: drowning in a regulatory soup?', *Journal of Law and the Biosciences*, 3, 2: 281–303. doi:10.1093/jlb/lsw018.

Nightingale, P. and Martin, P. (2004) 'The myth of the biotech revolution', *Trends in Biotechnology*, 22, 11: 564–569.

NYU School of Medicine (2018) 'Working Group on Compassionate Use and Pre-Approval Access'. NYU Langone Health, Department of Population Health: New York. https://med.nyu.edu/pophealth/divisions/medical-ethics/compassionate-use (Accessed 12 April, 2018).

O'Malley, P. (2009) 'Responsibilization', in A. Wakefield and J. Flemming (eds) *The Sage Dictionary of Policing*. Sage: Thousand Oaks, CA and London, 276.

O'Neil, C. (2016) *Weapons of Math Destruction: How Big Data Increases Inequality and Threatens Democracy*. Allen Lane: London.

Office of the Australian Information Commissioner (2017) 'Australian Red Cross Blood Service data breach', 7 August. https://www.oaic.gov.au/media-and-speeches/statem ents/australian-red-cross-blood-service-data-breach (Accessed 1 May, 2018).

Office of the Australian Information Commissioner (2018) *Notifiable Data Breaches: Quarterly Statistics Report: January 2018–March 2018*. https://www.oaic.gov.au/resources/privacy-la w/privacy-act/notifiable-data-breaches-scheme/quarterly-statistics/Notifiable_Data_Brea ches_Quarterly_Statistics_Report_January_2018__March_.pdf (Accessed 18 May, 2018).

Oudshoorn, N. and Pinch, T. (eds) (2003) *How Users Matter: The Co-Construction of Users and Technology*. MIT Press: Cambridge, MA.

Owen, M. (2012) 'Pharma 3.0'. *Aiim community*, 30 January. http://community.aiim.org/ blogs/mark-owen/2012/01/30/pharma-3-0 (Accessed 19 March, 2018).

Oxford Dictionaries (2016) 'Word of the Year 2016 is… *post-truth*'. *Oxford Living Dictionaries*. http://blog.oup.com/2016/11/word-of-the-year-2016-post-truth/ (Accessed 15 December 2016).

Partnership on AI (n.d.a) 'Founding partners'. https://www.partnershiponai.org/#s-foun ding-partners (Accessed 14 September, 2017).

Partnership on AI (n.d.b) 'Tenets'. https://www.partnershiponai.org/tenets/ (Accessed 14 September, 2017).

PatientsLikeMe (n.d.a) 'DigitalMe™'. https://www.patientslikeme.com/research/digitalme (Accessed 22 September, 2017).

PatientsLikeMe (n.d.b) 'How does PatientsLikeMe make money?'. https://support.patientsli keme.com/hc/en-us/articles/201245750-How-does-PatientsLikeMe-make-money- (Accessed 22 September, 2017).

PatientsLikeMe (n.d.c) 'About us'. https://www.patientslikeme.com/about (Accessed 22 September, 2017).

Penny, J. (2017) 'More than "slacktivism": we dismiss the power of politics online at our peril', *The Conversation*, 2 August. https://theconversation.com/more-than-slacktivism-we-dism iss-the-power-of-politics-online-at-our-peril-79500 (Accessed 22 September, 2017).

Pepper, J. (2012) 'Croydon man died in long haul op, inquest hears', *Croydon Guardian*, 26 January.http://www.croydonguardian.co.uk/news/9491936.Paraplegic_man_died_in_ long_haul_op__inquest_hears/ (Accessed 15 June, 2017).

Petersen, A. (1998) 'Sexing the body: representations of sex differences in *Gray's Anatomy*, 1858 to the present', *Body and Society*, 4, 1: 1–15.

Petersen, A. (2001) 'Biofantasies: genetics and medicine in the print news media', *Social Science and Medicine*, 52, 8: 1255–1268.

Petersen, A. (2002) 'Replicating our bodies, losing our selves: news media portrayals of human cloning in the wake of Dolly', *Body & Society*, 8, 4: 71–90.

Petersen, A. (2004) *Engendering Emotions*. Palgrave Macmillan: Basingstoke.

Petersen, A. (2005) 'Securing our genetic health: engendering trust in UK Biobank', *Sociology of Health and Illness*, 27, 2: 271–292.

Petersen, A. (2006) 'The genetic conception of health: is it as radical as claimed?', *Health: An Interdisciplinary Journal for the Social Study of Health, Illness and Medicine*, 10, 4: 481–500.

Petersen, A. (2011) *The Politics of Bioethics*. Routledge: New York and London.

Petersen, A. (2015) *Hope in Health: The Socio-Politics of Optimism*. Palgrave Macmillan: Basingstoke.

Petersen, A. (2018) 'Capitalizing on ageing anxieties: promissory discourse and the creation of an "anti-ageing treatment" market', *Journal of Sociology*, 54, 2: 191–202.

Petersen, A. and Bowman, D. (2013) 'Engaging whom and for what ends?: Australian stakeholders' constructions of public engagement in relation to nanotechnologies', *Ethics in Science and Environmental Politics*, 12, 67–79.

Petersen, A. and Krisjansen, I. (2015) 'Assembling "the bioeconomy": exploiting the power of the promissory life sciences', *Journal of Sociology*, 51, 1: 28–46.

Petersen, A. and Seear, K. (2011) 'Technologies of hope: techniques of the online advertising of stem cell treatments', *New Genetics and Society*, 30, 4: 329–346.

Petersen, A., Davis, M., Fraser, S. and Lindsay, J. (2010) 'Healthy living and citizenship: an overview', *Critical Public Health*, 20, 4: 391–400.

Petersen, A., MacGregor, C. and Munsie, M. (2015) 'Stem cell miracles or Russian roulette?: patients' use of digital media to campaign for access to clinically unproven treatments', *Health, Risk and Society*, 17, 7/8: 592–604.

Petersen, A., Munsie, M., Tanner, C., MacGregor, C. and Brophy, J. (2017) *Stem Cell Tourism and the Political Economy of Hope*. Palgrave Macmillan: Basingstoke.

Petersen, A., Tanner, C. and Munsie, M. (in preparation) 'Navigating the cartographies of trust: how patients and carers establish the credibility of online treatment claims', *Sociology of Health and Illness*.

Phillips, K. A., Deverka, P. A., Hooker, G. W. and Douglas, M. P. (2018) 'Genetic test availability and spending: where are we now? Where are we going', *Health Affairs*, 37, 5: 710–716.

Pickard, V. and Yang, G. (eds) (2017) *Media Activism in the Digital Age*. Routledge: Abingdon.

Pickering, A. (2002) 'Cyborg history and the World War Two regime', *Perspectives on Science*, 3, 1: 1–48.

Postelnicu, L. (2018) 'BMA backs health committee's calls to suspend NHS Digital/Home Office data sharing deal', *British Journal of Healthcare Computing*, 17 April.http://www.bj-hc.co.uk/bma-backs-health-committees-calls-suspend-nhs-digitalhome-office-data-sharing-deal (Accessed 8 May, 2018).

Powles, J. and Hodson, H. (2017) 'Google DeepMind and healthcare in an age of algorithms', *Health and Technology*, 7, 4: 351–367.

Price, R. (2016) 'The fact fake news "outperformed" real news on Facebook proves the problem is widely out of control', *Business Insider Australia*, 17 November. http://www.businessinsider.com.au/fake-news-outperformed-real-news-on-facebook-before-us-election-report-2016-11?r=UK&IR=T (Accessed 15 December 2016).

PwC (2014) *The Wearable Future*. Consumer Intelligence Series. PricewaterhouseCoopers: Los Angeles, CA. https://www.pwc.com/us/en/technology/publications/assets/pwc-wearable-tech-design-oct-8th.pdf (Accessed 8 March, 2018).

Quantified Self (2017) 'About the Quantified Self'. http://quantifiedself.com/about/ (Accessed 11 September, 2017).

Queensland Government (2017) *Digital Health Strategic Vision for Queensland 2026*. Queensland Government: Brisbane.

Rabeharisoa, V., Moreira, T. and Alrich, M. (2014) 'Evidence-based activism: patients', users' and activists' groups in knowledge society', *BioSocieties*, 9, 2: 111–128.

Redrup, Y. (2017) 'Aussies to get genome mapped at GPs', *The Australian Financial Review*, 12 September, 25.

Redrup, Y. (2018) 'Genome firm seeks backers', *The Australian Financial Review*, 13 March, 24.

Regalado, A. (2017) 'Google's AI explosion in one chart', *MIT Technology Review*, 25 March. https://www.technologyreview.com/s/603984/googles-ai-explosion-in-one-cha rt/ (Accessed 14 September, 2017).

Remerowski, T. (2014) Google™ World. Documentary. Centillion Productions.

Republic of Estonia Ministry of Social Affairs (2018) 'Personalised medicine > Clinical flagship projects'. https://www.sm.ee/en/personalised-medicine#Preliminary%20study (Accessed 10 April, 2018).

Riphagen, M. (2013) 'Supporting reflective learning for daily activities using an interactive dashboard', presented at 6th International Conference of Education, Research and Innovation, Seville, Spain, 18–20 November, 3239–3249.

Ritzer, G. (1998) 'Introduction', in J. Baudrillard, *The Consumer Society: Myths and Structures*. Sage: London.

Romano, A. (2018) 'How Facebook made it impossible to delete Facebook', *Vox*, 22 March. https://www.vox.com/culture/2018/3/22/17146776/delete-facebook-difficult (Accessed 7 May, 2018).

Rose, N. (1999) *Powers of Freedom: Reframing Political Thought*. Cambridge University Press: Cambridge and New York.

Rose, S. L., Highland, J., Karafa, M. and Joffe, S. (2017) 'Patient advocacy organizations, industry funding and conflicts of interest', *JAMA Internal Medicine*, 177, 3: 344–350.

Royal Free London (n.d.) 'New app helping to improve patient care', https://www.roya lfree.nhs.uk/news-media/news/new-app-helping-to-improve-patient-care/ (Accessed 24 August 2018).

Royal Society (2005) *Personalised Medicines: Hopes and Realities*. Royal Society: London.

Ruckenstein, M. and Schüll, N. D. (2017) 'The datafication of health', *Annual Review of Anthropology*, 46: 261–278.

SAI Global (2017) Store: SA HB163:2017 Digital Hospitals Handbook, Standards Australia. https://infostore.saiglobal.com/en-au/standards/sa-hb-163-2017-1919534/ (Accessed 23 April, 2018).

Samuel, G. N. and Farsides, B. (2017) 'The UK's 100,000 Genomes Project: manifesting policymakers' expectations', *New Genetics and Society*, 36, 4: 336–353.

Sanborn, B. J. (2018) 'HIMSS18 revenue cycle recap: patient-centric approach takes communication and flexibility', *HealthITNews*, 14 March. http://www.healthcareitnews.com/ news/himss18-revenue-cycle-recap-patient-centric-approach-takes-communication-a nd-flexibility (Accessed 19 March, 2018).

Schumacher, A. (2018) 'How blockchain technology can stop misuse of personal genomic data', *BioNews*, 9 April. https://www.bionews.org.uk/page_135208 (Accessed 10 April, 2018).

Schwab, K. (2017) *The Fourth Industrial Revolution*. Portfolio Penguin: London.

Schwartz, B. (2016) 'Google to boost mobile-friendly algorithm this May', *Search Engine Land*, 16 March. http://searchengineland.com/google-boost-mobile-friendly-algorithm -coming-may-244941 (Accessed 13 June, 2017).

Seetharaman, D. (2018) 'Facebook profit surges but usage declines', *The Australian*, 2 February, 23.

Senellart, M. (2008) *Michel Foucault: The Birth of Biopolitics. Lectures at the Collège de France 1978–1979*. Translated by G. Burchell. Palgrave Macmillan: Basingstoke and New York.

Sherbon, J. (2017) '"Better technology gives better patient outcome", Special report—digitalising government services', *The Australian Financial Review*, 11 April, 41.

Siegal, J. (2018) 'Facebook says Cambridge Analytica data breach was even worse than we thought', *BGR*, April 4. http://bgr.com/2018/04/04/facebook-cambridge-analytica-data-breach-87-million/ (Accessed 10 April, 2018).

Simonite, T. (2016) 'How Google plans to solve artificial intelligence', *MIT Technology Review*, 31 March. https://www.technologyreview.com/s/601139/how-google-plans-to-solve-artificial-intelligence/ (Accessed 14 September, 2017).

Simpson, J. M. (2017) 'Home assistant adopter beware: Google, Amazon digital assistant patents reveal plans for mass snooping', *Consumer Watchdog*, 13 December.http://www.consumerwatchdog.org/privacy-technology/home-assistant-adopter-beware-google-amazon-digital-assistant-patents-reveal (Accessed 22 March, 2018).

Siwicki, B. (2018a) 'Google, Oracle and others make precision medicine moves at HIMSS18', *Healthcare IT News*, 9 March. http://www.healthcareitnews.com/news/google-oracle-and-others-make-precision-medicine-moves-himss18 (Accessed 10 April, 2018).

Siwicki, B. (2018b) '"Alexa, call a nurse." Special Report: AI voice assistants are infiltrating US healthcare with early success', *Healthcare IT News*, 6 February.http://www.healthcareit.com.au/article/"alexa-call-nurse"-special-report-ai-voice-assistants-are-infiltrating-us-healthcare-early? (Accessed 19 March, 2018).

Siwicki, B. (2018c) 'Cerner, Salesforce to collaborate; Google showcases new Cloud Healthcare API', *Healthcare IT News*, 6 March. https://www.healthcareitnews.com/news/cerner-salesforce-collaborate-google-showcases-new-cloud-healthcare-api (Accessed 22 March, 2018).

Smith, A. (2015) 'U.S. Smartphone use in 2015', *Pew Research Center, Internet and Technology*, 1 April. http://www.pewinternet.org/2015/04/01/us-smartphone-use-in-2015/ (Accessed 3 March, 2018).

Smith, C. S. (2018) 'Siri, Noooooooo!', *The Australian Financial Review*, 19–20 May, 42.

Solon, S. (2017) 'Facebook can track your browsing even after you've logged out, judge says', *The Guardian*, 3 July.https://www.theguardian.com/technology/2017/jul/03/facebook-track-browsing-history-california-lawsuit (Accessed 3 March, 2018).

Srinivasan, R. and Fish, A. (2017) *After the Internet*. Polity Press: Cambridge.

Statistica (2018a) 'Number of active Facebook users worldwide as of 1st quarter 2018 (in millions)' Available by subscription from https://www.statistica.com.(Accessed 17 May, 2018).

Statistica (2018b) 'UK: smartphone ownership by age from 2012–2017'. Available by subscription from https://www.statistica.com. (Accessed 6 March, 2018).

Statistica (2018c) 'Distribution of Google's revenues from 2001 to 2017, by source'. Available by subscription from https://www.statistica.com. (Accessed 29 October, 2018).

Stephen, I. D., Hiew, V., Coetzee, V., Tiddeman, B. P. and Perrett, D. I. (2017) 'Facial shape analysis identifies valid cues to aspects of physiological health in Caucasion, Asian, and African populations', *Frontiers in Psychology*, 8: 1883. doi: 10.3389/fpsyg.2017.01883.

Stephens-Davidowitz, S. (2017) *Everybody Lies: What the Internet Call Tell Us About Who We Really Are*. Bloomsbury: London and New York.

Stevens, L. (2018) '"Inexcusable" mistakes made in Google DeepMind and Royal Free NHS data deal – study', *digitalhealth*, 16 March.https://www.digitalhealth.net/2017/03/deepmind-health-royal-frees-criticised-lack-patient-involvement/ (Accessed 5 May, 2018).

Suleyman, M. and Snow, R. (2016) *Co-designing a patient and public involvement and engagement (PPIE) strategy for DeepMind Health*. DeepMind Health: London. https://deepmind.

com/documents/44/DMH_PPIE_recommendations%20-%20rosamund%20snow.pdf (Accessed 8 August, 2018).

Sunstein, C.R. (2018) *#Republic: Divided Democracy in the Age of Social Media.* Princeton University Press:Princeton, NJ and Oxford, UK.

Swan, M. (2013) 'The quantified self: fundamental disruption in big data science and biological discovery', *Big Data*, 1, 2: 85–99. doi:10.1089/big.2012.0002

Swartz, J. (2017) 'Inventor of web fears for privacy', *The Australian Financial Review*, 13 March, 9.

Synoptek (2018) 'Healthcare cloud computing trends for 2018'. https://synoptek.com/industry-solutions/it-services-healthcare/healthcare-cloud-computing-trends/ (Accessed 11 May, 2018).

Taylor, P. (2018) 'Whose property?', *London Review of Books*, 40, 3: 25–26.

Thaler, R. H. and Sunstein, C. R. (2009) *Nudge: Improving Decisions About Health, Wealth and Happiness.* Penguin Books: London.

Thomas, D. (2018) 'Smartphones just aren't sexy any more', Financial Times insert, *The Australian Financial Review*, 5 March, 19.

Townsend, P. and Davidson, N. (1982) *Inequalities in Health: The Black Report.* Penguin Books: Harmondsworth.

Transparency Market Research (2017) 'Global digital health market: snapshot', https://www.transparencymarketresearch.com/digital-health-market.html (Accessed 23 April, 2018).

Tuffs, A. (2010) 'Stem cell treatment in Germany is under scrutiny after child's death', *British Medical Journal*, 341, 7780: 960–961.

Turkle, S. (2015) *Reclaiming Conversation: The Power of Talk in the Digital Age.* Penguin: New York.

Turner, L. (2012) 'Medical travel and global health services marketplace: identifying risks to patients, public health, and health systems', in J. R. Hodges, L. Turner and A. M. Kimball (eds) *Risks and Challenges in Medical Tourism: Understanding the Global Market for Health Services.* Praeger: Santa Barbara, CA.

Tzezana, R. (2017) 'Singularity: explain it to me like I'm 5-years-old', *Futurism*, 3 March. https://futurism.com/singularity-explain-it-to-me-like-im-5-years-old/ (Accessed 9 May, 2017).

UCL Partners (2018) 'DigitalHealth.London'. https://uclpartners.com/what-we-do/innovation/digitalhealth-london/ (Accessed 20 August 2018)

UK Biobank (2017) 'About UK Biobank'. http://www.ukbiobank.ac.uk/about-biobank-uk/ (Accessed 7 September, 2017).

US Food and Drug Administration (n.d.) 'Digital health'. https://www.fda.gov/medicaldevices/digitalhealth/ (Accessed 21 April 2017).

Van Dijck, J. (2014) 'Datafication, dataism and dataveillance: big data between scientific paradigm and ideology', *Surveillance & Society*, 12, 2: 197–208.

Wachter, R. (2017) *The Digital Doctor: Hope, Hype, and Harm at the Dawn of Medicine's Computer Age.* McGraw Hill: New York.

Walker, J. (2017) 'The cancer game-changer' (Inquiry), *The Weekend Australian*, 26–27 August, 17.

Wang, A. B. (2018) 'China's facial recognition cameras pick man out of crowd of 60,000', *The Sydney Morning Herald*, 14 April. https://www.smh.com.au/world/asia/china-s-facial-recognition-cameras-pick-man-out-of-crowd-of-60-000-20180414-p4z9kp.html (Accessed 5 May, 2018).

Wasserman, E. (2016) 'Telecom companies lose out to Google, Apple in med tech telemedicine race', *FierceBiotech*, 16 May. https://www.fiercebiotech.com/medical-devices/telecom-companies-lose-out-to-google-apple-med-tech-telemedicine-race (Accessed 19 March, 2018).

The Week (2018) 'Pros and cons of privatizing the NHS', *The Week*, 26 April. http://www.theweek.co.uk/nhs/63360/pros-and-cons-of-privatising-the-nhs.

Welch, H. G. (2011) *Over-Diagnosed: Making People Sick in the Pursuit of Health.* Beacon Press: Boston, MA.

White House (2018) 'The Trump Administration's plan to put you in charge of your health information', 9 March. https://www.whitehouse.gov/articles/trump-administrations-pla n-put-charge-health-information/ (Accessed 12 April, 2018).

Wilkinson, R. G. (1996) *Unhealthy Societies: The Afflictions of Inequality.* Routledge: London and New York.

Winder, D. (2018) 'Cloud still hangs over patient data sovereignty concerns', *digitalhealth,* 4 May.https://www.digitalhealth.net/2018/05/cloud-still-hangs-over-patient-data-sover eignty-concerns/ (Accessed 11 May, 2018).

Wong, C., Harrison, C., Britt, H. and Henderson, J. (2014) 'Patient use of the internet for health information', *Australian Family Physician,* 43, 12: 875–876.

World Economic Forum (n.d.) 'Healthcare: building a digital healthcare system'. http://rep orts.weforum.org/digital-transformation/healthcare-building-a-digital-healthcare-system/ (Accessed 3 May, 2017).

World Economic Forum (2016) The International Organization for Public–Private Coop-eration. http://www3.weforum.org/docs/WEF_Institutional_Brochure_2016.pdf (Acces-sed 20 August 2018).

World Economic Forum (2018) 'World Economic Forum Annual Meeting. Strategic Outlook: The Digital Economy'. https://www.weforum.org/events/world-economic-forum-annua l-meeting-2018/sessions/strategic-outlook-the-digital-economy (Accessed 24 April, 2018).

WHO (2005) *Resolutions and Decisions. WHA58.28 eHealth.* World Health Organization: Geneva. http://www.who.int/healthacademy/media/WHA58-28-en.pdf (Accessed 3 August, 2018).

WHO (2016) *Global Diffusion of eHealth: Making Universal Health Coverage Achievable.* Report on the Third Global Survey of eHealth. World Health Organization: Geneva. http:// www.who.int/goe/publications/global_diffusion/en/ (Accessed 3 August, 2018).

WHO (n.d.) 'Constitution of WHO: Principles'. http://www.who.int/about/mission/en/ (Accessed 19 April, 2018).

World Wide Web Foundation (2017) *Algorithmic Accountability: Applying the Concept to Dif-ferent Country Contexts.* World Wide Web Foundation: Washington, DC. https://web foundation.org/docs/2017/07/Algorithms_Report_WF.pdf (Accessed 3 August, 2018).

World Wide Web Foundation (2018) *The Invisible Curation of Content: Facebook's News Feed and Our Information Diets.* World Wide Web Foundation: Washington, DC. http://web foundation.org/docs/2018/04/WF_InvisibleCurationContent_Screen_AW.pdf (Accessed 7 May, 2018).

World Wide Web Foundation (n.d.) 'Our work'. https://webfoundation.org/our-work/ (Accessed 7 May, 2018).

Worthington, J. (2018) 'Digital drive behind change in treatment', *The Australian Financial Review,* 23 February, 7.

Xiuzhong, V. and Xiao, B. (2018) 'Chinese authorities use facial recognition, public shaming to crack down on jaywalking, criminals', *ABC News,* 10 March.http://www.abc.net.au/ news/2018-03-20/china-deploys-ai-cameras-to-tackle-jaywalkers-in-shenzhen/9567430 (Accessed 5 May, 2018).

Zero Childhood Cancer (2017) 'The Zero Childhood Cancer program'. http://www.zer ochildhoodcancer.org.au/page/14/the-program (Accessed 6 September, 2017).

INDEX

academic research 103–4
Accenture 87–8
ActiveHealth Management 88
advertising 29, 41, 101, 108; *see also* direct-to-consumer advertising
Aetna 88
aged care 83–4
ageing in place 83–4
algorithmic accountability 116–17
Algorithmic Accountability (World Wide Web Foundation) 117
algorithmic medicine 44–5; *see also* precision medicine (algorithmic medicine)
algorithms: advertising and 101, 108; big data analytics and 41–2, 43; health apps and 82–3; machine learning and 62–3; personal voice assistants and 113
All of US (Precision Medicine Initiative) 54–5, 64
Alphabet 93; *see also* Google
Alter, A. 109
Amazon 68, 86, 90, 113
American Medical Association (AMA) 83
Anxiety Disorder Association of British Columbia (AnxietyBC) 84
Apple: AI and 68-69; cloud computing and 91; colonization and monetization of healthcare and 93; facial recognition technology and 32, 114; gamification and 33; health insurers and 88; home and community care and 84–5
Apple Watch: detection of heart problems and 33

architecture of choice 40–2, 86
Aronowitz, R. 74–5
ARPANET 14
artificial intelligence (AI): care–technology relationship and 73–4; cloud computing and 90–1; deep learning and 69–70; expected impact of 24–5; precision medicine and 44–5, 62–3, 66–70; singularity and 20–1; *see also* machine learning
Australia: academic research in 103–4; artificial intelligence in 24; cancer screening programs in 75; data breaches in 111; Digital Health Strategy in 76–7; electronic health records in 77, 78, 79–81, 98, 99; genomics in 48, 54, 57–9; health insurers in 88; investment in digital health in 104; precision medicine in 47–8, 50, 54, 56–9
Australian Centre for Research Excellence in Digital Health 103–4
Australian Competition and Consumer Commission 41
Australian Council of Learned Academies (ACOLA) 47–8
Australian Digital Health Agency 2–3, 10, 12, 76–7, 78, 79–81
The Australian Financial Review (newspaper) 13, 76
Australian Genomics 54
Australian Research Council 39

Banister, S. 65
Baudrillard, J. 29

behavioural economics 4
behavioural theory 33
Berners-Lee, T. 14–15, 116–17
big data: algorithms and 41–2, 43;
    applications of 41–3; health data
    economy and 105–7; precision medicine
    and 7, 24–5, 44–5, 47–8, 54, 56–61,
    63–4; role and impact of 5, 12;
    see also DeepMind
bio-digital citizenship 8, 25, 28
bio-economy 38–9
biobanks 52–3, 56, 60, 64
bioethics 72
bioinformatics 9
biomedicine: concept of 45–6, 100;
    personalization in 48–9; see also precision
    medicine (algorithmic medicine)
biotechnologies 8, 49; see also stem
    cell treatments
blockchain technology 53, 86, 104
Bourdieu, P. 6–7
Brave New World (Huxley) 19
Browne, R. 19
Butler, J. 4

Cambridge Analytica scandal 52, 107, 108,
    112, 115–16, 117
Cancer Research UK 75
cancer screening programs 75, 98
CancerSEEK 51
Canguilhem, G. 46
Cardon, L. 50–1
care–technology relationship 72–4
Castells, M. 6–7, 28–9, 32
CCS Insight 88
Center for Humane Technology 109
Centers for Disease Control and Prevention
    (CDC) 83–4
China 24, 114–15
Choosing Wisely initiative 72
Church, G. 57
The Circle (Eggers) 27, 94
citizen empowerment. See empowerment
clinical trials 82–3
cloud computing 22-23, 41, 61, 90–2
cloud robotics 91–2
CloudUPDRS 82
Clynes, M. 17
Commonwealth Bank 76
community partnerships 2
compassionate access 35–7
conferences 103
confirmation bias 38
Consumer Watchdog 113
Corepoint Health 102–3

Cross-Over Health 93
cryptocurrencies 57, 58
Cukier, K. 105
customized medicine 47; see also precision
    medicine (algorithmic medicine)
cyber-balkanization 116
cyber-colonization 20
cybersecurity 13, 52, 92, 107–8
cyborg 17–18, 33

data activists 117–18
data breaches 52, 107, 108, 111–2;
    see also Cambridge Analytica scandal
dataveillance 110
deep learning 69–70
DeepMind 24, 36, 65–8, 93, 112
digital divide 14
The Digital Doctor (Wachter) 62, 77, 97–8
digital economy 4, 33
digital health: algorithmic accountability and
    116–17; concept and rise of 1–2, 9–12;
    data activists and 117–18; data breaches
    and 52, 107, 108, 111–12; effectiveness
    and efficiencies of healthcare systems and
    96–9; empowerment and 29, 69, 74, 86,
    96, 100–1; as Faustian bargain 107, 115;
    Fourth Industrial Revolution and 18–20;
    future dangers of 113–15; future of
    115–16; harvesting of personal data and
    107–10; health data economy and 105–7;
    main claims and issues in 3–9; optimistic
    portrayals of 15–8; promise of 12–3,
    95–6; quality of healthcare and 99–100;
    regulation of 118; resistance to 116,
    118–19; surveillance and 110; use of term
    1–2; utopian and dystopian visions of
    13–15; wealth creation and 102–4;
    see also networking of the self; digital
    healthcare economy; precision medicine
    (algorithmic medicine)
Digital Health Cooperative Research Centre
    103–4
Digital Health London 11
Digital Health Strategic Vision
    (Queensland) 33
digital healthcare economy: care–technology
    relationship and 72–4; cloud computing
    and 90–2; colonization and monetization
    of healthcare and 93–4; converged
    experience of risk and disease and 74–5;
    electronic health records and 77–81;
    health insurers and 87–9; home and
    community care and 81–5; personal voice
    assistants and 89–90; Pharma 3.0 and
    86–7; in policy and the media 76–7;

rise and impact of 71–2; self-tracking and 85–6; smartphones and 31
digital literacy 2, 29, 33, 64, 107
digital patient activism 34–6
Dinger, M. 58
direct-to-consumer advertising 4, 29, 39–40, 57
Donnelly, P. 59
driverless cars 20, 31

e-health. *See* digital health
echo chamber effect 101, 116
The Economist (magazine) 13
Eggers, D. 27, 94
electronic health records (EHR) system 9-10, 23, 77–81, 86, 96–9
empowerment 29, 69, 74, 86, 96, 100–1
Equifax 52
Estonia 60
Estonian Genome Project 60
European Union (EU) 41
Evanstad, L. 78–9
Everybody Lies (Stephens-Davidowitz) 5
expanded access. *See* compassionate access

Facebook: advertising and 41; algorithms and 42, 43; Cambridge Analytica scandal and 117; data breaches and 52, 112; harvesting of personal data and 107–8; Partnership on AI and 68; role and impact of 30, 33–4; stem cell treatments and 36
facial recognition technology 32, 114–15
Farr, C. 33
Fitbit 82–3, 88
Food and Drug Administration (FDA) 10
Ford, M. 21, 91–2
Foucault, M. 6–7, 46
Fourth Industrial Revolution 18–20, 24, 104
Fox, S. 61–2
Framework to Guide the Secondary Use of My Health Record System Data (Department of Health) 79
Frankfurt School 28; *see also* Fromm, E.
Friends of the NYU Working Group on Compassionate Use and Pre- Approval Access 36–7
Fromm, E. 6–7, 25, 26–8, 42–3, 109–10
The Future of Precision Medicine in Australia (Australian Council of Learned Academies) 47–8

gamification 33
Gard, C. 36

Gartner 4
Garvie, C. 115
genealogy 7
genetic tests 37–8, 50, 64
GeneWatch 53
Genome.One 57–9
Genomic Data is Going Google (Google) 61
genomics: artificial intelligence and 68; big data analytics and 54, 56, 95; biobanks and 52–3, 56; commercialization of data in 106–7; critiques of 61–2; public consent and 51; recent initiatives in 56–61; research initiatives and 54–6; rise and impact of 48–9; *see also* All of US (Precision Medicine Initiative); precision medicine (algorithmic medicine)
Genomics and Genome Editing in the NHS (House of Commons Science and Technology Committee) 51
Genomics England 48, 54–5, 106
Genomics plc 59
Germany 24
Gibson, I. 52
GlaxoSmithKline 50–1
Global Alliance for Genomics and Health (GA4GH) 54
Google: advertising and 41; algorithms and 42, 43; cloud computing and 91; deep learning and 70; facial recognition technology and 32; Fitbit and 82–3; Partnership on AI and 68; personal voice assistants and 113; *see also* DeepMind
Google Flu Trends 41–2
Google Genomics 61
Google-knowing 38, 101
governmentality 7
Greenfield, A. 30, 32
Guynn, J. 117

Haraway, D. 17
Harris, T. 109
Hassabis, D. 65
health apps 31, 82–6; *see also* smartphones
health data economy 105–7
health informatics. *See* digital health
health information 37–8
Health Information and Management Systems Society (HIMSS) 82
health insurers 87–9
Health Plus Care 103
health tourism 38–9
Health Wizz 86
Her (film) 27, 114
Hippocrates 48
Hodson, H. 112

Hosanagar, K. 38
hospitals 46, 72, 89, 90
How To Create a Mind (Kurzweil) 65
Human Genome Project 61–2
Humby, C. 105
Huxley, A. 19
hype cycle 4, 96

IBM 68–9, 91–2, 93–4
Illich, I. 72
Illumina 69
implantable technologies 20
India 24
information and communication
    technologies 8
Inside Airbnb 117
internet: access to 106; resistance to 116;
    utopian and dystopian visions of 14–16;
    see also social media
internet-balkanization 116
Internet of Things 7–8, 20
interoperability 77–8
Italy 93–4

Janssen 35–6
JASON 62, 82, 83
Jobs, S. 109

Keen, A. 14
Kelly, K. 85
Kelsey, T. 12
Kleiner Perkins 41
Kline, N. 17
Koene, A. 63
Kurzweil, R. 20, 24, 65
Kushner, J. 77–8

Legg, S. 65
libertarian paternalism 80
Lock, M. 62
Lucas, E. 110
Lynch, M. P. 38, 101

machine learning: care–technology
    relationship and 73–4; cloud computing
    and 90–1; precision medicine and 62–3;
    role and impact of 21, 44–5;
    see also artificial intelligence (AI)
Mann, S. 85
market research 102–3
Marx, K. 6–7
Mattick, J. 63, 95
Mayer-Schönberger, V. 105
McCoy, K. 117
McLuhan, M. 6–7, 25–6, 27–8, 38, 42–3, 109

McNamee, R. 118
Medibank 88
Medical Research Council (MRC) 53
medicines: forms of 45–6; personalization in
    48–9; *see also* precision medicine
    (algorithmic medicine)
Microsoft 68
Minion, L. 98, 99
Mol, A. 45, 72–3
Müller, M. U. 31
Mumford, L. 27
Musk, E. 24, 65

National Academy of Sciences (NAS) 47–8
National Electronic Health Transition
    Authority 10
National Fair Housing Alliance 117
National Health Service (NHS): DeepMind
    and 65–8; electronic health records and
    78–9; future vision of 11–12; genomics
    and 106; Genomics England and 48,
    54–5, 106; 'GP at Hand' service and 118;
    precision medicine and 59, 65–8; privacy
    and 110; private provision of healthcare
    and 74; public cloud computing and 92;
    public consent and 51
National Institutes of Health (NIH) 55,
    64, 106
Nebula Genomics 56–7, 58
neoliberalism 7, 8–9, 25, 29, 49, 73
network society 14, 28–9, 32, 90–1
networking of the self: compassionate access
    and 35–7; concept of 25–9, 42–3;
    digital architecture of 'choice' and 40–2;
    digital patient activism and 34–6; health
    information and 37–8; health tourism and
    38–9; stem cell treatments and 29, 36,
    39–40; technologies for 30–5, 89–90
neurotechnologies 20
New Global Digital Health Partnership 12
*Next Steps on the NHS Five Year Forward
    View* (NHS) 11
Nguyen, V.-K. 62

Office of the Australian Information
    Commissioner 111
100,000 Genomes Project 51, 55, 64
O'Neil, C. 42, 63, 116
Over-Diagnosed (Welch) 75
Owen, M. 87

P4 medicine 47; *see also* precision medicine
    (algorithmic medicine)
Park, J. 83
Parmenter, M. 76

Partnership on Artificial Intelligence to Benefit People and Society (Partnership on AI) 68–9
patient activism 35; *see also* digital patient activism
patient empowerment. *See* empowerment
patient engagement 2
patient forums 33–4
PatientsLikeMe 33–4
performative power 115–16
personal voice assistants 89–90, 110, 113–14
Personalised Medicines (Royal Society) 49–50
personalized medicine. *See* precision medicine (algorithmic medicine)
Pew Research Center 30
Pharma 3.0 86–7
post-truth 5
power 7
Powles, J. 112
preapproval access. *See* compassionate access
precision medicine (algorithmic medicine): big data and 7, 24–5, 44–5, 47–8, 54, 56–61, 63–4; biomedicine and 45–6; concept of 44–5; critiques of genome hype and quantification and 61–2; deep learning and 69–70; DeepMind and 36, 65–8; definitions and use of terms 46–8; machine learning and AI in 44–5, 62–3, 66–70; personalization in 48–51; public consent and 51–3, 64; recent initiatives in 56–61; research initiatives and 54–6; smartphones and 31; *see also* genomics
Precision Medicine Initiative (All of US) 54–5, 64
PricewaterhouseCoopers (PwC) 88–9
privacy: harvesting of personal data and 107–10; personal voice assistants and 110; precision medicine and 62; 'right to be forgotten' law and 41; smartphones and 32; *see also* data breaches
public consent 51–3, 64
Public Population Project in Genomics (P3G) Consortium 56

Quantified Self 85
quantified self movement 85–6
Quest Diagnostics 69

radio 26
Redrup, Y. 58
regulation 118
Remerowski, T. 41
responsibilization 29

'right to be forgotten' law 41
risk 74–5
robots 73–4
Royal Free London 67, 93, 112
Royal Society 49–50, 51
Ruckenstein, M. 110

SAI Global 103
Schüll, N. D. 110
Schumacher, A. 53
Schwab, K. 18–21, 24, 104
self-tracking 85–6
Shivon 56–7, 58
Simpson, J. M. 113
singularity 20–1
smartphones 30–5, 82, 89–90; *see also* health apps
Snow, R. 66
social media 14–15, 87, 116; *see also* Facebook
splinternet 116
Stamina Foundation 36
Start4Life 90
stem cell treatments 29, 36, 39–40, 96
Stephen, I. D. 114
Stephens-Davidowitz, S. 5, 59–60
stratified medicine 47; *see also* precision medicine (algorithmic medicine)
Suleyman, M. 65, 66
Sunstein, C. R. 80
surveillance 7, 14–15, 26, 110
Swartz, J. 15

Taylor, P. 93, 108
technological determinism 17
television 26
Telstra 87
Thaler, R. H. 80
3D printing 20
Transparency Market Research 102
Turkle, S. 109
Twitter 30
Tzezana, R. 20

UK Biobank 52–3, 64
United Kingdom: cancer screening programs in 75, 98; electronic health records in 78–9, 80, 98; genomics in 48, 51, 53–5, 59–60, 106; investment in digital health in 104; personal voice assistants in 90; precision medicine in 48, 51–3, 54–5, 59–60; private provision of healthcare in 74; public cloud computing in 92; *see also* National Health Service (NHS)

United States: data activists in 117; data
    breaches in 111; electronic health records
    in 77–8; genomics in 48, 54–5; personal
    voice assistants in 90; precision medicine
    in 47–8, 54–5; private provision of
    healthcare in 74
US Department of Health and Human
    Services 10

Vinge, V. 20

Wachter, R. 62, 77, 97–8, 105
The Wearable Future (PwC) 88–9
wearable technologies 8, 20, 32, 82–6, 88–9
Welch, G. 75
WikiLeaks 15

Williams, E. 15
Williams, J. 91
Wolf, G. 85
women 73
World Economic Forum 15–17,
    71, 104
World Health Organization (WHO) 2,
    99–100
World Wide Web Foundation 116–17
Worthington, J. 76
Wozniak, S. 117

YouTube 117

Zero Childhood Cancer 56
Zuckerberg, M. 118

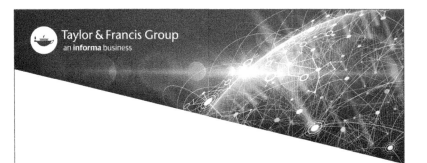

Made in the USA
Middletown, DE
13 January 2022

58581262R00084